THE PRACTICAL
ARCHAEOLOGIST

THE PRACTICAL
ARCHAEOLOGIST

How we know what we know about the past

JANE MCINTOSH

Facts On File Publications
New York, New York ● Oxford, England

THE PRACTICAL ARCHAEOLOGIST
How we know what we know about the past

Library of Congress Cataloging-in-Publication Data
McIntosh, Jane
The practical archaeologist
Includes index.
1. Archaeology. 1. Title
GN31.2M35 1986 930.1 85-29289
ISBN 0-8160-1400-0

This book was designed and produced by The Paul Press Ltd,
41-42 Berners Street, London W1P 3AA

Art Editor	Antony Johnson
Project Editor	Elizabeth Longley
Editorial	Mike Groushko
	Christopher Mole
	John Burgess
Art Assistants	David Ayres
Illustrations	Alan Suttie
	Antony Johnson (maps)
Art Director	Stephen McCurdy
Editorial Director	Jeremy Harwood

Typeset by Wordsmiths, Street, Somerset
Origination by South Sea International, Hong Kong
Printed in Singapore through Print Buyer's Database

The Paul Press wish to thank John Schofield and his colleagues at
The Museum of London for their invaluable help and advice during the
preparation of this book.

CONTENTS

—— PART 1 ——

WHAT IS ARCHAEOLOGY?

Opposite: *The god Vija Tai, was worshipped by the Mayan civilization which flourished in Central America between AD 1200 and 1450; here he is represented on a pottery censer found at Mayapan, Mexico.*

SWEET FOOD OF ANTIQUITY

'IN THE STUDY OF Antiquity,' wrote the English antiquarian William Camden (1551-1623) 'there is a sweet food of the mind well befitting such as are of honest and noble disposition.'

In all ages and all countries, man has been fascinated by his past. Today, many people argue that it is only by studying the past that we can properly understand the present and, perhaps, learn from the errors and achievements of our ancestors. A knowledge of their past is vital, too, to the self-respect of nations, as can be seen from the relatively large proportion of national budgets that many countries allocate to archaeological research.

Archaeology and History

Archaeology is often said to be the handmaiden of history. But the relationship between the two branches of study is not simply that of master and servant.

History depends on the availability of written records. Those are usually incomplete, and may well be biased or inaccurate, too. Archaeology, on the other hand, can reveal much that would ordinarily be left out of written accounts, especially the details of everyday life. It helps, therefore, to round out our view of the past, to make it more balanced.

What is more, history deals only with the past of literate societies, a tiny portion of man's story. The written records of ancient peoples such as the Greeks of Classical times tell us something about their illiterate neighbours and contemporaries. But most of what we know about these less-advanced peoples comes from archaeology. And archaeology is our only source of information about the millions of years of prehistory.

A Total Study

Archaeology is a total study. It involves analyzing everything that remains from the past, with the aim of reconstructing that past as fully as possible. Although some people regard archaeology as synonymous with excavation, it is far more than that. Excavation is only one of many of its processes.

Scientists carry out complicated analyses to date archaeological finds, to provide information on the sources of archaeological material, or to establish exactly how ancient artefacts were made. Field archaeologists use many scientific devices to locate and map ancient sites.

Botanists, zoologists and physicians contribute information about the diet of ancient man, the environment in which he lived and his state of health. Archaeologists also study contemporary societies to gain an insight into life in the past. Their investigations range from observations of the daily life of surviving hunter-gatherers to surveys of the contents of dustbins in modern America, to try to relate people's activities to the artefacts that are the main source of archaeological evidence.

Rummaging among the rubbish of the ages may seem a long way from Camden's 'sweet food of the mind'. But, as the pioneer of modern archaeology A.H. Pitt-Rivers (1827-1900) pointed out, it is the study of the ordinary, everyday things that helps us to reconstruct the past, far more so than rare, valuable objects that were unusual even in their own time and place.

The amazing achievements of our ancestors astound and fascinate us – the golden treasures of Tutankhamun, the jade princess of China, the vastness of the Pyramids. But in the end it is our common humanity that exerts the greatest appeal down the millennia – the man desperately stretching out his arms to protect his family as volcanic ash engulfed Pompeii, the 4000-year-old exercise books of Sumerian schoolboys, the crumbling remains of the flowers laid on Tutankhamun's coffin.

That is the ultimate attraction of archaeology. It is the patient, meticulous, scientific study of every man by the everyman that is in us all.

Imagine the surprise *of Howard Carter when he peered into the long-sealed outer chamber of Tutankhamen's tomb and saw this weird and wonderful golden couch (right), with its figures of the cow-headed goddess Hathor. Underneath, stored for all time, are clay containers holding mummified joints of gazelle and ducks, to sustain this Pharoah, who died so young, in the afterlife were he would have taken his place among the other gods.*

Archaeology was lifted *from pure treasure hunting to its proper level of scientific study by the work of a few great men. We are indebted to A.H. Pitt-Rivers for demonstrating the value of detailed and methodical research and on-site recording. The publication of his findings set a new standard and Pitt-Rivers showed scholars the great knowledge of the past that could be gleaned from observation of simple things, so often ignored in the early days of archaeology.*

THE ILLUSTRATED LONDON NEWS, FEB. 3, 1923.—169

MUMMIFIED FOOD FOR THE KING'S "KA": TUTANKHAMEN'S "LARDER."

THE "TIMES" WORLD COPYRIGHT, BY ARRANGEMENT WITH THE EARL OF CARNARVON.

CONTAINING MUMMIFIED JOINTS OF MEAT, HAUNCHES OF GAZELLE, LIVER, AND TRUSSED DUCKS—FOOD FOR TUTANKHAMEN'S SOUL: A PILE OF WHITE ROUNDED BOXES UNDER THE HATHOR-HEADED COUCH IN THE TOMB ANTE-CHAMBER.

ANTIQUARIANS AND NOBLE SAVAGES

THE ORIGINS OF ARCHAEOLOGY go back for more than 2500 years. Nabonidus, the last king of Babylon (he reigned from 556 to 539 BC), excavated the temple of Shamath at Sippur to try to find out who built it. Nabonidus's daughter Ennigaldi-Nanna collected local antiquities and displayed them in the world's first known museum, in the city of Ur, which was located near the Euphrates.

The Greek historian Thucydides (c. 460-395 BC) describes how the Athenians excavated ancient graves on the Aegean island of Delos and interpreted the artefacts they found in them in terms of the politics of their own day. Chinese historians, too, used ancient artefacts and the remains of ruined cities to try to build up a picture of their ancestors' way of life.

This interest in the past was common to all literate ancient societies, while even illiterate peoples maintained an oral tradition of the deeds of their forebears. So philosophers such as the Roman Lucretius (96-55 BC) and Yuan K'ang, who lived in China during the 1st century AD, drew upon some remembrance of their ancestors when they wrote about former technological epochs – the age of stone, the age of jade, the age of bronze – and contrasted those with what they saw as the degenerate age of iron in which they themselves were living.

Lucretius and other writers of classical Rome and Greece were aware, too, of more primitive peoples of their own day who still used stone or bronze tools. Their existence, to Roman and Greek eyes vigorous but barbaric, showed that the classical authors' notions of their own past were valid.

The Age of Antiquarians

From the collapse of the Roman empire in the 5th century AD to the end of the Middle Ages, scholarly interest in the past waned. People recalled only relatively recent events. Previous eras and the splendours of Greece and Rome were thought of only as legends, based around stories of mythical gods and heroes. The Bible provided the main framework for history.

Stone tools and implements were popularly thought to be thunderbolts. Prehistoric pots were believed, in central Europe, to have been spontaneously generated in the ground.

It was the Renaissance, from the mid-15th century onwards, that stimulated an upsurge of interest in Classical Greek and Roman art and architecture. In turn, this aroused a passion for collecting antique objects among the well-to-do.

A clay brick *found in Tell el-Mugayyar in modern Iraq, site of the ancient Chaldean city of Ur. It dates from the reign of Nabonidus, last king to rule before the Persian conquest. The cuneiform impression records the building of a temple dedicated to Ningal, wife of the moon god.*

Thucydides (right) *was one of the world's great historians, driven by a passion for the past of his own Greece and a desire to be as accurate as possible in recording it. He wrote of Athenian excavations on Delos and may well have seen this terrace of marble lions (above) which dates from the 7th century BC.*

By the 16th century, scholars were investigating Roman ruins in Italy, helping to feed the collectors' market. Excavations at Herculaneum and Pompeii, towns buried by the eruption of Mount Vesuvius in AD 79, yielded a rich supply of treasures from 1709 onwards.

Egyptian antiquities were transported to Europe. Mummies were particularly popular. In medieval times, powdered preparations made from mummies were believed to have formidable powers of healing, but by the 18th century that belief had waned and florid exhibitions of mummy dissection became a public entertainment. European travellers explored much of the Middle East, and produced richly illustrated volumes describing its ancient monuments.

Secrets of the Stones

In northern and western Europe, the monuments of antiquity were exhaustively studied and described in scholarly fashion from the 16th century. Prehistoric megaliths, impressive structures such as Stonehenge in England, were a particular focus of interest, and their origins were the subject of learned debate. They were variously interpreted as burial chambers, memorials, altars or temples associated with human sacrifice, built by Druids, Romans or Vikings.

Some students of ancient monuments enjoyed royal patronage. In 1533, John Leland was appointed antiquary to the king of England and, as such, examined ancient documents and old buildings. Since Leland's time, many monarchs have supported antiquarians and archaeologists – perhaps because royalty has a vested interest in the past to establish its ancestry and therefore its legitimate claim to rule.

Early antiquarians did not concentrate on the monuments alone, but also on the general surface features of the land around. The study grew into the science of topography, and it now plays a major part in archaeology. William Camden (1551-1623) was one of its pioneers. He observed patterns of ancient streets in fields of growing corn, noting that the crop grew more thinly where the thoroughfares had once been. Today, thanks to aerial photography, such patterns are a valuable clue to archaeologists seeking ancient sites (*see pages 34-35*).

The Childhood of Man

The discovery of America in the 16th century, and the exploration of Africa and the Pacific, gave added stimulation to antiquarian thought.

In the optimistic climate of the Enlightenment – the 18th-century Age of Reason in Europe – the primitive inhabitants of these newly found lands were regarded as 'noble savages', unspoiled examples of what mankind must have been like in its earliest days, before the Biblical Fall. Their lifestyle was taken to reflect that of the inhabitants of Europe before Roman times. So a study of their customs and way of living – part of what is now called anthropology – could illuminate the work of historians and archaeologists.

Contact between Europeans and the primitive peoples of America and elsewhere produced one immediate and significant insight. Many of the native inhabitants still used stone tools similar to those found all over Europe, and previously believed to be thunderbolts. The growing suspicion that these objects were, in fact, man-made in origin was thus confirmed.

From total destruction *in 79 AD until 1594, Pompeii and its 3 neighbouring towns (Herculaneum, Boscoreale and Stabiae) sank into oblivion. Then in the second half of the 19th century excavation began in earnest, revealing such wonders as this Temple of Apollo, unearthed from its grave of lava, and now sharing the horizon with Vesuvius, its one-time destroyer.*

ORDERING THE PAST

BEFORE THE TIME of the Greeks and Romans, the past was 'wrapped in a thick fog', according to Rasmus Nyerup (1759-1829), an eminent Danish antiquarian. 'Everything that has come down to us from heathendom … is older than Christendom,' he declared, but by how much 'we can do no more than guess.'

What was needed was a system to help dispel the fog – one that would divide the vast expanse of prehistory into workable chronological blocks, to which objects discovered by antiquarians and archaeologists could be assigned as appropriate.

The ancient Romans and Chinese had, in fact, created the basis of such a system with their ages of stone, bronze and iron. But although the theoretical significance of their approach was appreciated by some later scholars, it was not until 1819 that a coherent attempt was made to apply it to archaeological material.

In that year, the Danish National Museum reopened, with a totally novel reclassification of its prehistoric exhibits. Its curator, Christian J. Thomsen (1788-1865), had arranged their collection according to the substances from which they were made, following the three consecutive ages of stone, bronze and iron of which Lucretius had written nearly 2000 years earlier.

In 1836, Thomsen elaborated on this 'three-age' scheme of prehistory in his book *Ledetraad til Nordisk Oldkyndighed* (Guide to Nordic Antiquities). In it, he described the objects, burial rites and tomb architecture associated with each age, drawing on his own extensive familiarity with the material.

John Lubbock was one *of a long line of scholars seeking to make order of mankind's seemingly jumbled past. In his book* Prehistoric Times *(1865) he divided the Stone Age into two: Palaeolithic and Neolithic, in other words the Old Stone Age and the New Stone Age.*

Thomsen's study was translated into German in 1837 and into English in 1848. By the second half of the 19th century, his system had become widely accepted. It is still the foundation stone of archaeology's attempts to order prehistory, though it has been considerably refined.

Probing the Strata

Thomsen's assistant and eventual successor at the Danish National Museum was J.J. Worsaae (1821-1885). A meticulous and painstaking archaeologist, his work helped to show the validity of the three-age system.

Unlike many antiquarians of his day, Worsaae did not dig haphazardly into ancient sites in search of treasures. In excavating burial mounds and Denmark's peat bogs, a rich source of prehistoric objects, he worked carefully, taking note of the distinct layers he discerned as he dug downwards.

Worsaae recognized one of the fundamental principles on which archaeological investigation depends – that of stratigraphic succession. Like the geological strata laid down by the forces of nature over the ages, successive layers of archaeological material have accumulated in places frequented by man. Some are natural accumulations of soil and decayed vegetation, while others are the result of human activity. An archaeological site is therefore like a layer cake, in which the top layer is the most recent and the succeeding layers become progressively older the deeper you go. The period of time represented by each layer can vary considerably; in some burial mounds the layers may have been added within minutes of each other, while on other sites a deposit only a few centimetres deep can represent hundreds of years of human occupation.

By careful investigation, Worsaae was able to show that the Stone Age of Lucretius and Thomsen preceded an era in which most tools and implements were made of bronze. After the Bronze Age came an epoch in which everyday tools were iron, bronze being reserved for ornaments and luxury goods – the Iron Age that Lucretius had disparaged as degenerate.

While Worsaae conducted his pioneer investigations in Denmark, discoveries elsewhere showed that Thomsen's three-age scheme was valid for all Europe. But in France in particular, archaeologists found crudely chipped stone axes in addition to the polished ones regarded as typical of the Stone Age. That led them to conclude that there had, in fact, been two Stone Ages, for which Sir John Lubbock (1834-1913) coined new names: Palaeolithic for the earlier, or Old Stone Age and Neolithic for the later, or New Stone Age.

In caves and rock-shelters inhabited by Palaeolithic peoples, French archaeologists such as Edouard Lartet (1801-1871) discovered breathtaking wall-paintings. At first, few believed that prehistoric savages could have been capable of works of such technical skill and artistic vigour. It was not until the mid-1890s that evidence emerged to win over the sceptics: Palaeolithic art discovered at La Mouthe and Pair-non-Pair in France was found to be covered by undisturbed later deposits.

Four Ages of Man

As discoveries throughout Europe broadened knowledge of the artefacts of Thomsen's three ages, scholars tried to assess what the artefacts might imply about the development of human society. Researchers based their theories, at least in part, upon comparisons with the lifestyles of contemporary primitive societies. One of the leading scholars in this field was another Scandinavian, Sven Nilsson (1787-1883). He proposed the idea that mankind passed or was passing through four phases. In the earliest, corresponding to much of the Stone Age, men were savage hunters and fishers. During the second phase, they herded some of the animals they had formerly hunted, but most people remained nomads. In the third phase, they settled down and turned to agriculture, creating a surplus of food that could be traded. The development of coinage to simplify such trade was, with the emergence of writing, one of Nilsson's signposts to the fourth phase – civilization.

Nilsson's ideas were adopted and modified by anthropologists such as Britain's Sir Edward Tylor (1832-1917) and Lewis H. Morgan (1818-1881) in America. Towards the end of the 19th century, it became widely accepted that all human societies everywhere were following the same general course of development, although obviously they were not all in the same phase at the same time. Believers in the theory ascribed it to what they called the 'psychic unity' of man. Today's archaeologists no longer accept the concept of an inevitable course of human progress, but traces of the idea of man's essential unity survive in the work of those who seek to discover universally applicable general laws of human behaviour.

The cave paintings *at Lascaux, which were discovered by French schoolboys in 1940, revolutionized our view of the abilities of Paleolithic man, as the artistic skills that created this bison demonstrate.*

THE AGE OF MAN

UNTIL LESS THAN 200 years ago, the Old Testament version of the Creation of the world went unquestioned, at least in public, in western nations. Thinkers and religious leaders tried to put a date to the event. In 1650, Archbishop James Ussher of Armagh in Ireland calculated from the Bible that the Creation had taken place in 4004 BC – a view subsequently widely accepted by many practising Christians.

Given the state of knowledge at the time, Ussher's dating did not seem unreasonable. Historical events known about – from Biblical sources and the writers of Greece and Rome – could all be encompassed within it.

First Doubts Appear

As more was learned about antiquity and as the sciences of geology and palaeontology – the study of fossils – began to develop, the timetable of world events derived from a literal reading of the Bible posed increasing difficulties for those who believed in it.

The upsurge of interest in fossil-hunting in 18th-century Europe revealed more and more remains of unfamiliar beasts, birds, fish and plants, often deep in the ground. The orthodox explanation was that the creatures and plants had been destroyed by Noah's flood – thus reconciling them with the Bible. People who believed it came to be called 'catastrophists', or 'diluvianists', the latter from *dilivium*, the Latin word for flood.

However, the explanation did not satisfy everybody. Among the doubters was James Hutton (1726-1797), a geologist from Edinburgh in Scotland. Hutton is now sometimes called the father of modern geology, but in his own century and well into the following one he was vilified by many people as an atheist.

Hutton observed the natural processes that form and shape the landscape, and maintained that these processes had occurred in exactly the same way throughout the past and that they would continue to do so in the future. 'We find no vestige of a beginning, no prospect of an end (in nature)', he wrote.

The theory Hutton propounded is called uniformitarianism, and is now generally accepted. However, the catastrophists were not prepared to give up their case without a fight.

The Lower Rhine Valley *revealed itself to be rich in mammal fossils of the Pleistocene epoch. This engraving shows a typical excavation of the mid-19th century at one of the many cave sites which yielded remains of mastadons and other large mammals dating back to over 10,000 years ago. There were no hominid, or human, remains found at this level, but these sites provided invaluable information about European mammal habitation and migration patterns.*

Faced with a steady increase in the discoveries of different species of fossil animals and plants, they refined their ideas, still trying to reconcile them with the Bible. Perhaps, the catastrophists suggested, there had been another flood or similar disaster after God had created the world, but before He had created man. As all other living creatures appeared before man in the Biblical account, that would mean that some species had been destroyed even before Noah's flood.

Despite the efforts of the catastrophists, uniformitarianism gradually gained ground, as followers of Hutton expanded upon his ideas. In 1833, Sir Charles Lyell, another Scot, published his *Principles of Geology*. Lyell's masterwork was the most influential geological sourcebook of the 19th century. It gradually won scientific respectability for Hutton's thesis, establishing that the world began many millions of years before Ussher and the catastrophists said it had, and paved the way for the theory of evolutionary development of all living things.

The Diffident Iconoclast

In 1797, John Frere, an antiquarian living in Norfolk, England, wrote a description of observations he had made in a clay pit being dug at Hoxne in Suffolk. In a layer of sandy soil he had found fossilized bones of extinct animals. In the gravel layer below, there were shaped stones that, he conjectured, were primitive weapons, presumably from a distant age when metal was totally unknown.

Frere commented that the items 'tempt us to refer them to a very remote period indeed; even beyond that of the present world' – a evolutionary thought in the days when he was writing, as it went against the accepted ideas of Ussher and the catastrophists.

Little notice was taken of Frere at that time. But as the geological principle of stratification (that certain types of rock are formed in layers or strata, from which it is possible to draw conclusions about their age) gained acceptance, together with the archaeological principle of stratigraphy based upon it, scholars came to share Frere's opinion.

Investigations of several sites in Europe where fossils and human artefacts appeared together, particularly caves and river terraces, suggested that man had lived alongside creatures that were now extinct. This meant mankind, like the earth itself, was far older than the Bible-derived timetable would allow.

At first, the scientific establishment rejected the implications. But the turning point came in 1859, when a group of distinguished British scholars visited Abbeville in northern France to observe the work being carried out there by Jacques Boucher de Perthes (1788-1868). He had found flint tools associated with bones of extinct animals in local gravel pits. The British came away convinced of the validity of Boucher de Perthes' findings and endorsed them vigorously. As a result, most scholars came to accept mankind's great antiquity.

The Origin of Species

The revolution in 19th-century thinking in geology, started by Hutton and carried forward by Lyell and others, was accompanied by an equally massive upheaval in biology. It came to a head in 1859, when the British naturalist Charles Darwin published the book usually referred to as *The Origin of Species*.

Since the 18th century, scholars had been speculating that fossils were earlier links in a chain of evolution in which creatures gradually adapted to changes in their environment, rather than victims of Biblical floods. To Darwin, however, belongs the credit for working out the mechanism by which evolution takes place – natural selection. Individual members of a species vary in some of their characteristics, and those with variations best suited to their environment are the most likely to survive and reproduce (i.e. 'survival of the fittest'). The original variations become enhanced in succeeding generations, eventually leading to the evolution of a new species.

Various scholars quickly saw the implications the theory of evolution held for determining the origins of mankind, among them Thomas Huxley (1825-1895), who earned the nickname of 'Darwin's bulldog' for his vigorous championing of the idea. Darwin himself hesitated to enter the public controversy, but did so in 1871, with his book *The Descent of Man*.

In that work, Darwin contended, as Huxley and others had already done, that mankind had evolved from the same ancestors as present-day apes. For the theory to hold, however, there would have to have been at some stage of prehistory a creature representing an evolutionary 'bridge' between man's ape-like forebears and man himself. The search for the fossilised remains of this creature, the so-called 'missing link', united naturalists, geologists and fossil-hunting antiquarians.

Charles Darwin's view *of evolution as propounded in* The Origin of Species *(1859) challenged the traditional thinking of the time, both religious and scientific. Man became not a unique creation of an almighty being, but merely an animal at the top of a hierarchy that somehow left him related to primates such as the gorilla. Although the basis of Darwin's theory is still generally accepted, there are many questions left unanswered. For instance, nothing explains the widespread presence of discrete species and the total lack of linking species, which would show the existence of a true evolutionary process, thereby demonstrably proving Darwin's theory.*

Quest For the Missing Link

Peking Man *lived about half a million years ago. He was a hunter-gatherer who used crude stone tools and had discovered fire. He was also, apparently, a cannibal and regarded human brains as a delicacy. Peking Man stood about 1.56m (5ft) tall. His body was covered with hair though he probably clothed himself with animal skins for extra warmth.*

THE IDEA THAT MAN is descended from apes provoked two reactions in the second half of the 19th century. For some scholars, the search for man's earliest ancestors was akin to the legendary quest for the Holy Grail in its intensity. But others resented the implication that mankind is simply a superior sort of animal. Fundamentalist believers in the literal truth of the Bible rejected the theory of evolution.

In 1856, the skeleton of what is now known to be an early man was found in a limestone cave at Neanderthal, near Dusseldorf in Germany. It attracted great attention, but the most eminent pathologist of the day, Rudolf Virchow, declared that it came from a modern human who had suffered from arthritis and rickets.

However, in 1882 skeletons showing similar characteristics to the Neanderthal remains were discovered at Spy in Belgium, associated with the bones of extinct animals. Scholarly opinion had changed, and these were accepted as a form of early man. Their acceptance was reinforced by subsequent finds of such skeletons from other sites in Europe, particularly in France.

The type of skeleton is now called Neanderthal. It is thought that Neanderthal man lived throughout Europe and western Asia between 100,000 and 40,000 years ago. He was a variant of the species *Homo sapiens*, like ourselves. The western European, or classic, Neanderthals developed rather different physical characteristics from their counterparts in western Asia, and it is not clear whether or not they were direct ancestors of modern man. But our descent from Asiatic Neanderthal stock is now well-established.

The Java Apeman

The Neanderthals were too similar to modern man to be the missing link with the apes, so the quest was still on. In 1887, a young Dutch anatomist and surgeon, Eugene Dubois, set out upon it, heading for the East Indies.

Dubois did not choose his destination at random. Some scholars, including Virchow, had already speculated that the missing link would be traced in the tropics, home of all modern apes.

Amazingly, within four years of his arrival, Dubois found what he was looking for. In the fossil beds of Java he unearthed the skull and thighbone of a man-like creature, with a smaller brain cavity than modern man and a thick, bony ridge across the brows. The structure of the thighbone showed that the creature had walked upright.

The scientific world, however, was not ready to accept the Java fossil as an ancestor of man, and Dubois became mentally unbalanced battling in defence of his theory. It was not until the 1930s that the German anthropologist Gustav von Koenigswald found further examples of the creature in the Java fossil beds, and the achievement of Dubois was recognized.

The Java apeman is now known as *Homo erectus* (upright man). He lived between 1.5 million and 400,000/300,000 years ago. And he was not confined to Java, as later research was to show.

From the Dragon's Teeth

For centuries, Chinese apothecaries sold what they called dragon's teeth as a sovereign remedy for illness. In fact, what they believed to be the remains of ancient dragons were fragments of fossilized animals. Many were actually teeth, and in the 1920s Western scholars concluded that some on sale in Peking could have come from apemen.

They tracked the source of the teeth to Chou K'ou Tien, a huge cave 45km (28 miles) from Peking. Excavations between 1927 and 1939 yielded the remains of 45 apemen closely resembling those previously found in Java. Similar specimens have subsequently been discovered in many parts of the Old World, including Spain and east Africa.

Peking man used fire for cooking, warmth and defence against wild animals. He was also, it seems, a cannibal who systematically smashed the skulls of his fellows and ate their brains.

Child of the South

The scientific scepticism that greeted the Java apeman emerged again when the remains of a young man-like ape were found in 1924. They were identified by Professor Raymond Dart, an Australian, in a box of fossil-bearing rocks sent to him from Taung in South Africa. In modern times, no apes have lived in the region, so it did not seem a likely place in which to search for the missing link.

In addition, the skull, thought to be of a child about six years old, had teeth resembling those of a human, but a brain cavity no larger than that of modern apes. Scholars had for years reasoned that apes in man's lineage would have a large brain and apelike jaws and teeth. Their expectations had been fulfilled in 1912 by 'Piltdown man', allegedly found in Sussex in England, but shown in 1953 to be a hoax *(see*

Richard Leakey *and his wife, Meave, painstakingly pieced together the fragments of a human skull found near Lake Turkana, Kenya, in 1972. The skull belonged to* Homo Habilis – *nearly 2 million years old – the earliest hominid to make and use tools. Leakey's father, Louis Leakey, first discovered Homo Habilis in 1959; the work of the younger Leakeys reinforced Louis' claim that upright man was much older than previously believed.*

page 133), so the Taung child had no place in their scheme of things.

Dart named his discovery *Australopithecus africanus* (African ape of the south). By the 1940s enough specimens of *Australopithecus* had been found in Africa for scientists to accept them as part of mankind's family tree. However, it now appears they were cousins, rather than direct forebears, of man.

Today, two species of *Australopithecus* have been identified. *A. africanus* was small and slender, and lived 2-3 million years ago. *A. robustus* was sturdier and lived 1-2 million years ago. Both species walked upright.

The Leakey Achievement

The Kenyan archaeologist and anthropologist Louis Leakey had been searching east Africa for traces of man's early ancestors for 30 years when, in 1959, he was rewarded by finding the remains of a very robust *Australopithecus robustus*. He named it 'Dear Boy' in understandable gratitude. The following year, he and his wife Mary made an even more important discovery – the fossil remains of another creature living at the same time as *Australopithecus*, but much more manlike in appearance. Leakey called it *Homo habilis* (handy man). It flourished between 2 million and 1.5 million years ago.

The evidence now suggests that *Homo habilis* was the first hominid, the group of primates of which man is the only survivor, to make stone tools. It seems he was not averse to using them to kill his australopithecine cousins.

Enter Lucy…

At Laetoli, near the Olduvai Gorge in Tanzania, Mary Leakey and her son Richard made one of their most exciting finds, footprints preserved in hardened volcanic ash. They show that several hominids crossed the site nearly 4 million years ago (that is, perhaps 1 million years before *Australopithecus africanus*), walking upright.

A few bones of these creatures were also unearthed at Laetoli, but Hadar in Ethiopia was the site of the most spectacular finds. There, in November 1974, a French and American team led by Don Johanson and Tom Gray discovered nearly half of the skeleton of a hominid they nicknamed Lucy *(see page 145)*. This was remarkable because fossil hominids are rarely represented by more than a few teeth or bones.

By 1981, the remains of 13 individuals like Lucy, though less complete, had been unearthed at Hadar. These hominids are called *Australopithecus afarensis* (Afar is the region of Ethiopia in which Hadar lies). Some believe that *A. afarensis* is a direct ancestor both of man and of his cousins *A. africanus* and *A. robustus*.

FORTY CENTURIES LOOK DOWN

THE CIVILIZATION of Egypt was already nearly 3,000 years old when the country was conquered by Alexander the Great of Macedon in 332 BC. The massive memorials of the ancient kingdom fascinated the Greek invaders, but they treated them with some irreverence. The word 'pyramid', for instance, comes from the Greek name for a small cake, and the expression hardly fostered Egyptian self-pride.

Egypt became a Roman province in 30 BC, after the suicide of Queen Cleopatra, and it was the Romans who started the removal of the ancient treasures – a practice followed by subsequent invaders and visitors right down to the present century. The Romans took several obelisks, the tall pyramid-topped columns used as memorials.

Western European interest in Egypt flagged after the fall of Rome, but by the 16th century travellers were once again visiting the country, which had become part of the Ottoman Empire in AD 1517. The pyramids aroused wild speculation. Some people surmised correctly that they were tombs. But others looked for more fanciful explanations, attributing to them mystical and magical properties. A belief in the powers of the pyramids persisted into the 19th century, and vestiges remain today.

By the late 18th century, travellers from several nations had written detailed descriptions of many Egyptian monuments. However, one event in 1798 revived European fascination with Egypt on the grand scale – stimulating both scientific study and massive pillaging.

The French Invade

When French infantry under the command of Napoleon Bonaparte stormed ashore at Alexandria on July 2, 1798, their main aim was to emulate the army of Alexander the Great and subdue Egypt as a prelude to marching on India. But Napoleon's invasion had other purposes, too. With his troops and cannon, he brought another army – scholars excited by accounts of Egyptian antiquity and determined to record all aspects of it.

Napoleon's forces occupied Egypt for three years, until the British and Turks drove them out. In that time, the French scholars amassed enough information to fill a 19-volume work, *Description de l'Egypte*. As the volumes appeared, individual collectors and representatives of institutions such as the British Museum and the Louvre began a scramble to collect antiquities.

Many of the collectors were sincerely interested in Egypt's past, but even so they caused untold damage. One of the worst offenders was the Italian Giovanni Battista Belzoni (1778-1823), who shamelessly destroyed antiquities in his quest for papyri. 'Every step I took I crushed a mummy in some part or other,' he wrote of one of his forays.

A Champion Appears

The indiscriminate damage done by the Egyptologists, as the collectors came to be called, aroused the anger of the French antiquarian, Auguste Mariette (1821-1881) who waged a campaign against it.

It was an uphill struggle at first. Even Said Pasha, the ruler of Egypt, could barely be restrained from joining in the pillage. But eventually Mariette persuaded the Egyptian authorities to set up a national antiquities service to control excavations and the export of relics, and, in 1857, to put him in charge of it. He acquired the sole rights to excavate in Egypt, and fought long and hard to establish a museum of antiquities at Boulak, later moved to Cairo.

Napoleon saw himself as 'Great' in the tradition of Alexander. But as well as being a conqueror of other cultures, he took upon himself the very special role of recording and preserving the history of one of the world's greatest civilizations, that of ancient Egypt. His military campaign of 1798, which ended in the battle of the Nile, included among its personnel historians, artists and linguists; their job was to observe, record and interpret the ancient monuments and artefacts. Perhaps the greatest and most significant of these finds was the Rosetta Stone whose decipherment was the breakthrough in understanding the hieroglyphic writing system of the ancient Egyptians. All the material the expedition gathered was published in the 19-volume Description de l'Egypte.

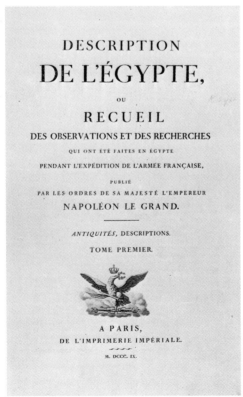

DESCRIPTION

DE L'ÉGYPTE,

ou

RECUEIL

DES OBSERVATIONS ET DES RECHERCHES

QUI ONT ÉTÉ FAITES EN ÉGYPTE

PENDANT L'EXPÉDITION DE L'ARMÉE FRANÇAISE,

PUBLIÉ

PAR LES ORDRES DE SA MAJESTÉ L'EMPEREUR

NAPOLÉON LE GRAND.

ANTIQUITÉS, DESCRIPTIONS.

TOME PREMIER.

A PARIS,
DE L'IMPRIMERIE IMPÉRIALE.

M. DCCC. IX.

Mariette's policies were largely followed by his successor, service, Gaston Maspero (1846-1910). During his directorship, an extraordinary cache of royal mummies was discovered near the temple of Hatshepsut at Deir-el-Bahri. Maspero revoked the monopoly of excavation, and among the beneficiaries was the Englishman Sir William Flinders Petrie (1853-1942).

Petrie was employed by the Egypt Exploration Fund, set up in 1882, to promote scientific excavation and restoration of monuments and to publish the results. He was a meticulous and prolific excavator.

Tomb of the Boy-King

The Valley of the Kings at Thebes is a dry water-course on the west bank of the Nile, and the burial place of the rulers of Egypt during the New Kingdom, from 1567 to 1085 BC. The existence of the tombs was known to the Greek and Roman rulers of Egypt, but over the centuries, robbers removed most of the treasures. In 1902, an American, Theodore M. Davis, was granted the right to excavate in the Valley. His team, including the Englishman Howard Carter (1873-1939), found a series of hitherto-untraced tombs, some rich in funeral ornaments.

After several successful years of exploration, Davis decided that the Valley had yielded all of its secrets. But Carter was convinced there was more to find, and with the financial support of Lord Carnarvon, he continued the excavations.

For six frustrating and fruitless years, Carter systematically surveyed the Valley floor. In 1922, during what was to have been his final season, an undisturbed tomb entrance was discovered. Lord Carnarvon was sent for from England, and Carter waited for his arrival before opening the tomb. His patience was rewarded, for inside was one of the most magnificent archaeological treasure-stores ever found.

The tomb was packed with precious objects, including gold figures and masks and precious jewellery. Investigation showed the tomb was that of the young, obscure king Tutankhamun, who ruled for nine years until 1352 BC, dying when he was about 19 years old. Unlike the other graves in the valley, his had not been pillaged centuries before – although there was evidence that it had been entered and resealed.

The treasures from it are on display in Cairo, but the work of describing in full all the artefacts found in the tomb is still going on. Carter himself spent 10 years alone just in removing them.

Tutankhamun's tomb *lay for centuries hidden and protected under the rubble created by the construction of the tomb of Rameses VI. Then, in 1922, the determined archaeologist, Howard Carter discovered the entrance. Just 3 months later, he was looking into the burial chamber itself. Below we see Carter, arm outstretched, and Lord Carnarvon, standing, looking into the innermost of the 3 gilt shrines which contained the royal sarcophagus. Inside this was the young king's mummy, its face overlaid with the magnificent mask of solid gold (right) which has come to be so familiar.*

VOICES FROM THE PAST

AMONG THE DISCOVERIES that most excited antiquarians and explorers from the 17th century onwards were the written records of ancient civilizations. If they could be deciphered, they would give a vivid new insight into the life and times of their authors.

Ancient, unfamiliar writing – on mud tablets, inscribed on the walls of palaces, fortresses and tombs, or on early forms of parchment or paper – present archaeologists and language experts with a problem somewhat like cracking a secret code.

The code-breakers have to look for clues. Does the language resemble any other known tongue? Do the symbols used represent letters of an alphabet, as they do in Latin and Greek and the scripts of modern western civilization? Or do they denote syllables, as some do in modern Japanese, or whole words, as in the picture-writing of the earliest-known scripts, found in the Middle East and dated to around 3500 BC?

The number of different symbols gives some guidance. If there are relatively few of them in the corpus of texts, the writing is likely to be alphabetic. But if there are hundreds or thousands, the script is probably syllabic or derived from picture-writing, or a mixture of both like various types of modern Chinese.

Some ancient writings have so far defied all attempts by scholars to decipher them – even when computers are used. The inscriptions of the Indus civilization, which flourished in southern Asia from about 2300 to 1700 BC, still remain a riddle, for example. Patient detective work has unravelled other ancient tongues – of Egypt, the Near East, Homeric Greece, and the Mayan civilization of central America.

Scholars anticipated that the Mayan writings would be priestly discourses on astronomy, a subject in which the Maya were known to be expert. Instead, translation revealed a grim record of dynastic struggles, violent wars and bloody triumphs, fundamentally changing the previous view of the Maya as a peaceful theocracy.

Riddle of the Glyphs

The Rosetta Stone was the most important discovery made by the French scholars who accompanied Napoleon during his invasion of Egypt. It is a slab of basalt found in 1799, on which a decree set out by King Ptolemy V in 196|BC is inscribed.

The decree is in three scripts – two forms of old Egyptian and one of Greek. The Greek

Jean-Francois Champollion *(1790-1832), the French Egyptologist, took 14 years of painstaking work to produce the first complete decipherment and translation of the Rosetta stone – the key that unlocked the mysteries of Egyptian hieroglyphs. By matching the hieroglyphs making up the name Ptolmys (Ptolemy) to their Greek equivalents, Champollion was able to work out the sound which each symbol represented.*

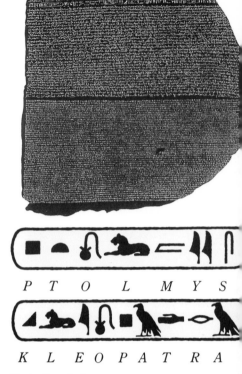

P T O L M Y S

K L E O P A T R A

writing was, of course, familiar to the scholars, so it gave an invaluable guide towards translating the Egyptian scripts – one of which uses picture symbols called hieroglyphs. The other is cursive, a style devised for speedier writing than was possible with the ornate hieroglyphs.

Attempts at decipherment started with the proper names. In the hieroglyphs, scholars agreed, those names would appear in cartouches, carved representations of clay seals. Some progress was made, but the scholars were considerably hampered by the mistaken assumption that the hieroglyphs were ideographic – that is, each symbol represents a complete word. In fact, as we now know, the glyphs are phonetic; each symbol denotes a sound.

The man whose intuition solved the riddle was Jean-Francois Champollion (1790-1832), a remarkable French-born linguist who, from 1809, devoted all his available time to the study of Egyptian manuscripts and inscriptions. Champollion had an intimate knowledge of Coptic, a language derived from ancient Egyptian. He was the first person to suspect that the hieroglyphs might be phonetic.

Examining the cartouches, Champollion was able to assign phonetic values to a number of symbols, enabling him to identify many personal names. Painstakingly, Champollion built up an

Old

With

A god

Egyptian *hieroglyphs included over 700 signs, such as those above.*

phabet from the inscriptions in the cartouches.
n 1823, the breakthrough came. Champollion
ealized that his alphabet of symbols formed the
reater part of the main text outside the
artouches of the Rosetta Stone. Could it be, he
vondered, that they were used phonetically
here, too?

Champollion tried the theory, and it worked.
Recognizable Coptic words sprang out at him
rom the text. He was able to produce the first
ull translation of the Rosetta Stone. But
Champollion's work drew mixed reactions. It
vas fully vindicated only in 1866, more than 30
ears after the Frenchman's death, when
nother bilingual inscription, the Decree of
Canopus, was translated using his system.

Victories of Darius

High upon cliffs near Behistun in what is now
western Iran is a lengthy inscription in three
ancient languages. It dates from the time of
Darius I, ruler of Persia from 521 to 486 BC.
The inscription includes an account of Darius's
victory over rebels against his authority, and
other events in his life.

Its decipherment was largely the work of a
brilliant British army officer and archaeologist,
Sir Henry Rawlinson (1810-1895). Perched on a
adder 100m (325ft) up the cliffside and aided by
a helper he described as 'a wild Kurdish boy',
Rawlinson copied the inscription, to try to
decipher it at his leisure.

The three languages – Old Persian,
Babylonian and Elamite – are written in
cuneiform (wedge-shaped) scripts typical of the
ancient Near East. Old Persian resembles
Avestan, the language in which the holy text of
the Zoroastrian religion is written, and that had
been translated by the mid-18th century.

Other scholars had already been working on
Old Persian, and had shown that its cuneiform
symbols are alphabetic. Independently of them,
Rawlinson deciphered the alphabet and was the
irst to translate the Old Persian text of
Behistun. Armed with that, he moved on to the
Babylonian inscription, which contains many
more symbols and was clearly syllabic.

As with the ancient Egyptian language, work
started with the proper names. By the 1850s,
many scholars were successfully reading
Babylonian.

Rawlinson did not attempt to decipher the
third language of the inscription, Elamite, which
was completely unknown. Excavations in the
ate 19th century revealed the hitherto-

unsuspected existence of the Sumerians who
spoke it, and yielded a body of texts that enabled
work on its decipherment to begin.

Forerunner of Greek

Linear B, the script on tablets found during
excavations at Knossos on Crete from 1899,
presented more problems for would-be
translators than either ancient Egyptian or
Babylonian had done. The language was
completely unknown. There were no bilingual
texts, nor any clues from recorded history about
what the tablets might contain.

An American scholar, Alice Kober (1907-
1950), eventually concluded the language was
inflected – that is, the word endings varied
according to the case of the nouns or the tense of
the verbs. She assembled an impressive array of
words that looked the same except for their
endings, and suggested grammatical values for
their endings.

After Alice Kober's death, her work was
continued by a Briton, Michael Ventris (1922-
1956), and by the early 1950s he had built up a
complete picture of the interrelationships of the
different symbols. What was lacking was any
idea of how they had been spoken.

Ventris eventually identified what seemed
likely to be the names of Cretan towns and
started trying some – Amnisos, Knossos,
Tylissos. The approach worked, and it gave him
the crucial key to the symbols. But it did more.
To Ventris's amazement, it revealed that the
language of the Linear B texts was a form of
ancient Greek, an idea that scholars had firmly
rejected many years before.

The Sumerians
*abandoned picture-
writing for cuneiform
symbols in the 3rd century
BC. A stylized picture of
grain (left) was drawn
sideways, then reduced to
four simple strokes. The
cuneiform tablet (above),
dating from 2050 BC, is a
receipt for a large number
of bronze and copper tools.*

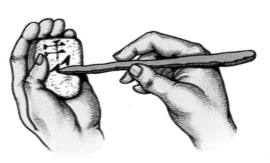

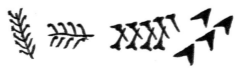

PALACES AND ROYAL GRAVES

CLAUDIUS RICH (1787-1821) owed his appointment as British Resident (diplomatic representative) in Baghdad, in his early 20s, largely to his extraordinary aptitude for languages. Although he spent most of his term of office in skilful diplomacy he found time to collect antiquities and to make detailed surveys of some of the ruins of Iraq, including the ancient cities of Babylon and Nineveh.

Rich's early death robbed archaeology of a fine scholar. But his collection of antiquities laid the foundation of the British Museum's Oriental Department, and the tradition he established of giving hospitality and encouragement to antiquarian-minded travellers was continued for many years by his successors in Baghdad and Iraq's second city, Mosul.

Among those who benefited from this hospitality was the English antiquarian and explorer Sir Austen Henry Layard (1817-1894). While in Mosul in the 1840s, he met the recently arrived French scholar Paul-Emile Botta (1802-1870) and visited his excavations.

Botta was looking for Nineveh, an important city of the Assyrian empire, which reached its height in the 8th and 7th centuries BC. The ruins of Nineveh were thought to be somewhere near Mosul, on the River Tigris.

The Kuyunjik mound in Mosul, which later turned out to be part of Nineveh, was Botta's first target for excavation. However, he soon transferred his attention to nearby Khorsabad. His discovery there of the spectacular remains of the palace of Sargon II, king of Assyria from 721 to 705 BC, prompted the French government to give him further generous financial support to continue excavations of the site.

Layard, meanwhile, had privately been given funds by the British Ambassador in Istanbul, Sir Stratford Canning, to excavate at Nimrud, also near Mosul. There he found two Assyrian palaces, which he thought were remnants of Nineveh. But Layard continued investigating Kuyunjik, claimed by the French as 'their' site.

In 1847, Layard found a corner of a building under the mound. Intensive excavations between 1849 and 1851 revealed that he had located the massive palace of Sennacherib, ruler of Assyria between 705 and 681 BC, conqueror of Babylon, and the man who rebuilt and extended Nineveh. Within the palace was Sennacherib's great library, providing a wealth of information about Assyrian life. Sennacherib's palace was in Nineveh itself, so Layard had succeeded where Botta had failed.

Destructive Digging

The British and French archaeologists who worked in Mesopotamia – the land between the Rivers Tigris and Euphrates, now mostly in Iraq – in the 1840s and 1850s did so under a handicap. The people and institutions financing their expeditions, among them the British Museum and the Louvre in Paris, expected instant and spectacular finds.

Despite any qualms among the excavators, that meant that the excavations were, in effect, little more than well-documented looting expeditions. Rivalry between France and Britain made it vital to stake national claims to sites by quickly digging into them. In the process, much information was destroyed.

Matters became even worse after the outbreak of the Crimean War in 1853. The officially sponsored British and French archaeological teams were recalled, leaving the field clear for illicit plundering by independent operators who were totally unhampered by scholarly considerations and motivated by sheer greed and the desire for profit.

This limestone slab, *comes from excavations a Nineveh, ancient capital of the Assyrian Empire. I was here that Sennacheri built his great palace. Looking at the three registers on the slab, from top to bottom, we see building materials being transported by boats on th River Tigris to the proposed site, which was surrounded by woods. In the site itself, workmen are moving a colossal bul from a quarry. The men shown atop the statue are actually alongside it and are carrying stonecutting tools. The wooden poles on the wheeled carts, above and behind, would have been used both to rol the statue and as general building material.*

Even after the teams returned from 1872, the independent ransack continued. But at least, towards the end of the century, archaeologists themselves began to employ more scientific techniques in the course of their work.

Babylon laid bare

By 1900, American and German archaeological teams were working alongside the British and French in Mesopotamia.

Robert Koldewey (1855-1926) excavated Babylon, which became the dominant city of Mesopotamia under its great lawgiving king Hammurabi in the 18th century BC. For 14 years from 1899, Koldewey carefully laid the site bare to reveal the stratigraphy and the ground-plans of ancient buildings. His fellow-German Walter Andrae (1875-1956) adopted the same approach at Assur on the River Tigris, the principal city of the Old Assyrian period.

During the early 20th century, archaeologists' attention began to shift from the relatively recent, massive and splendid cities to an earlier period in Mesopotamia's past. They sought information on the rise of civilization there and on the beginnings of agriculture.

Meanwhile, excavations continued at Nimrud, Nineveh and Khorsabad. Other ancient sites were uncovered, including Susa, capital of the Elamites and, for a time, of the Persian. At Mari in Syria, a French team discovered the remains of a palace, dating from before 2000 BC.

Links with the Bible

The earliest chapters of the Old Testament are largely set in Mesopotamia, and for that reason excavations there captured the imagination of scholars and the general public. This was never more so than in 1872 when a British Museum employee, George Smith (1840-1876), discovered among the museum's collection of clay tablets what appeared to be an incomplete account of the Biblical Flood.

When news of Smith's discovery became public, there was great excitement. The *Daily Telegraph* newspaper sponsored an expedition to the Near East to seek the missing portion of the tablet. Smith led the expedition and, incredibly, found what he was looking for just five days after beginning his work, in the piles of debris which had resulted from previous excavations of the Kuyunjik mound.

Ur, near the River Euphrates in what is now south Iraq, is familiar to students of the Bible as the home of Abraham. The site was excavated by Sir Leonard Woolley (1880-1960), revealing royal graves and also the bodies of people sacrificed, apparently willingly, to accompany their kings.

Woolley worked painstakingly to preserve the artefacts he found, and he even recovered a vanished object. Recognizing a series of small holes as traces of decayed wood, he filled them with plaster of Paris; the result was a cast of a wooden harp.

George Smith *(above) made one of the great contributions to archaeological and Biblical scholarship when, in 1872, after finding a partial account of the Flood, he led an expedition to the site of ancient Nineveh (left), where he successfully recovered the missing portion - in just 5 days.*

SCHLIEMANN'S ODYSSEY

THE *ILIAD* and the *Odyssey*, Homer's epic accounts of the siege of Troy and the wanderings of Odysseus, have enthralled people since they were composed more than 2500 years ago. In modern times, they were widely assumed to be just myths of ancient Greece, or at least a vague, highly embroidered version of the Greek past.

Heinrich Schliemann (1822-1890), a German self-made millionaire, was an exception. For decades, he was convinced that the world so poignantly depicted by Homer was a real one, tied to actual geography and genuine historical events. Schliemann was gripped by the immediacy of Homer's tale.

His fortune made, Schliemann retired from business and set out to prove that his belief was more than just a romantic notion. He went to Turkey, followed the topographical details Homer supplied and, in 1870, dug into a mound at Hissalik that his researches convinced him must be Troy. It was.

Schliemann's first excavation was energetic rather than scientific. But in subsequent work he was assisted by Wilhelm Dorpfeld (1853-1940), a German regarded as one of the finest field archaeologists of the day. After Schliemann's death, Dorpfeld continued the excavations.

The two also excavated Homeric sites on the Greek mainland – Mycenae, Tiryns and Orchomenos. As each spectacular find emerged, Schliemann kept the fascinated public aware of it through newspaper reports and rapid publication of results. Schliemann was in no doubt that at Troy he had located the treasures of Priam, the king killed when the city fell to the Greeks, or that graves containing exquisite gold work at Mycenae were those of Agamemnon and other semi-mythical Trojan War figures.

The story of *Heinrich Schliemann is one of a man driven by an obsession, a dream of finding Troy, the great city of legend, supposedly destroyed in antiquity. Schliemann kept his dream alive through a long, successful business career, during which he amassed the fortune that left him free to devote the remaining third of his life to archaeology – and his search. He astounded the world when he unearthed the walls of the city (below) in 4 periods of excavation, beginning in 1871 and continuing until his death in 1890.*

Later research has shown that many of Schliemann's finds are several centuries older than the dates he ascribed to them. Even so, his achievements were remarkable. He revealed the existence of Bronze Age civilization in the Aegean, and inspired many archaeologists to investigate it. And he certainly demonstrated most dramatically the potential archaeology possesses to illuminate the past.

Recreating the Bronze Age

From the 1890s, Schliemann's successors in the eastern Mediterranean began to build up a firm picture of the Bronze Age civilization he had identified. This was named Mycenaean, after Mycenae, and flourished from about 1600 to 1200/1150 BC.

The Mycenaeans evidently traded with ancient Egypt, and that helped in ascertaining when they had been at the height of their powers. Sir Flinders Petrie, who had done so much for Egyptian archaeology (see page 18), identified Egyptian pottery on a visit to Mycenae. From that, it was relatively easy to calculate the dates of the Mycenaeans. Petrie also brilliantly recognized hitherto unfamiliar pottery that had been found in Egypt as of Aegean origin – amazingly, even before examples of an identical style had been discovered in the Aegean zone itself.

Mycenaean influence was considerable in the eastern Mediterranean, from mainland Greece to Cyprus and the islands of the Aegean, and as far west as Italy. And Mycenaean rulers were obviously wealthy as well as powerful. Bodies found by Schliemann at Mycenae were heavily decked in gold jewellery.

From about the 15th or 14th century BC, chieftains lived in increasingly magnificent palaces such as those at Mycenae itself, Tiryns and Pylos. When these leaders died, they were buried in what are known as *tholos* tombs – dry stone, beehive-shaped structures with a long entrance passage.

While archaeologists fired by Schliemann's work were busy tracking down the Mycenaeans, others, including Dorpfeld at this time, were examining the classical age of Greece through excavations at Samothrace and at Olympia, home of the ancient games which were held every four years in honour of Zeus, father of the Greek gods. Meanwhile, on Crete the British archaeologist Sir Arthur Evans (1851-1941) was unearthing remnants of a civilization even older than that of the Mycenaeans.

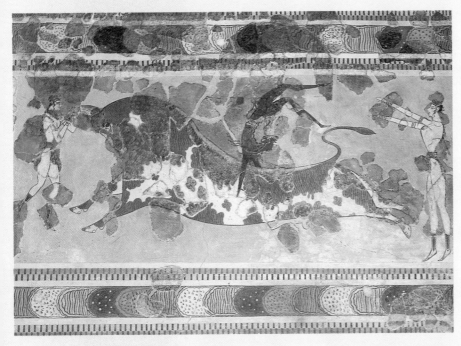

The finds at *Knossos paint a rich picture of a vibrant and prosperous civilization. The colonnaded halls and corridors of the great palace (above) are a striking feature. External colonnades would almost certainly have been surmounted by a motif of horns, recalling the bull cult that was so central to Minoan life. Scenes showing dancers with bulls (left) are common on the frescoes from Knossos and other Minoan sites.*

IN GREEK LEGEND, Minos was a king of Crete who kept a monster called the minotaur – half-human, half-bull – in a labyrinth in his palace. This creature was the offspring of the king's wife, Pasiphae, and was the result of her coupling with a white bull sent to her by the god Poseidon as a form of revenge against her family. Minos spent the final years of his reign living in a massive labyrinth, with Pasiphae and her strange love-child living at the centre. Archaeological research has shown that, like Homer's tales of Troy, the story was based on vague memories of a genuine past.

Schliemann himself had looked to Crete for the antecedents of Mycenaean civilization, but did not carry out excavations there. In 1899, Evans did – digging into an ancient mound at Kephala (Knossos). He discovered the remains of a palace far older than those of the Mycenaeans.

Beautiful frescoes, a throne and a massive granary containing enormous storage jars indicated that the palace had belonged to a wealthy ruler of a highly developed civilization. Evans named it Minoan, after King Minos.

An Egyptian stone figure with a dated inscription found in the great eastern court of the palace showed Evans that the Minoans had had contacts with Egypt long before the Mycenaeans did. Extensive work has shown the Minoan civilization to have reached its zenith between about 1950 and 1450 BC. After that, Knossos and most of Crete were controlled by the Mycenaeans.

In addition to the British venture, excavations at Knossos and elsewhere on Crete were carried out by French, German, American and Greek teams. Together, they built up a vivid picture of Minoan life. Palaces, settlements and tombs were found throughout the island.

Excitingly, those provided at least part of the answer to one mystery. Stylized sculptures of bull's horns and other depictions showed that the Minoans made a cult of the bull – perhaps the origin of the minotaur legend. The maze-like passages of the palace at Knossos could represent the labyrinth in which the beast was reputedly kept.

However, archaeological research revealed a new mystery, too. The Minoan civilization collapsed in around 1450 BC, but no one is yet sure why. One theory is that it was destroyed by the eruption of the nearby island-volcano of Thera, now Santorini – itself the home of an advanced society strongly under Minoan influence. But the Santorini eruption was in about 1500 BC. It showered Crete with volcanic ash, and, at about the same time, many of Crete's buildings were damaged by fire. Scholars are still puzzling over the cause of the Minoans' collapse, but it is probable that the Mycenaeans played some part. The eruption provided a magnificent bonus. On Thera (Santorini), huge drifts of volcanic ash engulfed whole areas, preserving buildings and their contents in good condition. Excavations are still going on. The exquisite frescoes in these houses have added further intimate details to our picture of life in the Minoan world.

SECRETS OF THE NEW WORLD

WHEN THE SPANISH and Portuguese conquered the Aztec and Inca empires of Central and South America in the 16th century, they collected a great deal of information about the cultures of their new subjects. Despite this, the European invaders gradually came to think of the native American Indians as a poor and barbaric race, incapable of great works of construction or the other hallmarks of civilization.

For that reason, the impressive ancient monuments of the Americas were attributed to a more or less unlikely collection of foreigners – the Vikings, the Welsh, the Chinese, the Phoenicians and the lost tribes of Israel. The tendency was particularly marked in North America, where many pioneers eased any qualms they might have felt about oppressing or slaughtering their victims by regarding them as unenlightened savages.

Nevertheless, as early as 1590 Jose de Acosta, a Spanish Jesuit, was arguing that the Americas had been colonized from Asia in prehistoric times via a land-bridge that had once connected the extreme north of the continents. His contemporary Diego de Landa (1542-1579) noted a continuity of culture between the ruins of the ancient Maya civilization in Central America and the art-forms of the Indians who populated the region in his day.

Relics of the Redskins
Early European settlers noted the burial mounds and earthworks of North America. But few were investigated until the mid-19th century, when conscientious antiquarians began to create the scientific basis of American archaeology.

In 1848, Ephraim Squier and E. H. Davis published their study of the mounds of Mississippi and Ohio. It showed that there were different types of mounds – those used for burials, others in the effigy of a beast or bird, and some that had been platforms for temples.

But the study revealed little about the people who had erected them, and Squiers and Davis concluded that the mound-builders were not native Americans. The antiquarians were wrong. We now know that the mounds were the work of settled farming communities hundreds of years before the arrival of Columbus and, even earlier, of settled hunter-gatherers who were part of a complex trading network.

Other scholars investigated the pueblo villages of flat-roofed stone or clay houses in the south-western United States, first built nearly 1000 years ago. The villagers' predecessors in the region had lived in pit-dwellings, and those were excavated, too.

The Earliest Americans
Jose de Acosta's belief that America had been colonized from Asia in prehistoric times gradually gained limited acceptance among scholars. In the 17th century, for example, the physical similarities between American Indians and the Mongoloid peoples of Asia were cited as further evidence of the theory. But it was not until the 19th century that de Acosta's view became widely held. And it was the early 20th century before solid archaeological clues to when the colonization took place started to emerge.

The search for the earliest American caught the public imagination, so much so that a whole army of tricksters claimed to have found his remains. In this climate of fraud, serious scholars had to exercize rigid scientific discipline, particularly as the most eminent physical anthropologist of the day, Ales Hrdlicka (1869-1943), declared magisterially that early man had not been present in America. Proof that he was began with the discovery in 1925 of an arrowhead with the bones of an extinct type of bison, at Folsom in New Mexico.

Subsequent finds at a number of sites present unimpeachable evidence of the existence of 'palaeo-Indians' who arrived across the land-bridge from Asia and gradually spread southwards. But precisely when that happened is still a matter of fierce controversy. The available archaeological evidence indicates that people were living in the far north more than 25,000 years ago, and that some had moved

Serpent Mound, *Ohio, USA, is typical of the many burial mounds and earthworks built in North America between 1000 BC and 600 AD. The precise significance of these mounds remains a mystery, but they were probably linked with religious and mythical practices.*

further south before the way was blocked by ice-sheets 18,000 years ago. When the ice-sheets began to retreat 4,000 years later, colonization developed on a large scale.

In Search of Lost Cities

While many American antiquarians were primarily concerned during the 19th century with relics of their own country, some looked further south. One of them was John Lloyd Stephens (1805-1852), who was a prominent lawyer, writer and amateur politician.

He and the talented English artist Frederick Catherwood (1799-1854) were intrigued by rumours of long-lost cities in the Yucatan peninsula of Central America. Between 1839 and 1842, they braved the jungle and its suspicious or hostile inhabitants to investigate, finding five – Copan, Quirigua, Palenque, Uxmal and Chichen Itza. All were virtually unknown, except to the local Indians.

Four of the cities had been built by the Maya, whose civilization reached its heights from about AD 300 to 900. The fifth, Chichen Itza, also bore traces of Maya building, but it was predominantly a city of the Toltecs, the warrior culture that flowered during the 300 or so years following the Maya's decline.

The Mystery of Tiahuanaco

European archaeologists became fascinated in the 1870s by the Inca civilization of the Andes. From 1877, they excavated sites in Peru – including the pilgrimage centre of Pachacamac.

The German linguist Max Uhle (1856-1944) was in charge at Pachacamac. By studying

pottery and sculpture, he identified four chronological periods in Peruvian history prior to the downfall of the Incas. The classifications, modified only slightly, are still used today, and Uhle is acknowledged as the founder of Peruvian archaeology.

Uhle also helped to prepare the first authoritative book about one of the most mysterious of the Andean ancient sites, Tiahuanaco in Bolivia. Its vast and impressive ruins include the magnificent Gateway of the Sun. The site is thought to have been a religious centre, and perhaps a powerful city-state, too. Local tradition says that Tiahuanaco was already in ruins when the Inca empire was at its height and, thanks in part to Uhle's chronology, it has been shown that Tiahuanaco represents a period well before the Incas. Modern dating indicates that the site was occupied from about 1500 BC, and was at its zenith between AD 300 and 700.

The Temple of Inscriptions, *at the Mayan city of Palenque, Mexico, dating from the 7th century AD, was discovered in 1949. It contains a massive, elaborately carved sarcophagus and a wealth of grave goods. Palenque was abandoned in 810 – the beginning of the Mayan collapse.*

The Gateway of the Sun *found at Tiahuanaco, Bolivia, built about AD 600, is the most spectacular surviving monument of the mysterious Andean civilization which pre-dated the Incas by several hundred years.*

LURE OF THE ORIENT

THE MAGNIFICENT MONUMENTS of India intrigued and impressed European travellers from the 16th century onwards, and several made detailed records of them. In 1784, the foundation of the Asiatic Society of Bengal put their work on a firm footing. The society aimed to inquire widely into the arts and sciences of Asia, and its members published papers on coins and literature, as well as on ancient inscriptions and manuscripts and on archaeology.

One of the society's most eminent members was James Prinsep (1799-1840). He succeeded in deciphering the Brahmi and Kharoshti scripts of ancient India, thus making available a wealth of new background information, in particular on the empire of Ashoka, who ruled most of India in the 3rd century BC.

The formation of the Archaeological Survey of India in 1861, under the direction of General Sir Alexander Cunningham (1814-1893), promoted further study of the sub-continent's history, notably of the sites associated with Buddhism, the main religion of India for many centuries. Architectural surveys by James Fergusson (1808-1886) and James Burgess (1832-1916) provided excellent, accurate and detailed reports of many of these sites.

However, it was not until the appointment of Sir John Marshall (1876-1956) as director-general in 1901 that excavation and conservation came to form an important part of the

This view of the citadel *at Mohenjo Daro, as seen from the north-west, shows the 'college' in the immediate foreground. This is another of the highly developed building complexes situated on the western mound of the site. This mound was on higher ground, well above the water table, and therefore not only in a better state of preservation, but also far easier to excavate.*

Mohenjo Daro, *first excavated in 1922, proved itself to be an important site of the Indus civilization, only just identified the previous year. The citadel, one of its two characteristic mounds, contained the great bath complex (shown above), used for ritual ablutions. It may also have served as the residence of the priests.*

Archaeological Survey's work. Aspects of Marshall's excavation techniques have been criticized by people who subsequently investigated sites he had uncovered (*see page 31*). But he undoubtedly widened the Survey's field of activities.

In the 1920s, its archaeologists began excavating the ruins of Mohenjo Daro and Harappa, in the north-west of the sub-continent. They were the chief cities of the Indus civilization, which reached its height between about 2300 and 1750 BC. The excavations dramatically revealed the unsuspected antiquity of Indian civilization, which scholars had previously thought evolved much later, well into the 1st millenium BC.

One of the most remarkable attributes of the Indus peoples was their skill in town-planning. Their cities and towns were laid out on two mounds. The lower mound was the residential part of the town, divided into a neat grid pattern of two-storeyed houses with courtyards.

On the upper mound there were municipal and religious buildings. The great bath at Mohenjo Daro, which was probably used in religious rituals, is among the most magnificent of these.

Cleanliness was obviously extremely important to the Indus civilization. Most houses in Mohenjo Daro and Harappa had bathrooms and latrines, from which waste was carried off

y a highly developed system of covered drains
unning through the city.

Caravans of Silk

During the last years of the 19th century,
cholars were intrigued by ancient manuscripts,
ome in unknown languages, originating from the
esert region of Chinese Turkestan. Sir Aurel
tein (1862-1943), an archaeologist of Hungarian
irth and British nationality, determined to
stablish their significance. Following the trail of
he manuscripts, he uncovered a remarkable
orld in the wastes of central Asia, during three
xpeditions between 1900 and 1916.

In ancient times, this now-barren region lay
n a great trade route linking east to west. Along
travelled merchants bringing luxuries such as
hinese silk to India and, eventually, to Rome,
reece and the Near East. In the opposite
irection, Buddhist missionaries carried their
aith so successfully to China, at about the same
me that Christianity was spreading through
urope, that Chinese Buddhists were soon
ppearing as pilgrims in India.

Stein explored and excavated Buddhist caves,
emples and houses, the caravanserais where
ravellers and their pack-animals rested, and the
uard-posts at the limit of China's Han empire.
t Miran, he found a Buddhist shrine decorated
a a style reflecting the meeting of east and west,
nd at Tun-Huang he investigated the Hall of
000 Buddhas. There, Stein made what, to him,
ere his most important discoveries – a series of
ilk temple banners and a vast cache of sacred
uddhist manuscripts.

But at other sites the dry desert air had
reserved a wealth of more ordinary artefacts.
hey ranged from goods made of felt to ancient
ooden chopsticks and a unique form of guitar,
he strings of which were broken.

China Reawakens

he Chinese developed an interest in their past
uring the centuries immediately before the time
f Christ, studying artefacts and ruins that were
ncient even then. But gradually what had been a
udding science stagnated into mere hoarding of
ld objects. Active interest in archaeology lay
ormant and was rekindled in China only around
he turn of this century.

One of those responsible for the reawakening
as a Swedish geologist, J. Gunnar Andersson
1874-1960). In 1921, he discovered a Neolithic
illage at Yang Shao, in central China.
xcavations showed that the inhabitants were

cultivating crops, mainly millet, more than 5000
years ago. Stone axes and decorated pottery
were also found.

Yang Shao alone would have assured
Andersson's place in the history of archaeology.
But he was also responsible for another great
discovery when, in 1926, the excavations he had
initiated at Choukoutien yielded teeth of one of
our early ancestors, Peking Man (see page 16).

Between 1928 and 1935, teams led by
Chinese archaeologists excavated a series of
sites around Anyang. They were drawn to the
area initially because some local farmers had
found inscribed bones that were used in
divination by the ancient Chinese. The work
started in 1928 continues today – revealing the
extraordinary wealth and technical expertise of
the earliest known Chinese civilization. For
Anyang was the last capital of the Shang
dynasty, rulers of part of what is now China from
about 1850 BC to 1030 BC, and was a royal city
for some 300 years.

Finds made there include several royal tombs
containing not only the remains of the monarch,
but also the skeletons of many victims of human
sacrifice. There are beautiful ivory carvings,
and splendid weapons and ceremonial vessels of
bronze. Shang craftsmen had also developed an
advanced technique for casting complex bronze
objects in elaborate piece-moulds; this was a skill
which was totawlly unknown elsewhere in the
world during that era.

The bronze works *of
the Shang Dynasty
demonstrate its high level
of sophistication and
artistic development. This
fan ding, or sacrificial
food vessel, was excavated
in 1950 at Anyang, the
ancient Shang capital
until about 1100 BC. It is
approximately 22cm
(9 in) high and the
quality and detail of the
relief dates it to the late
Shang Period, just prior
to the Chou conquest.*

DIGGING UP THE PAST

A poignant reminder *of the power and influence of nature in man's history. This cast is from Pompeii and the victim was one of several beggars who were struck down by the Vesuvian eruption, just outside the Nucerian Gate to the east of the city. A bag, still full of alms, was found next to him. The shape itself was reconstructed by pouring plaster of Paris into the cavity which remained in the ash which hardened around the decomposing body. Many such casts have been made of the 2000 inhabitants killed in AD 79 and the images they present give us a very clear picture of daily life in a typical Roman town.*

DURING THE LATER l8th century and throughout most of the l9th century, excavation was a popular activity, combining entertainment with treasure-hunting. In England, for example, the well-to-do hired labourers to dig trenches through ancient burial mounds. When the trench had almost reached the level at which finds could be expected, the gentry appeared to watch the final stage. Valuable and 'interesting' artefacts were removed, and everything else was ignored or even destroyed. The site was then abandoned or ploughed over.

The same was true throughout the civilized world. The kings of Naples sponsored forays into the volcanic materials covering Pompeii and Herculaneum in search of statues. European explorers – and archaeologists – dynamited their way into Egypt's pyramids and tombs. In Mesopotamia, rival expeditions sank holes into mounds simply to establish their claim to dig at the site later.

There were some lights in the darkness. Thomas Jefferson, president of the USA from 1801 to 1809, exercised great care when he excavated a burial mound in Virginia in 1784 to try to settle arguments about who built it. He did not manage to resolve the dispute, but his patient work established that it had been built in a series of stages, with six layers of bodies, buried at different times, each separated from the other by layers of soil and stones.

Half a century later, in Denmark, the young J.J. Worsaae was equally meticulous. While still in his teens, Worsaae began gaining the experience on which he based his principles of pre-excavation surveys, stratigraphy and recording of all finds (*see page 12*). But Worsaae, like Jefferson, was unusual among his contemporaries, and it took many years for his approach to gain general acceptance.

Probing Pompeii

One sign of a changing trend in archaeology came in 1860, when the Italian Giuseppe Fiorelli (1823-1896) took over responsibility for the investigations at Pompeii. His immediate predecessors had already abandoned the random digging of the first statue-hunters, but Fiorelli imposed a new discipline. He was deeply interested in the everyday lives of the inhabitants of the long-buried city, and to learn as much as he could about their existence, he painstakingly excavated remains of the ancient *insulae*, the Roman tenements, block by block and layer by layer.

That was only the first of Fiorelli's innovations. He also developed a method of pouring plaster into cavities in the ash which had buried Pompeii when Vesuvius erupted in AD 79, and subsequently hardened. When the plaster set and the surrounding ash was removed, Fiorelli was left with a cast of the shape of the cavity itself.

The shapes were often instantly recognizable as organic material that had decayed after the ash had engulfed it – bodies of humans and animals, furniture and wooden structures. Fiorelli's casts recreated their external appearance in minute detail.

German Precision

From the 1870s, German archaeologists contributed greatly to the development of a scientific approach to archaeology. Ernst Curtius (1814-1896) carried out excavations at Olympia in Greece to an extremely high standard. One of those who trained under him there was Wilhelm Dorpfeld, who later lent his expertise to Schliemann's work at Troy (*see pages 24-25*).

In Mesopotamia, Robert Koldewey and Walter Andrae adopted similarly rigorous methods. They were the first to succeed in tracing courses of ancient mud-brick. The bricks were identical in composition to the soil surrounding them, and because of this had not been detected by earlier excavators.

Andrae also pioneered the use of the deep sounding form of exploratory excavation – that is, digging deeply in a relatively small area to establish the stages in the development of a site. It enabled him to trace the history of the Temple of Ishtar in the Assyrian city of Assur back to its origins as an early Sumerian shrine.

In Turkestan, Hubert Schmidt (1864-1933), a pupil of Dorpfeld, foreshadowed modern archaeological methods in his excavations of the mounds of Anau, the site of settlements from the later Stone Age to the Iron Age. He employed experts from other scientific fields to do detailed analyses of human and animal bones, remnants of cultivated grain and metal objects as they were uncovered.

The General's Principles

Many people of many nationalities contributed to the development of a truly scientific approach to archaeology throughout the course of the 19th century. But the man who is generally credited with making the first real steps towards establishing scientific base of archaeology was a British general, Augustus Henry Pitt-Rivers (1827-1900).

In 1880, Pitt-Rivers inherited a large estate including part of Cranborne Chase in Dorset – an area of England which is particularly rich in both prehistoric and ancient monuments. Retired from the army after a distinguished career and with a considerable fortune at his disposal, Pitt-Rivers set about excavating the monuments on his own lands.

He approached this task with rigid military discipline. Each site had to be excavated in full. The precise location of every artefact had to be recorded. Pitt-Rivers insisted that no relic was too trivial to consider; on the contrary, he asserted, for the true archaeologist, everyday objects are more valuable as a guide to the past than precious ones are.

Pitt-Rivers also developed and extended the layer-by-layer stratigraphic excavation techniques which were first used by Worsaae. He published his findings quickly and in comprehensive detail, in a four-volume study that is regarded as exemplary even today.

But Pitt-Rivers's methods were not adopted by other archaeologists overnight. Nearly 30 years after the general's death, Sir John Marshall was excavating sites in India in his capacity as director-general of the Archaeological Survey – a post to which he had been appointed because of his supposed knowledge of current excavation techniques (see page 28). Yet according to Sir Mortimer Wheeler (1890-1976), a major figure in the development and dissemination of scientific excavation techniques, Marshall dug the sites 'like potatoes'.

Wor Barrow *(left and below), a typical Neolithic barrow, or burial mound, in Dorset, was excavated in 1883 by Pitt-Rivers. Although the techniques employed were rather crude, the carefully kept research notes are an early example of fine archaeological recording. Three layers were unearthed: a Roman layer about 51cm (20½ in) deep; a Bronze Age layer to a a depth of 75cm (2½ ft); and a Stone Age layer down to 2.4m (8ft). Below that he found layers of chalk. The position of each skeletal remain or artefact was meticulously indicated on a scaled plan of the site.*

PATHS OF EVOLUTION

Since Darwin's *theory of evolution, scientists have been seeking to reconstruct mankind's past, especially looking f[or] 'missing links' which would testify to leaps up the evolutionary ladder. Unfortunately, dedicati[on] to scientific truth can become victim to the need for recognition and acclaim. Here we see scientists examining the Piltdown skull, with its human skull and ape-lik[e] jaw 'discovered' by Dawson in 1912. It was not until newly available advanced dating techniques were applied t[o] the remains in 1953 that [it] was shown to be a forgery. The bones were, in fact, modern.*

AS ARCHAEOLOGICAL KNOWLEDGE has accumulated, scholars have become increasingly aware that mankind's development around the world has not followed a single evolutionary course in which progress was inevitable. Civilizations not only rose, but fell, sometimes to be replaced by others. Nor could stages be defined in which progressively more civilized features emerged. The most striking anomaly was the extraordinary cave art during the Upper Palaeolithic era in Europe. It seemed inappropriate to such a primitive phase and was not subsequently built upon, but lost.

In the face of such evidence, intellectual opinion moved away from the theory of uniform stages and inevitable progress. Two contrasting views came to replace that theory, and dominated the study of European prehistory until recently. The false dichotomy is gradually being dispelled.

One school of thought held that inventions and advances took place in one specially-favoured area of the world, and spread out. Its most extreme exponents, the 'hyperdiffusionists', were led by Sir Grafton Elliot Smith (1871-1937), the prominent Australian physical anthropologist and anatomist. His study of the processes used in Egyptian mummification convinced him that Egypt was the favoured area. Such techniques, the building of megaliths, metallurgy, and civilization itself had all developed in Egypt, in Elliot Smith's opinion, and were spread by the Egyptians to areas in which they visited or settled.

At the opposite extreme were the nationalist[s,] a school of European archaeologists who insisted that the development of mankind in Europe had been a wholly indigenous process. That led to national rivalries and, in its more chauvinistic form, to the unfortunate acceptance of several hoaxes such as Piltdown Man (*see pag[e] 133*) and Glozel (*see page 143*). Both answered a yearning for national priority in major developments – Piltdown, for the British, in the search for man's earliest ancestors, and Glozel, for the French, in the origins of civilization.

At the furthest fringe of nationalism, Gustaf Kossinna (1858-1931) reversed the diffusionist[s'] routes and distorted archaeological data to demonstrate, falsely, that a 'pure master race' o[f] Aryans was responsible for the development of civilization throughout Europe.

The Lure of Chronology

Whatever their views on the mechanisms behind cultural changes, archaeologists of the late 19th and early 20th century were preoccupied with establishing regional sequences of development based on changes in artefact types. The relative chronology of these types was determined from their stratigraphic relationships in excavations.

In France, rich in Palaeolithic material, Gabriel de Mortillet (1828-1898) proposed a series of chronological stages based on variations in stone tools and to some extent in associated fauna. This scheme was refined by the great French Palaeolithic archaeologist, the Abbe Breuil (1877-1961). He made particular use of 'type fossils' – artefacts equivalent to the animal fossils chosen by geologists to characterize stratigraphic chronological divisions.

Other scholars subdivided the later epochs of the European past. Foremost among them was the Swedish archaeologist Oscar Montelius (1843-1921), who proposed divisions of the Neolithic period in northern Europe, each characterized by different forms of stone tools and megalithic tombs. Similar systems devised by others were based on typological changes in pottery, bronze and iron swords, stone and bronze axes and so on.

These schemes were generally applicable only to a particular region, but some attempts were made to produce broad syntheses of European prehistory. Joseph Dechelette (1862-1914) did so in France, as did the *Reallexicon der Vorgeschichte* edited by Max Ebert (1879-1929) in Germany.

The American Approach

American archaeologists, in the first half of this century, were just as preoccupied by chronology as their counterparts in Europe but approach was rather different.

Dendrochronology – the use of the annual rings of certain trees in dating (*see page 135*) – enabled the age of many Pueblo villages in the south-west of the USA to be determined quite precisely. Since many American sites had shallow deposits lacking stratigraphy, relative chronology often depended on seriation, or sequence-dating – the chronological ordering of groups of artefacts on the basis of similarities in their composition (*see pages 130-31*). But stratigraphy was not ignored, and played a part, for example, in the work of Alfred Kidder (1855-1963) at Pecos in Texas.

Another major difference from Europe was that archaeology in America developed alongside anthropology, in some respects as a junior branch of it. As a result, many archaeologists focused their attention on the cultural history of groups of surviving American Indians, such as the pueblo-dwellers of the south-west and the horse-riding Plains Indians. Little attempt was made to consider broad overall trends in American prehistory.

One exception was the 'archaic hypothesis' proposed by Herbert Spinden (1879-1967). He envisaged a basic American culture, practising farming and making pottery, that spread throughout the continent of North America from the Valley of Mexico. Although the pattern of development was later shown to be far more complex than Spinden himself had thought, his hypothesis was an important stimulus to the growth of American archaeology.

This site is *typical of Pueblo cliff dwellings in the south-western United States. They are remarkably sophisticated structures to have been developed by a civilization we consider primitive. Because the environment is hot and relatively free from rainfall, the degree of preservation both of the homes and their contents is high. As a result, modern archaeologists have been able to create a fairly full picture of the lives of this ancient Indian people.*

How Cultures Spread

THE VIEWS OF Elliot Smith and the hyperdiffusionists remained popular for several decades. But by the 1930s, a less extreme theory of the diffusion of culture was becoming accepted among archaeologists in Europe.

The man with whom this change in attitudes is most often associated is Gordon Childe (1892-1957), an Australian who settled in Britain. Childe, who had an amazing grasp of European languages, studied both excavated material and publications from all over Europe. In 1925, he produced a major synthesis which represented the fruits of his research, in his book *The Dawn of European Civilization*.

Childe introduced the important concept, already in vogue among some German archaeologists, of 'archaeological cultures'. Such cultures are ethnically or socially distinctive groups that can be distinguished from each other by their characteristic artefacts. Variations in the non-functional aspects of artefacts are taken as an expression of variations in cultural conventions. Childe's extensive body of work fostered a pan-European view of the past and counteracted the narrow preoccupation with regional chronologies. It also concerned itself with the mechanisms behind major technological and socio-economic changes in prehistory.

Oriente Lux

Like the hyperdiffusionists, Childe believed that many innovations in human development had originated in the Near East, among them farming, metallurgy and urban life. They had spread from there to Europe, and ultimately throughout the whole of the Old World. But Childe disagreed with the hyperdiffusionists about how the process of diffusion had actually taken place.

The hyperdiffusionists contended that the natives of the lands to which the Egyptians introduced the benefits of civilization had previously been existing in a condition of low savagery. Childe argued that the prehistoric societies of Europe were vigorous and independent, adapting developments and inventions that had spread from the Near East to their own cultures and needs.

Thus, according to Childe, the manifestation in Europe of new ideas and technology from the east was essentially European. This view of development came to be called 'modified diffusionism', and went part of the way towards reconciling the hyperdiffusionist and nationalist schools of archaeology.

5000 years of History

Childe's modified diffusionist approach eventually gained wide acceptance among western European archaeologists. It was attractive because it offered a partial solution to the question of chronology that continued to preoccupy scholars in the years between the two World Wars.

Historical records give a firm chronology for the Near East back to 3000 BC. Datable Egyptian material in the Aegean had allowed Sir Flinders Petrie and Sir Arthur Evans to give historical dates respectively to the Mycenaean and Minoan Bronze Age civilizations. Using the same method of cross-dating, though on less reliable ground, Childe and others attempted to date prehistoric cultures which had existed in the rest of Europe.

Two key links were perceived as being highly significant from their point of view: the megaliths of western Europe, some of which resembled Aegean tombs, and the apparently striking similarities between the finds from sites with early metallurgy in the Balkans and those from datable Troy.

The acceptance of Near Eastern origins for many of mankind's advances made it possible for European archaeologists to date their material. If, however, the Near East had been denied its priority, for pre-war archaeologists, all possibility of dating European prehistory would have vanished.

Looking at the Landscape

Not every archaeologist remained obsessed by chronology during the inter-war years. Some turned their attention to the factors that lay behind the Near East's emergence as a birthplace of farming and cradle of civilization, while others looked at the environmental conditions affecting patterns of prehistoric settlement.

Meanwhile, science had given archaeologists an important new tool, in the form of aerial photography. The earliest air photo had been taken from a balloon over Paris in 1858, and by the 1900s scholars were taking a bird's eye view of many ancient sites.

The greatest pioneer of aerial photographs was O. G. S. Crawford (1886-1957). In 1928, he co-authored *Wessex from the Air*, a classic photographic study of one of England's richest archaeological areas. It revealed a host of hitherto unsuspected sites, as well as unnoticed features of known ones.

Aerial photography
*has provided
archaeologists with a
valuable tool for studying
ancient sites. The
technique was pioneered
by O.G.S. Crawford (left)
who began taking
photographs from balloons
around the turn of the
century. Crawford was
co-author of the classic
work* Wessex from the
Air, *published in 1928.
The book contains more
than 300 aerial
photographs, including
Hod Hill (far left), an
Iron Age fort captured by
the Romans in AD 63.*

Careful Techniques

During the inter-war years, excavation
principles and techniques were steadily refined,
in line with the growing awareness of the kinds
of information that could be recovered from the
soil. Massive walls and glorious artefacts ceased
to be the main targets of investigation.

In particular, delicate methods were needed to
uncover the prehistoric settlements of Europe,
where the main traces of occupation were
complicated horizontal spreads of postholes and
pits. Among the pioneers was Werner Buttler
(1907-1940), who excavated the great German
Neolithic settlement of Koln-Lindenthal.

Not all archaeologists absorbed the lessons of
such careful excavators and their predecessors.
In 1954, Sir Mortimer Wheeler, the doyen of
20th-century field archaeology, denounced the
incompetents in his manual *Archaeology from the
Earth*. Wheeler, whose field experience spanned
more than half-a-century, was particularly harsh
on the then widespread practice of digging by
fixed levels. He eloquently argued the case for
excavation by stratigraphic deposits, the working
method now generally accepted by archaeologists
worldwide (*see pages 76-7*).

THE DATING REVOLUTION

The discovery *of the technique of radiocarbon dating by Professor W.F. Libby, in 1949, radically changed the face of archaeology. Now scientific method could accurately date objects which before could only be placed in time by a careful balancing of their provenance (where they were found) and what else was known about the site and similar objects. Here Professor Libby is shown with the Nobel Prize he won in 1960.*

IN 1949, PROFESSOR Willard F. Libby (1908-), a chemist at the US Institute for Nuclear Studies in Chicago, announced a discovery that was to win him the Nobel Prize and to precipitate a revolution in archaeology. He had found a method of obtaining the absolute age of organic archaeological material by measuring the level of the radioisotope carbon 14 it contains, hence the method is called radiocarbon dating.

Previously, all dates for prehistoric Europe had depended on the assumption of the chronological priority of the Near East, held by diffusionists such as Gordon Childe. Now Europe could be dated independently, and that assumption challenged.

The Near Eastern historical chronology, in any case, went back only to about 3000 BC, and dates before then had been a matter of conjecture. Radiocarbon dating is accurate on material up to 40,000 years old.

Scholars had argued that farming communities had emerged in the Near East in around 4500 BC, and that farming had reached Britain in about 2000 BC. Carbon-14 dates at Jericho and at Durrington Walls in England suggested that agriculture began in the Near East at least 2000 years earlier than originally thought, and before 2500 BC in Britain. The findings were initially greeted with disbelief. But by the 1960s, enough consistent carbon 14 dates had been obtained to win general acceptance both for this extended Neolithic chronology and for the reliability of radiocarbon dating itself.

The technique has given archaeology a much broader perspective. Because it can provide relatively precise dates for material from all over the world, it allows archaeologists to compare the stages of human development in different regions at the same time. For instance, it has demonstrated that farming began in the millennia which followed the end of the last Ice Age in the Near East, south-east Asia and Central and South America.

Not When, but Why?

Radiocarbon dating released archaeologists from a narrow preoccupation with dating. Since the question 'when?' could now often be answered, other questions began to assume more importance, in particular 'why?'.

That had become a more urgent concern because radiocarbon dating had itself upset the generally accepted picture of the past. In particular, it showed that the period of time between the earliest farming settlements and the development of urban communities was far greater than anyone thought. Recognition of that fact gave new impetus to efforts to determine how and why the transformation from village to town took place.

Similarly, scholars tried to find out why, in different regions of the world, people should have taken to farming at about the same time. Part of the cause is generally accepted to have stemmed from environmental changes which followed the end of the last Ice Age, but archaeologists are still endeavouring to assess the impact of those changes on the inhabitants of other regions where farming settlements did not emerge then.

In areas such as Australia and the New World that are not linked to the historical chronology of the Old World, radiocarbon dating made it possible to establish and date cultural sequences. That, for example, enabled scholars to understand for the first time the pattern of man's colonization throughout the world during the last Ice Age.

A Widening Interest

Radiocarbon dating was not the only major development in archaeology in the years immediately following the Second World War, although it was undoubtedly the most significant. American archaeologists, especially, began to move towards the innovative idea of carrying out regional surveys, instead of the traditional approach of simply concentrating on individual archaeological sites.

Such surveys, which document the history of human settlement within a given region, throw light on changing trends in population growth and distribution, and on the very definite impact environment has on human settlement patterns. These surveys have become a vital part of archaeological research today.

The wide-ranging and detailed aerial photography carried out for military reasons during the war also benefited archaeologists, particularly as many of them were enlisted as air photo interpreters during the hostilities. Aerial photographs of North Africa, for example, revealed the position of the Roman frontier zone, with its extensive building works. In Italy photos showed a crowded landscape of ancient settlements in the Tavoliere region, a notoriously backward area in recent centuries. In addition, thousands of Etruscan tombs that had escaped the ravages of earlier treasure-hunters were suddenly revealed.

It might be *said that archaeology is the determined search for details of mankind's past. In some cases, the past is revealed within a relatively short period, as here when it took just two centuries; but it was only the advance of underwater archaeological techniques that made it possible. In 1749, the Dutch East Indies ship* Amsterdam *was wrecked off Hastings and sank in 9m (30ft) of quicksand seabed. Recovery was impossible until 1965 when a limited excavation showed the presence of many objects. A foundation set up by the Dutch government undertook the work in earnest and has sponsored surveys of the site since 1975. Here we see Dutch scientists recording details of the structure (above) and taking samples of wood from the ship (left).*

ARCHAEOLOGY TODAY

RADIOCARBON DATING was the first major breakthrough in establishing the timetable of the past, and most scholars welcomed it. But some had doubts, and those doubts increased as discrepancies between carbon-14 dates and known historical dates began to emerge.

Dendrochronology, or tree-ring dating, (see pages 134-35) was used to cross-check radiocarbon techniques, and as a result they have now been modified and their accuracy considerably improved. The results of this cross-checking drove the final nails into the diffusionist coffin so far as Europe is concerned. Carbon-14 dating has definitively shown that the supposed links between the Near East and Europe, by which civilization was claimed to have spread, are chronologically impossible.

Conventional radiocarbon dating has thus been of great importance to archaeology. But it has drawbacks. It can be performed only on organic remains, of which relatively large samples have hitherto been needed, and its range of around 40,000 years confines it to the most recent chapters of the human story.

Recent scientific developments partly offset these shortcomings. New scientific equipment allows carbon-14 dates to be obtained from smaller samples, and promises to extend the date-range considerably, probably to 100,000 years (see page 138).

Other physical dating techniques have been developed, too – many of them by-products of research into radioactivity. Some have strange-sounding names. T-L, for example, is used to date relatively recent pottery. K/Ar, fission track and USD dating all depend on radioactive decay, and reach back into the far-distant past.

The result of these advances is that archaeologists now have a timescale against which man's evolution can be viewed. The timescale can be stated confidently for most parts of the world. And it is far longer than had previously been imagined.

Detective Work

Aerial reconnaissance has been used by archaeologists since the turn of the century, and geophysical surveying devices have been in archaeological use since the 1940s. But, like radiocarbon dating, these techniques have been considerably refined and extended.

Infra-red has been added to the photographic repertoire, and a whole range of electrical, magnetic and sonic instruments have been borrowed from the earth sciences and modified, or developed specifically for archaeology. Sonic instruments have proved particularly useful in underwater detective work.

The importance of the past concealed beneath the waves has long been recognized, but until the development of the aqualung in the 1940s it could generally be investigated only in particularly favourable circumstances. Now many of the constraints have been removed, and the underwater world of ancient wrecks and submerged settlements has suddenly been opened up to view (see pages 98-9).

This aerial view *clearly shows the outline of the Badbury Rings, th remains of a hill fort in south-west England which dates back to the Iron Age. The last, or outer, ring may not have been added until just before the Roman invasion in 43 AD. The total area of the site is jus over 7 hectares (18 acres,*

*The underwater
archaeologist must be as
exact in recording of data
as his ground-level
counterpart. Here we see a
scientist surveying the
wreck of one of the many
ships which foundered off
the coast of Canada. After
pinpointing the precise
location of each piece of
wreckage with his
equipment, he then
records its precise co-
ordinates on a grid plan of
the whole site.*

An All-round Approach

Archaeology has tended to concentrate on artefacts, man-made relics of the past. But the information artefacts are expected to yield has expanded greatly. In addition, modern scientific aids have provided much new data on ancient technology and sources of raw materials. So we can now build up a better picture of patterns of prehistoric trade, communications networks and industrial exploitation of the landscape.

Attention is increasingly focused, too, on such topics as subsistence economics and the landscapes around past settlements, to find out how ancient man obtained food to support himself. Efforts are being made to recover the remains of plant and animal material that formed part of his diet, and to study the environment to see where he obtained it. One result has been a growing awareness of just how much man modified his surroundings even in remote times.

To help them in this task of relating early societies to their environment and their neighbours, archaeologists have borrowed approaches from geography. Those include site territorial analysis, to establish the economic reasons lying behind patterns of settlement, and various theoretical models of economic and political geography.

Maths and Computers

Mathematics is another discipline that archaeologists have utilized for techniques, and computer technology is a great boon. Not only does it enable large amounts of information to be recorded, sorted and retrieved in seconds. It also imposes a requirement to use standardized recording systems.

Archaeological analyses have, thanks to the computer, become much more rigorous. Artefacts that were once classified largely by intuition can now be assessed according to mathematically-derived criteria.

Statistical and mathematical techniques are used to assess distribution patterns of archaeological material, both at a given site and throughout a region. Computer simulations can also provide theoretical models of possible developments from a given archaeological starting-point.

'New Archaeology'

The borrowings of equipment and techniques from other disciplines sparked off a debate that raged in the early 1970s and has smouldered on ever since. Essentially, it asks: can archaeology be regarded as a science?

Some people argue strongly that it cannot, and that in the proliferation of scientific aids archaeologists risk losing sight of the humans behind the artefacts. Others assert that archaeologists have for too long expected their data to have self-evident meaning, and that it is time their underlying assumptions were specifically stated and tested for validity.

These 'new archaeologists' advocate, among other things, the scientific approach of formulating hypotheses and collecting test data. The drawback is that archaeological tests often cannot be repeated, and not all of the variables can be tightly controlled. Nevertheless, a more rigorous approach to collecting and analyzing information can only be of benefit.

And some scientific techniques do lend themselves to archaeology. They include experiments with ancient forms of technology, which have provided valuable insights into, for example, manufacturing techniques, farming, building methods and navigation. Another approach is ethnoarchaeology, involving the study of present-day ethnographic groups (societies whose distinguishing characteristics are scientifically describable). Their activities and any material traces may establish the possible significance of ancient artefacts.

Science and technology may be helping, but they have also brought disadvantages. The increasingly rapid pace at which man is modifying his environment poses a growing threat to any surviving remains. Happily, many governments and private organizations have responded generously, by sponsoring archaeological investigations of threatened sites. The burgeoning popularity of archaeology among the general public means that professional archaeologists can call upon a plentiful reserve of interested amateurs who can provide invaluable assistance in the field.

Opposite: *Evidence of the past is all around us – we have only to allow ourselves to become aware of it. Here a Bronze Age burial mound has been preserved within a modern field of wheat in Wiltshire, England.*

THE ARCHAEOLOGICAL LANDSCAPE

ARCHAEOLOGISTS ARE frequently asked 'How did archaeological material end up underground?' There are many possible answers, stemming both from natural processes and from human activities.

When, for instance, a house is abandoned by its occupants, it gradually collapses; the roof falls in and the walls start to crumble and decay. Plants and living creatures, wind and rain, snow and frost or intense sun all contribute to its disintegration. The slow accumulation of soil from the decay of vegetation gradually raises the ground level, and the last remnants of the house eventually become buried beneath a soil layer of increasing thickness.

Other natural forces may be involved in burying archaeological sites. Soil eroded from higher ground nearby can be deposited on them, or they can be buried by soil carried in from elsewhere by the wind or deposited by floods. In deserts or by the seashore, the site may be covered by wind-blown sand.

Sometimes, natural disasters may cause the archaeological remains to be engulfed. Ash or lava flows from volcanic eruptions can overwhelm sites – Pompeii, for example, was buried by ash from Vesuvius. Earthquakes may smother a settlement in debris.

The Hand of Man

Nature is not alone in covering the works of man. Man himself often plays a part. Abandoned buildings are frequently demolished down to their foundations and any useful material is removed. Then new buildings may be constructed on the razed debris of the old, sometimes incorporating the material saved from their predecessors.

Through this process of destruction and renewal, settlements gradually rise above the level of their earliest occupation. Sometimes the results are dramatic. In the Near East, some favoured sites, occupied for thousands of years, have become enormous mounds, built up gradually from the decayed remains of myriad mud-brick houses.

When a structure decays or is demolished, its foundations are the part of it most likely to survive, because they are set into the ground. Post-holes, ditches, sunken floors, pits and foundation trenches are among the commonest archaeological finds. So are floors originally laid at ground level and the lowest courses of walls.

It would be a mistake, however, to imagine that all archaeological remains are below ground.

Many structures are built of materials that resist decay or degradation, and these are likely to survive above ground for a considerable time.

Churches and castles, half-ruined but still standing, are a familiar sight in Europe, where the much older megalithic tombs and monuments of the Atlantic coastal region also survive. Earthen structures may also endure for millennia, as the prehistoric barrows of Europe and the impressive mounds in the shape of animals and birds in the eastern USA have done.

Forces of Destruction

The same natural processes that preserve the traces of many archaeological sites by burying them can totally destroy others. For example, sites on hilltops or slopes may be entirely obliterated by erosion. Floods, changes in the courses of rivers and the action of glaciers can have a similarly destructive effect.

Man is even more active than nature in erasing evidence of the past and in recent times the rate of destruction has accelerated. Modern agricultural machinery penetrates the soil to depths spared by earlier farm implements. Road-building and other industrial activities in the countryside are equalled in their destructive potential by urban rebuilding and the spread of towns. The heritage of our past demands immediate investigation, before all traces of it vanish completely through the combined and uncontrollable forces of man and nature.

Armchair Beginnings

Fieldwork usually begins in the comfort of an armchair at home, or in a local library or public records office. Maps, both modern and less recent, can give clues to interesting sites. So can records of past land transfers and similar transactions, and other historical documents. It is useful to study place names and any accounts of earlier archaeological discoveries in the locality. Aerial photographs can give details of landscapes of the past.

Once an interesting-looking site has been traced, the area should be visited and explored. If further archaeological evidence is found, detailed surveys can begin.

The twin-towered ruins *of the 12th-century church of St Egbert in Kent, England, are built upon and use many of the same materials from the Roman Fort Regulbium which was built in 225 and occupied until the 4th century. The Roman fort slipped into the sea as the cliffs were eroded.*

THE ROMANCE OF MAPS

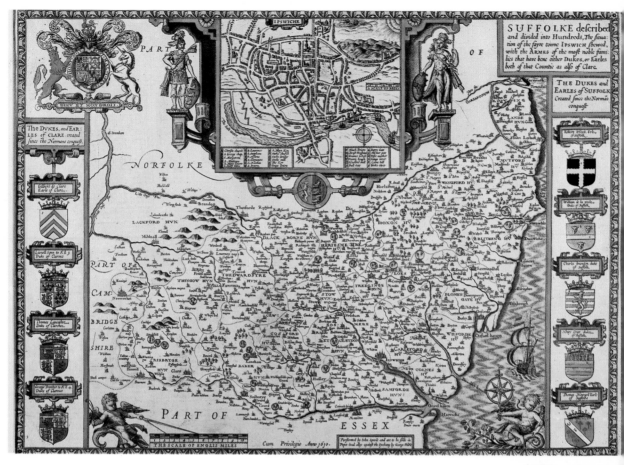

LARGE-SCALE (1:10000 or 1:10560) modern maps contain a lot of information that is useful to archaeologists. Many features of the landscape may still survive as partial ruins – castles, churches and other old buildings, barrows, megaliths and earthworks. Those are often marked on maps.

In other cases, the feature may have virtually disappeared, but its former existence may be signalled by a name. In England, for example, the word 'park' associated with a piece of land can indicate that it was once a deer park or the grounds of an estate. The name 'camp' may refer to Roman remains.

Maps also provide a detailed picture of modern field and parish boundaries, hedgerows and woodlands, roads and paths and other features of the present-day landscape. Irregularities or anomalies in them may be a clue to a feature of archaeological interest. For

example, an abrupt change in the line of a hedge or field boundary may be to avoid a structure which has since disappeared. Small ponds or ditches may be the last remains of a medieval moat, or an old abbey fishpond, or the race of a watermill. A clump of isolated trees in a field may mark the site of an ancient structure, which might be a barrow, a deserted house or something as mundane as a medieval rabbit warren.

Villages occupied in medieval times but later deserted can often be discovered by studying features on the map. Frequent clues are unusual shaped fields, isolated churches, and a series of paths or tracks which apparently converge on nowhere in particular. Parish boundaries apparently without an associated village may also indicate an abandoned settlement.

Modern town maps are also informative, because many of the streets are likely to follow

A 17th-century map
Suffolk, England, show
the division of the county
into 'hundreds' and the
names of the nobility. O
maps can provide useful
information for the
archaeologist but they
should be treated with
caution because their
accuracy varies and they
are often selective in the
details they include.

utes that date right back to the original
ttlement. Town streets, like rural boundaries,
so contain clues to former features such as
fensive walls, open markets or land once
longing to a churchyard or cemetery, manor
castle. For instance, circular castle defences
ill show up as an anomaly in a basically linear
reetplan. Curving parallel streets may once
ve been separated from each other by a town
all. In ancient towns and cities, street names
ay indicate the occupations of those who once
ed or traded there, or commemorate a former
ature or a person who once owned the land.
  Although many features of the present
ndscape reflect the past, much has also
anged, particularly since the later 19th
ntury. Earlier maps can therefore provide
otentially valuable additional information. But
ey should be treated with caution, because
eir accuracy varies and they are often selective
the details they include. Large-scale estate,
he and enclosure maps showing boundaries
d land-use are the most helpful.

ocumentary Evidence

he reading and interpretation of old documents
the preserve of the historian. But the contents
eld information of vital concern to
chaeologists, either by revealing the existence
hitherto-unknown archaeological sites or,
uch more commonly, by assisting in the
terpretation of archaeological material. For
xample, it may be difficult to distinguish
tween the earthworks constructed on
edieval estates and those of later formal
rdens without documentary help.
  However, documents are not always easy to
terpret accurately, so it is helpful to seek the
vice of a historian. The Domesday Book,
mpiled in England during the 11th century,
ovides a good example of some of the pitfalls
waiting the incautious archaeologist. As a
rvey of the land conducted for William I, it
ems a suitable source for studying the
stribution of later 11th-century settlements.
ut in some instances a village name may refer
a group of settlements lumped together, or a
ortion of a village divided for administrative or
her reasons. In other instances, villages have
ifted their location or changed their name.
  Despite such drawbacks, documentary
urces have their place. Surveys and inquiries
at give information on the economic
gnificance of the man-made landscape are of
rticular interest. Land charters, some dating

from before AD 1000, give archaeologists an
additional insight into how land holdings were
organized in the past. Many such documents are
preserved in public records, or in the archives of
ancient land-owning institutions.
  Although archaeologists need to rely on
historians to assess ancient documents, the
archaeologist may in turn be of service to the
historian in dating or authenticating historical
material and providing significant information
about its context. Archaeological data can help to
check the truth or relevance of documentary
statements. For instance, the conventional
picture of Vikings raping and pillaging, derived
from the writings of the clerics who were their
main victims, is in marked contrast to the
impression from archaeological evidence of
generally peaceful Viking colonization.

This page from
The Domesday Book,
*compiled in 11th-
century England and
written in Old English,
clearly demonstrates the
difficulty which is often
encountered in the study
and interpretation of
ancient material. It is
advisable to have the
advice of a historian when
researching such
documents.*

KING ARTHUR – MAN OR MYTH?

THE SHADOWY FIGURE of King Arthur exerts a powerful fascination for people of all nationalities. The legend surrounding him and his court at Camelot first became a source of popular literature in l2th-century France; and Arthur and his ideals, in our own time, were used as a symbol by President Kennedy who inspired a whole generation with it. But did Arthur exist, and, if so, how much of the legend has a basis in fact?

The full answer will never be known. Nevertheless, the quest for Arthur provides a good example of how archaeological and historical sources can complement each other to build up a picture of the past, and of how scholars in the two disciplines sift fact from fiction.

The Historian's Arthur

Scanty and dubious historical records establish the existence of Arthur, albeit not as a king, but as chief warlord of the Britons resisting invasion by Anglo-Saxons after the Roman occupation of Britain had ended in about AD 410. From the writings of the fiery 6th-century monk Gildas, from tables for calculating the date of Easter in which contemporary events were recorded as marginal notes, and from heroic poetry with possible early 6th-century roots – all known to us only from later copies of copies – we gather that Arthur was the victor in 12 battles. They included Cat Coit Celidon, probably fought somewhere in the Caledonian Forest of the Southern Uplands in Scotland, and his last and most important victory, at Mount Badon.

There he resoundingly defeated the Anglo-Saxon (English) invaders and won a respite from their encroachment, bringing a peace that was still holding when Gildas wrote. But the penetration resumed, and the English grip on Britain was assured when they defeated the Britons at the battle of Dyrholm in 577. Arthur himself had fallen some decades after Badon in a battle between British forces at Camlann.

Documentary discrepancies make Arthur's dates uncertain. Badon could have been fought in either AD 490 or 518, and Camlann in AD 511 or 539. And the exact location of neither battle is known – both Bath and Badbury Rings in Dorset have been suggested as possible locations for the site of Mount Badon.

The Romancer's Arthur

Other elements of the Arthurian legend, we can see from the documents, are anachronisms, added in medieval times as the romantic associations of Arthur developed. His status as a warlord was transmuted into that of High King, and his mobile defensive force became medieval heavy cavalry. A court at Camelot was attributed to him as a necessary kingly base.

Camelot first appears in the romance *Lancelot, le chavalier de la charette* by the 12th-century French poet

The hillfort at *South Cadbury is one of many places held to have been Camelot where the legendary Arthur held his court. Excavations in the late l960s found evidence that during the Arthurian period (late 5th-early 6th centuries AD) the old Iron Age site was strengthened, and saw active use as a military base.*

Chretien de Troyes, where its location remained vague. Medieval writers suggested Winchester, Caerleon and other places in the south and west of Britain. But in the early sources Arthur is not associated with any site in particular, nor is he said to have had an established base anywhere in Britain.

The Archaeologist's Arthur

What substance can archaeology add to the shadowy historical figure of Arthur? The answer is nothing to Arthur himself or to the other individuals of his age, for the information archaeology offers is generally impersonal. But to the tantalizingly incomplete historical snippets that have survived, archaeology can add a great deal, as excavations and surveys continue to reveal the remains of daily life as it existed in the aftermath of the Roman retreat from Britain.

Among the pottery finds in a number of Celtic British sites have been found sherds of several types of imported ware. Fragments of red ware bowls and amphorae indicate a trade linking Britain with the eastern Mediterranean, while blue-black bowls came from a somewhat closer source in France. Unlike the undistinguished native pottery, these fragments are relatively easy to date with some precision. They show that in the late 5th and 6th centuries AD a number of inhabitants of Britain retained some degree of contact with Europe, and that they were affluent enough to be able to afford goods imported from the continent.

So far, such pottery remains have been found in only one Roman town, Ilchester in Somerset, implying that few towns continued to be inhabited for long after the Romans left. On the other hand, the discovery of these wares in a number of long-abandoned Iron Age hillforts, the defences of which sometimes bear indications of 5th- or 6th-century refurbishment, reinforces the picture gained from written sources of the development of petty kingdoms.

Excavations within hillforts such as Dinas Powys in Wales and Castle Dore in Cornwall have yielded remains of structures that could be chieftains' halls. Among other finds at the site were abundant animal bones – which would seem to indicate feasting on a large scale – and some occasional evidence of metalworking and other industry. The hillfort at South Cadbury (*see pages 72-3*), while it follows the same pattern, is on a larger scale.

Although Gildas wrote of the peace that followed the battle of Mount Badon, both documentary and archaeological evidence show this to have been rather localized. Abundant finds of Germanic pottery, jewellery and other artefacts in south, north and eastern England attest to Anglo-Saxon advances and consolidation.

Nevertheless, archaeology does seem to confirm the check to the Anglo-Saxons observed by Gildas. Pottery of the type common in south-eastern England in the early 6th century, as well as other Saxon material, is virtually absent from the Upper Thames valley. There is also evidence of Anglo-Saxons from Britain settling in western France and Belgium and even returning to their ancestral lands in Germany. 'King' Arthur's achievement was therefore substantial, despite the ultimate failure of the Britons to stem the Anglo-Saxon tide.

A BIRD'S-EYE VIEW

Ancient structures, *such as buildings, walls, even street plans, leave their mark on the landscape by their very presence underground. For this causes alterations in soil depth which, in turn, are reflected when crops or plants grow. Often these alterations are only visible from above. This aerial photograph of a field of ripe wheat was shot near Petranell, south-east of Vienna. Clearly shown is the distinctive outline of a Roman legion's castrum, or encampment.*

ANCIENT WALLS, ditches and roadways continue to affect the landscape even when surface traces of their presence are not obvious. They alter the pattern of the soil below ground, causing variations in soil depth which, in turn, affects plant growth. Generally, even surface traces are only clearly seen from the air.

Low bumps and shallow hollows representing relics of the past show up clearly to an aerial observer by the shadows they cast, particularly when the sun is low and shadows are elongated. The remains of the banks and ditches of ancient earthworks can be seen, as well as the last vestiges of stone structures such as demolished abbey buildings, and the house platforms and hollow streets of deserted medieval villages. Medieval strip ploughing created patterns of ridges and furrows which have also survived in many areas and show up well as shadow sites.

Thin snow or frost can enhance surface variations. So can the differential melting of snow or flooding, which picks out slight depressions. The micro-environmental preferences of plants such as buttercups may give definition to low walls or shallow ditches.

Stripping and Soil Marks

Archaeological features that have left no trace above ground can sometimes be spotted from the air as soil marks, either when the top-soil is stripped, for instance in preparation for building development, or when land is deeply ploughed. Stripping is similar in some respects to the actual process of excavation; the truncated remains of pits, ditches and old foundations are exposed briefly as upper layers of the soil are removed. The machinery used in stripping inevitably churns the ground, making it hard to see the soil marks when close to them. From the air, however, soil which has been recent churned is more readily distinguishable from ancient remains.

The soil marks exposed by stripping delineate the remains themselves, producing a recognizable outline. By contrast, soil marks resulting from the disturbance of underground features by ploughing are far less clear-cut. The features are displaced by the turning of the earth and the dragging of the plough. That often results in quite dramatic zigzag or dogtooth effects, with material from the disturbed pit, ditch or building remains often contrasting sharply with the surrounding plough soil. But it may make the form of the underlying structure difficult to determine.

Soil marks suggesting the presence of an archaeological feature need to be investigated quickly, preferably by carefully controlled excavation. The fact that these marks exist at all shows that the buried remains are in the process of being destroyed.

Pointers from Plants

Patterns of plant growth, visible from the air, provide a very important clue to the existence of underground remains. Cereal grains, in particular, are exceptionally sensitive to deficiencies in moisture and nutrients, especially in the early stages of the growing season. In a dry spell, they grow best over buried ditches and pits, which are deeper and retain moisture, and poorly over buried walls and stone structures where moisture is lost and plants can take only shallow root.

Seed sown over pits and ditches germinates
re rapidly than that elsewhere, and the young
nts show up as patches of green against the
erwise bare earth. These precocious plants
main darker than the rest during the growing
son. Their lush growth is more prolonged and
they ripen later, remaining green while the
rounding crops turn golden. They also grow
er, and therefore cast shadows which help to
ine buried features.

Although deep-rooted plants such as cereals
duce the best cropmarks, some root crops,
h as sugar beet, and pulses, such as peas,
y also be useful indicators. Grass will become
ched or die over obstacles such as walls; it
survive longest over pits, ditches and other
ep-soil features. Cropmarks vary widely in
bility. Whether or not they stand out clearly
ends on the amount of rain in the growing
son, and also on when during the season it
s. Some soil types, such as gravels and chalk,
duce cropmarks which are more distinct than
se of other soil types.

terpreting Aerial Photographs
o types of photographs can be taken from the
– vertical, or overhead, shots and oblique, or
led, pictures. Vertical photographs can be
nned directly on to maps, although there is
ly to be some distortion of the image at the
ges. Pairs of vertical shots with a 60 per cent
erlap can be examined using a stereoscopic
wer; the landscape relief jumps startlingly
o three dimensions, emphasizing every bump
l hollow.

Oblique shots are much more difficult to map,
they generally show the archaeological detail
ch more clearly. Computer programmes have
en devised to adapt details from oblique
otos to two-dimensional maps, but
haeologists who have no access to a
mputer must resort to using tried-and-true but
orious conversion techniques.

Interpretation of aerial photographs requires
siderable skill and experience. Some modern
tures of the landscape, such as 'envelope'
ughing patterns, superficially remain when
en from the air. So do geological features such
rost cracks in the subsoil. A practised eye
distinguish these from genuine
haeological remains, but the site may need to
examined or local farmers consulted.

The interpretation of archaeological remains
ies heavily on a knowledge of the form of
haeological structures of many different

dates. Certain distinctive features often provide
clues; a short linear earthwork, for example,
may be positively identified as one side of a
Roman camp if its line is broken by a gateway of
characteristic form.

Frequently, aerial photographs show traces of
only a fraction of the remains below ground. A
more complete picture may emerge by
comparing several photographs of the same area
under different land-use, or taken at different
times of the year or in varying weather
conditions. Even with the most detailed aerial
view, however, many features are impossible to
interpret. A ring ditch, for instance, may be the
remains of a Bronze Age barrow, an Iron Age
hut circle, a Roman tower, a medieval windmill
or an element of a more recent formal garden.

New Horizons
Standard aerial photography usually relies on
black-and-white film, partly for economy, but
also because it usually heightens contrasts more
satisfactorily. Interestingly, other photographic
and related techniques are now being
investigated for their potential usefulness.

False-colour infra-red photography can be
used to show up cropmarks, but in general the
results are no better than conventional photos.
Infra-red linescan, which picks out contrasts in
ground temperature, because of the presence of
buried features, may one day prove helpful.

High altitude and satellite photographs can
reveal interesting features. Their resolution
tends to be poor, so sites are hard to pick out.
Radar has been used in surveying the jungles of
lowland Central America, and has transformed
our understanding of the Mayans.

Barbury Castle, *an
Iron Age hillfort in
Wiltshire, was excavated
in 1886. It was a source of
great archaeological
interest and finds include
excellent examples of the
work of Iron Age
blacksmiths: an anvil, 5
sickle blades, 3 spear
heads, a knife and rings
used in chariot or cart
construction. There is a
record of a number of
coins having been found
during an earlier
excavation, but they have
since disappeared. Roman
period finds included a
silver spoon, engraved
with the name of the
owner, Verecunda, and
an exceptionally fine
ornate brooch. Running
through the centre of the
site is the 40 mile long
Ridgeway, one of the great
prehistoric track routes of
Britain. No one is sure
how its date relates to that
of the hillfort itself.*

KNOWLEDGE OF the first civilizations of the ancient world accumulated and was studied on a comparative basis, it became clear that these civilizations fitted a pattern. All depended upon irrigation agriculture to sustain the needs of their populations. But there was one apparent exception to this seemingly inviolable rule – the Classic Mayan civilization of the Yucatan peninsula, which reached its height over a thousand years ago.

The area today is cultivated by slash-and-burn agriculture, locally called *milpa*. Archaeologists assumed that the same primitive agricultural technique was used during Classic Mayan times, 1500 years ago. But could *milpa*, which is capable of supporting far fewer than 100 people per square kilometre of cultivated land, really be the basis of a state which appears to have had quite high population densities?

One of the first indications that it could not have been came in the 1950s, when the University of Pennsylvania surveyed the area of Tikal, the principal Mayan ceremonial centre. The results of their survey showed that Tikal had been too heavily populated to have had enough room for the *milpa* plots necessary to feed all of its inhabitants. Nor, in fact, was there enough land for this purpose between Tikal and the next centre of any significance, Uaxactun, 18 km (11 miles) to the north. Scholars suggested that crop rotation might have allowed more intensive farming, and that the ramon, or breadnut tree, may also have been cultivated. But even this well-thought out explanation failed to account satisfactorily for the density of population which was indicated at Tikal, and archaeologists continued to remain puzzled.

Fields and Canals

A series of startling discoveries in the 1970s provided the answer to the mystery. Archaeologists found permanent field systems on man-made terraces on the hillsides of Quintana Roo, near Tikal. These productive permanent fields were traced only in the one area, but in 1972 Puleston and Siemens noticed signs of ancient canal systems on the Candelaria river. The finds convinced archaeologists to survey the area from the air.

The survey covered a large portion of Yucatan, and used both aerial photography and side-looking radar. New and surprising details were revealed. The canal network was found to spread over a wide area, and the swamps that occupy about half of the Mayan heartlands were criss-crossed with drainage channels. Between these channels, had been laid a grid of raised fields, forming the basis for a highly productive agricultural system.

Ground investigations confirmed the features noted from the air. And a new examination of the Mayan centres revealed the significant fact that almost all of them were on rivers, near lakes or on the edges of swamps. All of the largest sites, including Tikal, were beside swamps.

The raised field system had thus provided the agricultural base for the Classic Mayan civilization. On the evidence found at one major Mayan centre, Mirador, such farming methods could have begun even earlier, during the late Preclassic period.

With the help of aerial photography, an archaeological mystery had been solved. And the theory that the rise of early civilizations depended on intensive agriculture based on water control was once more apparently vindicated.

These two sites in the north-west Yucatan peninsula, demonstrate the scale and grandeur of Mayan civilization. Their temples, such as the one at Dzibakhaltun (left), are typified by the long, banked row of steps leading up to the large square structure where, presumably, religious ceremonies were carried out. The palace facade from Kabah (right), is from the end of the Classic Mayan period and shows the distinctive ornate detail of that time.

The Visible Past

EXPOSED REMAINS of the past are generally investigated by fieldwalking, a popular weekend activity among amateur archaeological groups. The best conditions for fieldwalking are, unfortunately, often uncomfortable – after rain, when objects have been washed clean and are visible, and during the winter, when vegetation is low and crops have not yet started growing.

The area to be investigated may be divided into blocks to be allocated to the participants, using hedgerows and similar features as boundaries. Ideally, large areas should be subdivided. The fieldwalkers pick up the archaeological remains they notice, or a representative sample, and note where dense concentrations of archaeological material occur.

Typical finds include a variety of sherds of pottery, flint and stone artefacts, coins and other small metal objects, and pieces of building material, for example brick, daub or tile. Such material often indicates that the remains of a building lie below the ground, although sometimes it may simply have been dumped on the site. Other tell-tale signs of disturbed occupation deposits include fragments of hewn stone and scatters of charcoal.

Dense concentrations of pottery and worked flint also suggest an occupation site, but isolated pieces more probably reached the field mixed with domestic refuse once used as manure. Dense scatters of firecrazed flint suggest that there are mounds of the same material underground. In Britain, these generally dates from the Bronze Age, but no one is yet sure of their purpose.

Worked flint and stone may belong to any period, but they can often be dated by their form, i.e. shape and techniques of manufacture. Waste flakes and microliths (small flint tools) may be less chronologically distinctive and can at times be misleading. For example, in Cyprus fieldwalkers have on occasion been deluded into identifying archaeological sites on the basis of dense scatters of flint chips, actually made quite recently and set in threshing sledges (boards which were dragged over harvested grain).

Coins, though exciting to the finder, are not generally useful sources of archaeological information. They can be lost in any place where people walk, so finding one may not, in itself, denote an archaeological site. Similarly, small metal objects may just be evidence of ancient carelessness, although they can sometimes indicate a disturbed burial, particularly if human bones are also present.

Checking the Terrain

Fieldwalking enables archaeologists to compare the anomalies previously noted on maps or in aerial photographs with the appearance of the landscape itself. Slight undulations may be the remains of ploughed out barrows, ancient ditches or medieval villages. Variations in the colour of the soil or the luxuriance of the vegetation, sudden changes in the line of hedgerows or field boundaries, and curiously shaped bodies of water may also indicate the presence of archaeological features.

Sometimes the date of field boundaries can be determined by inspection on the ground. The way a wall is built may indicate how old it is. And it is now thought possible to date hedgerows

The Sutton Hoo
treasure, excavated in 1939, was the richest find in Britain and a good example of how easily the past might have been lost. The ancient barrows had been plundered for treasure and this one, in fact, had been tunnelled into. Only luck prevented the robbers from digging below ground level where the treasure lay within an old Viking-style long ship. This was the only intact burial among the ten or so barrows on the site.

castle. Around a church, an area filled with a maze of houses without gardens is likely to represent later building over a medieval market place. Small details may be revealing: for example, a crack in the side of a house could be the result of subsidence that occurred because it was built over an infilled moat.

Urban reconstruction and maintenance offer opportunities for archaeologists. Trenches for drains or telephone cables, foundation holes, demolition projects and other such disturbances provide a welcome glimpse of what still survives below the surface and allow details of the past to be noted. However, sites revealed in these ways are usually glimpsed only briefly before they vanish underground again – or, are destroyed completely, as is often the case – unless the developer is unusually sympathetic to archaeology and can postpone his work to allow further investigations. In an ideal world, all large-scale construction projects would be preceded by a detailed archaeological survey, using all the techniques available, to establish a record of what is likely to be destroyed. After an assessment, provision could then be made for the excavation of some of the more interesting sites and a little bit of man's history would be preserved for future generations.

The evidence collected *by fieldwalkers is invaluable in creating as detailed a picture as possible of the past. This material was gathered in 1984 from an Iron Age settlement at Kondrajanhalli, in South India, and consists mainly of the type of potsherds from which reconstructions can be made, i.e. rim and base sherds from which diameters of the top and bottom respectively can be determined. Also are 3 interesting pieces in the bottom row to the right: a grindstone and polished stone axe and, to their left, the knob of a lid.*

curately simply by counting the number of ferent species of plants in a 30m (32½yd) retch; a new species will colonize the hedge out each 100 years.

Valking the Streets

enty of information can be gained by the urban ldworker versed in the nuances of changing chitectural styles. Modifications made to a ilding are usually more obvious from the side back, or inside, than from the front.

The layout of town or city streets frequently flects elements of the original plan of the ttlement, even if all or many of the buildings e relatively modern. A circular area among ear roads may once have been the bailey of a

LOOKING MORE CLOSELY: 1

OBSERVATIONS MADE while fieldwalking allow you to establish in general terms whether an area is archaeologically interesting. If it is, you will certainly want to explore further. First, however, a more detailed survey should be made, and some sort of site plan drawn.

Any 'bumps or hollows' you have discovered in the landscape should be carefully mapped, so that their shape can be compared with known earthworks, possibly giving clues to their age and nature. In some circumstances, a full-scale survey may be made, using many of the techniques discussed in the following section (*see pages 62-101*). But it is possible to carry out a rapid study with very little equipment.

At the simplest level, a freehand sketch plan will give a rough idea of the nature of the site. A rather more accurate method is to use a technique known as 'offsetting' to draw a scale plan of the site (*see Figures 1 and 2 on the page opposite*). This requires some basic items of surveyors' equipment – including ranging rods marked off in metres or feet (easy to make yourself from straight battens or poles of wood), metal or wooden pegs, several tape measures, and some balls of string.

The first step is to establish a base line running through the major axis of the site, marking it with pegs and a cloth tape measure. Next, take 'offsets' at right angles from the base line through all the main features of the site, using the ranging rods and tape measures to gauge distances (*see Figures 1 and 2 on the page opposite*). To ensure the offsets are at right angles to the base line, a compass, set square or T-square should be used. Make a note of all measurements, including that of the base line. Once the measurements have been completed, a scale plan of the site may be drawn.

The accuracy of this method is entirely adequate for archaeological purposes. The thickness of pencil lines imposes real limitations, in any case. At a scale of 1:500, the pencil line represents about 25cm (1in).

After completing the plan, study the site again to make sure that what you have drawn really resembles it. Record prominent landmarks such as buildings and field boundaries, so that the plan can be correctly related to a map of the area. Photographs from different angles provide a valuable additional record.

Once a thorough study of the surface of the site has been made, it is time to begin investigating what lies beneath the ground. This is the subject of the next chapter.

Offsetting *is a method of measuring a site or feature within a site, so that its shape can be represented on a diagram. A 'base line', running through the centre of the area is established and a series of straight lines, or 'offsets', are run out from the base line to the edges of the area. The points where they fall along the edge can be connected and the result will reflect the outer contours of what is being mapped. The only equipment needed is pegs and a tape measure or string (with measurements clearly marked) to define the base line, and a tape measure with which to determine the offsets. One person stands at the edge of the site (A), holding the tape; another stands at the base line (B) and moves the other end of the tape until it forms a right angle with the base (C), i.e. when the distance between A and the base line is shortest. Offsets continue to be formed until there are enough point to connect.*

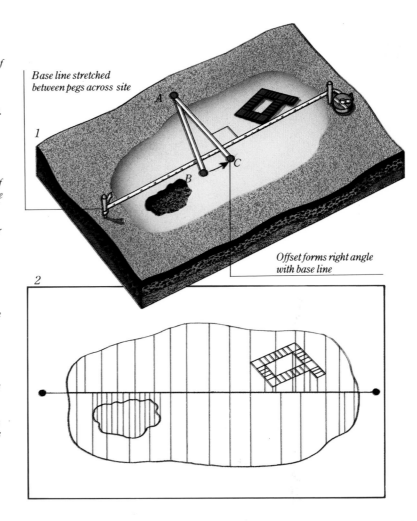

Base line stretched between pegs across site

1

Offset forms right angle with base line

2

A base line has been stretched across the site shown at left, in preparation for taking offsets. The offset method is most useful on small sites such as this one. Tape measures are also used in a similar way to make plans of archaeological sites after excavation has begun (far left).

LOOKING MORE CLOSELY: 2

Mechanical Aids

Many instruments, some originally developed for geophysics, can be used to help to detect buried archaeological features. One category depends for its effectiveness on the fact that the electrical resistance of soil decreases if it is damp. Soil within filled-in pits or ditches retains moisture for longer than the earth around it, while that above solid stone structures such as walls dries out more quickly.

The electrical resistance of the soil is measured with a resistivity gauge such as the Martin Clark meter, through probes inserted into the ground at regular intervals. A related survey technique relies on induced polarization – the physical phenomenon in which electromagnetic radiation waves are restricted to certain directions of vibration. The methods of measurement resemble those of the resistivity meter, and the results can be slightly better.

Buried features not only affect the electrical resistance of the soil, but they also produce

small local variations in the strength of the Earth's magnetic field. For example, the magnetic susceptibility of pits and ditches filled with organic material is greater than that of the surrounding soil, while roads and walls have decreased magnetic susceptibility. The variations can be measured with a magnetometer, of which there are several types. They can also detect fired clay structures, such as hearths and kilns, and iron.

The most commonly used instrument is the proton magnetometer. However, it suffers background interference from electric trains and magnetic storms. This problem does not arise with the differential fluxgate gradiometer or with the proton gradiometer, which in any case is far less expensive than the other two.

Magnetic surveys are generally carried out over a previously laid out grid. They can be impeded by thick vegetation and cannot be performed at all near overhead cables, iron fences and built-up areas, or over igneous bedrock, so resistivity surveys have to be used in those situations. Resistivity is the more reliable of the two techniques for detecting stone structures and for tracing linear features, while magnetic surveys can more easily locate small isolated features such as pits and iron objects.

The results of such surveys should be plotted on a map of the site. One way is to draw the equivalent of contour lines linking all the points where similarly anomalous resistance or magnetic readings were obtained. Another is to use dots of different sizes and shades to denote different degrees of variation from the norm.

Metal Detectors

Electromagnetic devices, of which the simplest is the metal detector, are also helpful in detecting buried features. They identify magnetic anomalies and are a supplement to the magnetometer, but do not penetrate so deeply. The two electromagnetic devices that are most widely used in archaeology are the pulse induction meter and the soil conductivity meter.

A metal detector can be a handy survey instrument, giving quick general results. The irresponsible use of metal detectors has quite rightly been condemned by archaeologists and others; holes dug to retrieve often quite unexciting bits of metal not only remove archaeological objects from their context, but also waste the surrounding archaeology too.

Unauthorized use of metal detectors on protected archaeological sites is illegal in many

The two *main geophysical surveying instruments used for detecting buried objects – the resistivity meter and the magnetometer – are compared in the diagram below. The black section of the arrows represents an average background reading; diagonal stripes represent a stronger magnetic field or electrical resistance; vertical stripes indicate lower magnetism or resistance. In this example, the resistivity meter records only the pit and the wall, while the magnetometer also detects the iron axe and the hearth. Neither can pick up minor features such as the post hole.*

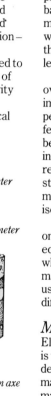

Magnetometer

Resistivity meter

Iron axe

Wall

Hearth

Pit

Post hole

‖‖‖‖	*Negative*
⫽⫽⫽	*Positive*
■	*Average reading*

...ountries. Items found by people using metal ...etectors are unlikely to be the finder's legal ...roperty; they may belong in law to the owner of ...he land, or to the state, depending on national ...egislation.

Techniques on Trial

...dvanced geophysical surveying techniques ...sing neutron scattering or gamma rays have on ...ccasion been tried by archaeologists, but the ...esults have not been very satisfactory. Ground-...enetrating radar seems more promising and has ...een used to map Etruscan tombs. Echo-...ounding is currently being investigated, but its ...rchaeological usefulness has yet to be proved. ...onic devices such as side-looking sonar have, ...owever, been employed to great effect in ...nderwater prospecting, for example in the ...earch for Henry VIII's long-lost warship *Mary ...ose* (see page 105).

...*Dowsing* – in which a hazel or other twig held ...bove the ground is said to twitch in the ...resence of underground water or buried objects ...is of debatable value in the detection of ...rchaeological features. Accurate results are ...laimed by a number of fieldworkers, though the ...uthor's limited experience of archaeological ...owsing has not been convincing.

...*Bosing* is another technique of varied ...sefulness. The ground is thumped with a ...vooden mallet or lead-filled canister or even ...ith the foot, and the resultant sound noted. ...filled ditches and pits should produce a more ...esonant sound than the surrounding ...ndisturbed soil.

Probing the Ground

...Once an underground site has been located, ...urther information can be obtained, at some ...estructive cost, by using a *probe* or an *auger*. ...he probe is a long metal rod with a T-bar ...andle, which is driven into the ground. The ...epth it reaches before encountering bedrock or ...n obstruction allows a profile to be obtained of ...uried structures, pits or ditches. The auger is ...imilar, but it has a corkscrew end which brings ...p small samples of soil when driven into the ...round for a short distance.

...Both devices risk damaging archaeological ...bjects underground and their use is therefore ...est confined to answering specific questions. ...or example, they can provide information on ...he depth and extent of features located by other ...neans. An auger survey made across part of the ...omerset Levels in south-west England

A soil scanning radar *is a modern geophysical instrument which can detect archaeological remains buried under the ground. The machine at right, developed by the Englishman Mike Gorman, was used in the Sutton Hoo excavation (see page 90).*

successfully traced the course of the Abbott's Way, a late Neolithic wooden track now buried beneath peat.

The Essential Record

Prospecting and field surveys are often carried out prior to an excavation. Because every archaeological feature of the landscape cannot be excavated in full, in most cases the field survey is the only archaeological record of sites that may subsequently be destroyed. It is therefore vital that the results of these surveys should be made generally available.

A brief report on what has been found, should be offered to a local archaeological journal - or to a national one if the results are sufficiently interesting. At the same time, the complete details should be written into a separate, much longer report which, with the material collected, should be offered to some suitable public body for safekeeping and the reference of others. The local museum is an obvious candidate, but in countries such as Britain where local government employs archaeologists to collate such material they may be more suitable recipients.

TWO KINGS AT WAR

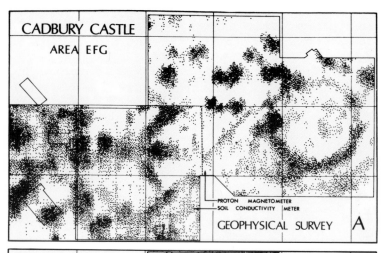

CADBURY CASTLE
AREA EFG

PROTON MAGNETOMETER
SOIL CONDUCTIVITY METER

GEOPHYSICAL SURVEY A

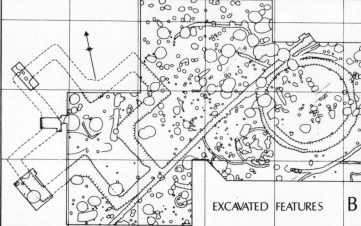

EXCAVATED FEATURES B

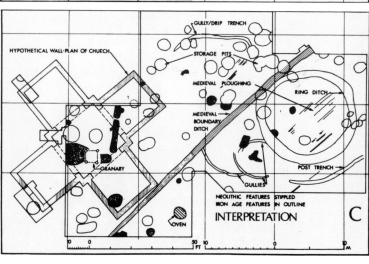

GULLY/DRIP TRENCH

HYPOTHETICAL WALL-PLAN OF CHURCH

STORAGE PITS

MEDIEVAL PLOUGHING

RING DITCH

MEDIEVAL
BOUNDARY
DITCH

GRANARY

POST TRENCH

GULLIES

NEOLITHIC FEATURES STIPPLED
IRON AGE FEATURES IN OUTLINE

OVEN

INTERPRETATION C

50 0   50 10   0   10
    FT   M

PAINSTAKING PRELIMINARY RESEARCH, drawing on the work of earlier investigators and on advanced technology, preceded two of the most romantic archaeological assignments to be undertaken in Britain in recent years. The first was at Cadbury Castle in Somerset, a spectacular Iron Age hillfort that, since the 16th century, had been identified with the fictional Camelot of King Arthur. The second led to the raising of the *Mary Rose*, a principal warship of Henry VIII's battlefleet, which sank in Portsmouth harbour on its maiden voyage, July 19, 1545.

The two investigations provide excellent examples of how modern archaeologists work in the field and the way in which their research puts flesh on the bones of history. They also demonstrate quite clearly that there is no real substitute for excavation.

The Fortress of Cadbury

John Leland, the King's Antiquary, first linked Cadbury Castle to Camelot in 1542, apparently drawing on a strong local tradition connecting the hillfort with King Arthur. Little evidence was found to support such a link until fieldwalking in the 1950s yielded a few sherds of the imported wares characteristic of the late 5th and 6th centuries AD. The finds rekindled interest in Cadbury, and in the 1960s Professor Leslie Alcock began excavations.

One of his objectives was to excavate a portion of the massive defences, to establish whether they had been strengthened or modified in Arthurian times. He also hoped to discover Arthurian structures. However, the area within the defences was large, amounting to some 7.2 hectares (18 acres), and the problem was to decide where promising remains might lie. Aerial photos of cropmarks were not good enough for detailed mapping.

So a geophysical survey of the site was carried out, using magnetometers and electromagnetic instruments, including the highly developed soil conductivity meter. Results were plotted by the dot density method.

An archaeological *survey of Cadbury Castle took place in the late 1960s. Here we see a detailed study of one area. The geophysical survey (A), done by testing for differences in soil temperature and electrical resistance, indicated the possible presence of buried features. When comparing this with a diagram of what the actual excavation later revealed (B), the value of the technique is obvious. Equally obvious is how much more a proper excavation can uncover. The interpretation (C) of the nature of the structures is the next stage of fieldwork.*

In 1967, a promising area was excavated. The results were most interesting. The large-scale features, including wide postholes, had shown up in the survey. But smaller details such as stake holes had not. The Arthurian-period timbered hall discovered in 1968 had only shallow foundations and it was due more to good fortune than to the survey that it was found at all.

The comparison between what the survey showed and the results of actual excavation made it clear that, while geophysical surveys may reveal the overall pattern of subsurface features, the relationships between those features cannot be determined without excavation. A series of parallel and transverse lines plotted in the survey were at first tentatively identified as rectangular halls. Excavation showed they were, in reality, a field ditch, a line of pits and part of the walls of an unexpected Late Saxon cruciform church.

Search for the Mary Rose

As Henry VIII's fleet was preparing to set sail from Portsmouth to do battle with the French, the *Mary Rose* heeled over and sank. Attempts in the following years to raise her failed. The wreck remained visible for some time, but gradually became buried by silt on the seabed.

In 1836, John and Charles Deane, pioneer divers and marine salvage experts, encountered portions of the *Mary Rose* that were briefly exposed. They salvaged some guns and other material, but subsequently the wreck was again lost to view and its location forgotten.

In 1965, however, members of the British Subaqua Club led by the journalist Alexander MacKee, with the archaeologist Margaret Rule, renewed the search. Using a naval chart of 1841 marking the spot where the Deanes had discovered the *Mary Rose*, they dove and prospected with a magnetic compass and an underwater magnetometer. Disappointing results made it seem likely that the ship was too deeply buried to be detected by ordinary means.

In 1967, however, the searchers enlisted the help of Professor Harold Edgerton of the Massachusetts Institute of Technology, who conducted a survey using a sonar sidescanner and a sonic 'pinger' device. These instruments detected an anomaly beneath the seabed in the search area and a slight mound above it. The following year two high-technology sub-bottom profilers were used to crosscheck the site. The results were encouraging enough for excavation to begin in 1969 of what is now one of the most famous wrecks ever investigated.

11 October, 1982 saw *the culmination of years of research and a major triumph for archaeology: the Tudor warship* Mary Rose *is here being lifted out of the waters of the Solent, near Portsmouth, where it lay buried for over 4 centuries. The ship is sandwiched between a carefully designed 150-ton cradle and a 60-ton lifting frame, supported by 3 legs (a fourth had already been removed). The ship had to drain slowly and although the first timbers were visible at 9:03 a.m., the entire structure did not emerge until late that afternoon. Repairs were then carried out on the lifting frame and it didn't reach the harbour until 10:00 p.m.*

EXCAVATION

Opposite: *One of the greatest urban excavations of this century took place in the 1970s, at York, England. Among the finds were the remains of a Viking settlement which occupied the site about 1000 years ago.*

THE UNDERGROUND WORLD

Projects in rescue archaeology allow the archaeologist to excavate and record a site that is being cleared for subsequent development. Just such an opportunity was given to the Museum of London, in the mid-1970s, when an old churchyard was being cleared in the City of London (that is, the square mile that was the original city itself). Fortunately, since nothing was scheduled to be built in the near future, the Museum was able to take two years to excavate. Burials, such as the one we see here, had begun in the early Middle Ages and continued until sometime in the 16th century, after which the graveyard was not used. In short, a perfect place to do a controlled study of the skeletons, both for a comparison of burial methods and a statistical analysis of the population. When the actual analyzing is complete, we should have detailed information on physical aspects of the Middle Ages, including ratio of the sexes; average height; disease, deformity and causes of death.

TO UNDERSTAND THE PURPOSE of archaeology and archaeologists, we must project ourselves back in time, imagining the things that people are likely to have done and the traces these things will have left behind.

Burials, for instance, generally leave distinctive signs in or on the ground. In the distant past, when a grave was dug, the body buried in it was often clothed and wearing jewellery (coffins were less frequent), while around the corpse were placed a few personal possessions and other tokens for life in the afterworld. When such a grave is investigated, the archaeologist is likely to find the skeleton, jewellery (if present) and some trace of the clothes in which the corpse was buried.

There will also be traces of grave offerings. Pieces of pottery and stone and metal tools generally survive, while animal bones within the tomb may indicate what was eaten as the last sacrificial meal.

Externally, the grave itself is usually distinguishable; the disturbed soil of what archaeologists term the grave fill normally looks different from the undisturbed soil around. Graves are often further marked by something erected above them, from a simple headstone to the impressive barrows of antiquity.

A Wealth of Buildings

The diverse structures that peoples of all kinds have built for themselves, their animals or their gods offer a wealth of material. Stone buildings generally provide the most substantial remains. This may be simply a foundation or as much as a few courses of their walls.

Floors, too, are important. Stone structures often have well-made floors, like Roman mosaic pavements. Less imposing buildings may have floors of beaten earth, or be covered with clay or some other durable material.

Brick structures are reasonably long-lasting, though mud walls are quite difficult for the archaeologist to detect. As they are constructed of bricks made from local clay, they are often virtually indistinguishable from the surrounding earth. Spraying the area with water, however, may reveal mud bricks more clearly.

Wooden structures leave varying traces. Where the roof was supported by substantial posts, these were generally set into large postholes. Though the timbers may have long since decayed, the postholes should remain, filled with packing material that often included stones. In many instances, the soil that accumulated when the post rotted differs in appearance, so a 'ghost' of the post is visible.

Other wooden structures were built using closely packed, slender uprights driven only a short way into the ground. These may remain as stake-holes, small holes whose fill often contrasts with the surrounding soil. The shallowness of such foundations means that, on site that has been disturbed by ploughing, for instance, they are unlikely to survive. The same is even more true of the remains of timber-framed structures, which were built entirely above ground with no foundations. However, with care and in favourable circumstances, their outlines may be detected by seeing how they have compacted the soil beneath them.

Where structures have left little or no detectable trace, an outline may be discovered by making a careful study of how artefacts and other remains are distributed. Establishing details of the distribution of domestic equipment – or even something as mundane as where refuse was stored – can reveal the position of both outer walls and internal partitions.

The Purpose of Pits

Many early excavators supposed that prehistoric people often lived underground, so pits were frequently identified as 'pit houses'. However,

This striking mosaic comes from Cirencester in the English Midlands, site of the ancient Roman town of Corinium, second in size only to London. The town was prosperous and yielded many finds, including examples of some of the best mosaics of the 2nd century AD, of which this, from a substantive town house, is just one. This is, in fact, a section of a large mosaic depicting the seasons and shows Pomona, goddess of autumn. It was made entirely from local stone: brick and tile (red), limestone (cream and white), sandstone (earth colours) and blue lias. Because the mosaics are composed of hard material and lay protected some 1-2 m (1-2 yd) below ground they are exceptionally well-preserved.

most were actually used for storage or rubbish disposal. Their sites stand out clearly in contrast to undisturbed soil around.

Saxon *grubenhauser* ('grub huts') – sub-rectangular hollows in the ground found in England and Germanic Europe – were for a long time accepted as pit dwellings. Now, however, it is thought that the hollow was actually an underground cellar or air-space, covered by the plank floor of an above-ground hut.

For true pit dwellings, we have to turn to the south-west United States. Here, the ancestors of the builders of great multi-storeyed pueblos lived in semi-subterranean houses with wooden superstructures. When the brick pueblos were built, the underground structure was retained as a holy *kiva*, or shrine.

Defending the Home

Defensive works surrounding individual houses or whole settlements were frequently composed of banks and ditches, as well as of stone or wooden walls. The impressive effects that can be achieved simply by enhancing naturally occurring features with artificial banks and ditches can be seen clearly in the many hillforts of Europe, of which Maiden Castle in south-west England is a superb example.

Time has softened the contours of these forts. The ditches have been partly filled with soil. Like many of the features already mentioned, ditches can be distinguished because their fill contrasts with the surrounding soil.

Banks seldom vanish entirely, but remain as a low bump. Well-preserved examples may yield traces, in the form of postholes and stakeholes, of a superstructure. Other ramparts combined stone and wood in their construction in a variety of ways, among them the timber-laced *murus gallicus* that presented such an obstacle to Julius Caesar in his conquest of Gaul.

A number of similar timber-laced ramparts have been partially preserved, particularly in Scotland, as 'vitrified forts'. Here, nature has come to the aid of archaeologists; the timber was destroyed in fires fanned by strong winds to such a temperature that the stonework was melted and transformed into a substance which resembles glass in appearance.

Stone fortifications, like stone house walls, stand the ravages of time better than timber ones do, and it is not unusual to recover several of their courses, assuming they have had only the forces of nature to contend with. In many instances, both domestic and defensive walls have been exploited by later peoples as a convenient quarry for building materials. When stone or brick has been removed, the former presence of the wall may be indicated by a 'robber trench'.

Maiden Castle, in Dorset, *dates back to 300 BC as a hillfort and is one of the largest such fortifications. Two centuries later it was strengthened and held out until 43 AD, when it was taken by Vespasian, who massacred all the defenders. It was then abandoned, except for a Roman shrine built 3 centuries later.*

Clues from the Context

THE TRACES OF standing structures and holes in the ground together represent a large proportion of what the excavator will encounter on-site. But there are also associated material remains, the very nature of which may be most informative. Distinctive artefacts provide the archaeologist with much of the evidence he will need for dating, and details about technology, trade and other aspects of daily life.

Another reason for the importance of material remains is perhaps less immediately obvious. It lies in the information to be obtained from the relationship between a find and its context. We have already seen that the overall distribution of material on a site can provide outlines of structures that have since vanished. Looking in more detail at how the material was actually distributed, we may hope to discover additional information about the function of particular areas within the site or within buildings on it.

Because context is so vitally significant to archaeologists, they bitterly resent destruction wrought by treasure-hunters who disturb archaeological sites. It is not, as many imagine, purely a spoil-sport attitude. The removal of an object from its context means that all the information it could have yielded about that context has been lost, and the full significance of the object may never be understood.

Reading the Signs
A large jar found during excavation could have been made for one of many purposes. Its context suggests what the specific one might have been. For example, if it was discovered with several others of similar proportions in an area obviously set aside for them, it would seem likely that it was used for storage. If careful excavation reveals pollen or other plant remains, those may lend support to the conjecture.

Further support for this view would be provided if the jars were found close to the area set aside for cooking. That area could be indicated by the presence of a hearth, and in some cases by more complicated cooking facilities. Around the hearth may be grouped other pieces of kitchen equipment, particularly coarse pottery vessels, their bases blackened from frequent exposure to the fire.

Another area of the house may contain a pair of small postholes, not apparently integral to the stability of the building. What might they represent? Here again, the associated material can provide valuable clues. If, nearby, a number of curious triangular clay objects with a hole in the top corner are discovered, these may well be loom weights. The postholes are therefore likely to be those from the frame of an upright loom.

A find of stone or metal instruments for scraping skins, on the other hand, might lead us to identify the postholes as the remains of the uprights from a frame on which animal skins were stretched to cure. Other possibilities include that of a meat-drying rack, known in a number of modern hunter-gatherer sites and now identified in several later Palaeolithic caves.

Whatever the interpretation, meticulous study of associated material is vital in helping to formulate it. Thus the information that can be recovered separately from structural remains and from artefacts and other material evidence is greatly enhanced by careful observation of the relationships between them.

Sifting the Soil
Much of what the archaeologist excavates can broadly be termed structural – walls and floors, postholes and pits, banks and ditches. But the surrounding soil is equally important. Each layer on a site, down to the bedrock, tells something about the human activities that have taken place there in the past, or, indeed, the lack of them.

Some of the layers are natural accumulations, formed by the decay of vegetation and of any organic materials left by man, or deposits of soil introduced by wind, water or erosion. Others are man-made, such as a layer of rubble or debris where inhabitants of a settlement have razed old structures to create a flat ground surface on which to rebuild. Sites occupied at one time by settlements may become the fields or gardens of succeeding generations, in which a man-induced natural soil builds up.

In all but the earliest sites, the bedrock marks the limit of archaeological material. When investigating the extremely remote past, archaeologists rely heavily on the processes of geological upheaval to reveal the evidence that interests them. That is one of the main reasons so many early Palaeolithic sites are known in the Rift Valley of Africa, where disturbances to the Earth's crust have resulted in the exposure of enormous blocks of land once buried many tens of metres below the ground.

One of the joys of excavation is the unique experience each site offers. Houses and streets and courtyards, wells and rubbish pits, roads and fortifications, fields and animal enclosures, cemeteries and megaliths – the variety of evidence of man's activities is infinite.

This reconstruction of the vertical excavation of 4th-century Roman workshop in England shows the archaeological evidence obtained from each level. The site, near Bristol, had been abandoned for some 1500 years, although on-site evidence suggested that it had been dug into once since then, perhaps by people searching for building stone.

Throughout the process of excavation, careful checks are made on the stratigraphy of the site as the various layers of soil are removed. In this, as with most digs, the bedrock marks the downward limit of investigation. Some very early sites, however, may be in or under bedrock, as a result of geological changes since they were occupied.

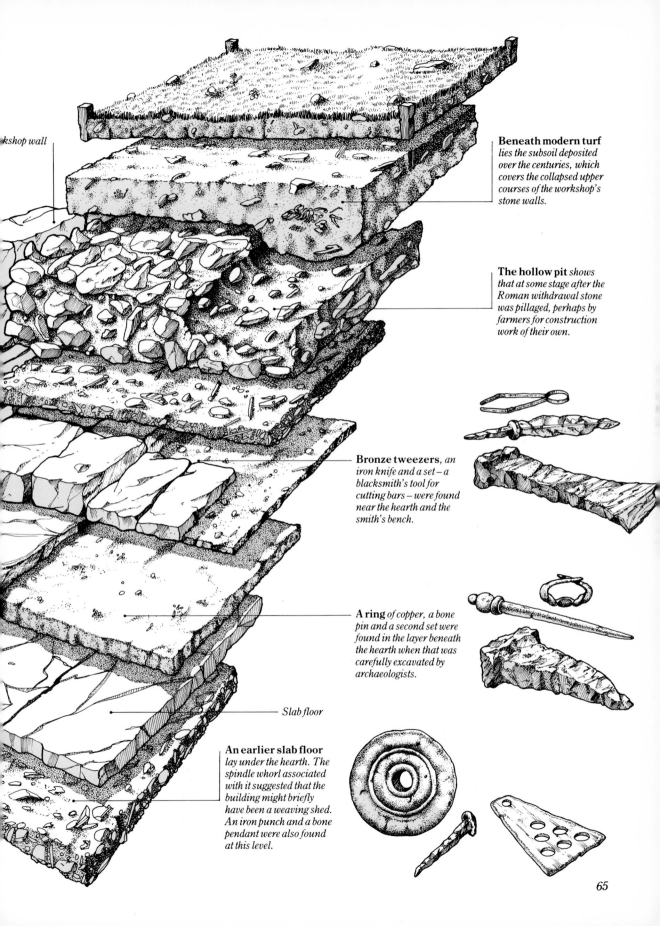

kshop wall

Beneath modern turf *lies the subsoil deposited over the centuries, which covers the collapsed upper courses of the workshop's stone walls.*

The hollow pit *shows that at some stage after the Roman withdrawal stone was pillaged, perhaps by farmers for construction work of their own.*

Bronze tweezers, *an iron knife and a set – a blacksmith's tool for cutting bars – were found near the hearth and the smith's bench.*

A ring *of copper, a bone pin and a second set were found in the layer beneath the hearth when that was carefully excavated by archaeologists.*

Slab floor

An earlier slab floor *lay under the hearth. The spindle whorl associated with it suggested that the building might briefly have been a weaving shed. An iron punch and a bone pendant were also found at this level.*

To Dig or Not to Dig

WHY DO ARCHAEOLOGISTS excavate sites? In the 19th century the answer would have been a simple, relatively straightforward one – to recover artefacts and structures, the relics of past ages. Gradually, however, the business of excavation became more skilful and its objectives more sophisticated; a mid-20th century archaeologist might well have said that he dug to discover the relationships between the relics of the past as much as to discover the actual relics themselves and to find out what happened and when.

Today's archaeologist, building on the foundations laid by his predecessors, will probably tell you that he digs to answer specific questions about the past. This, he will argue, requires a more thorough approach to excavation than ever before. An extreme exponent of this viewpoint will maintain that sites should be excavated only if they can be expected to answer specific questions of interest to the archaeological community.

At the opposite extreme, there are archaeologists who deplore any excavation except on threatened sites. In the frequently quoted words of Sir Mortimer Wheeler, 'excavation is destruction' and the rescue excavation lobby argues that there is no justification for digging any site that is not going to be disturbed or destroyed anyway. Save other sites for future archaeologists whose techniques will be better, they say – just think how we complain about the way in which our less scientific archaeological predecessors treated the sites they excavated.

Who is right – the research excavator or the rescuer? Are the viewpoints indeed mutually exclusive? Surely not; the answer must lie in some compromise between the two extremes.

The Threat of Progress

Archaeological sites are today threatened to an extent that they have never been before. The rate of rural and urban development and expansion is increasing due both to technological innovations and to social demands. Public funding of archaeological work has increased in many countries in an attempt to deal with this, but inevitably there are limits, even when state funds are supplemented by private generosity. Consequently, the resources can never hope to match the threat, and, inevitably, some sites will be destroyed without record.

Archaeology may even be of use to contemporary planners, for it may reveal hazards below ground that the developer will be grateful to avoid. A prior knowledge of important and interesting sites may also be used to argue for the re-routing of roads or modifications in the layout of structures, to allow these sites to be preserved for the public to see. In the United States an assessment of the threat to archaeology is mandatory in advance of any construction programme for which a federal permit is required, with the result that the archaeological landscape is being intensively explored and much of it conserved.

The Unknown Factors

Another argument in favour of well-planned rescue excavations is that the contents of a site can never entirely be predicted in advance. If they could, what would be the point of excavating it?

The research archaeologist may come to his site with a lot of well-formulated questions about the Neolithic henge he has noted from an aerial photograph. But what about the unexpected Iron Age temple or the Saxon wooden church whose remains he uncovers above his henge? He is not justified in digging through those just because they are outside his immediate area of interest. It is his duty to excavate what he finds, to the best of his ability within the budget available, because the evidence may be of vital interest to his colleagues studying the Iron Age or the Saxons. In this sense, there is no such thing as a purely research excavation, because rescuing unwanted evidence from archaeological destruction becomes almost inevitable.

Despite the many arguments in favour of concentrating available resources on sites whose destruction is imminent, there is some justification for conducting research excavations. Certain questions can be answered only by excavating particular sites that are not threatened. Some archaeologists also believe that proper training of excavators and the advancement of excavation techniques can be satisfactorily achieved only in the unhurried atmosphere of a research excavation.

Those can be extremely long-term projects. For example, the slow and meticulous open-plan excavations at Wroxeter, a Roman city in Shropshire, central England, have resulted in the discovery of traces of small timber buildings which have probably been missed on many similar sites dug at greater speed. At this rate, however, it would take 200 years to completely excavate Wroxeter.

Excavations at Coppergate, York (⟨ in the late 1970s an 1980s, uncovered a wealth of remains fr Viking times. The s discovered when the of a bank were bein deepened. A remark well preserved 8th-c Anglo-Saxon helme (below), known as ⟩ Coppergate Helmet, among the remains

RESCUING YORK

IN THE MID-1960s, it was recommended that inner and outer ring-roads should be built around the ancient English city of York, to cope with traffic problems. The threat to York's archaeology posed by the inner ring-road was obvious, and a preliminary investigation into its implications was commissioned.

The results convinced the British government to provide full financial backing for an archaeological unit to excavate affected areas of the city. There were also generous contributions of time and money, and various developers made planning modifications.

York was an important settlement in Roman times, when it consisted of a legionary fortress and a civilian settlement, on opposite sides of the River Ouse. In the Viking era, it was a substantial and prosperous town, but in the later Middle Ages it declined.

Results of the York Archaeological Trust's first year of work lived up to the highest expectations. Excavation of the St. Mary's Hospital site revealed details of its evolution over the centuries from a church to a hospital for aged chaplains and finally to a school. In the low-lying Lloyd's Bank site, waterlogged Viking leatherworkers' houses were uncovered, their plank walls and floors excellently preserved, along with a wealth of fascinating organic remains.

Most exciting was the chance discovery of the remains of a Roman bath-house, complete with a monumental sewer. Development of this site could be halted only briefly, so the archaeologists spent a frantic two weeks in digging. The bath-house was encased in the development, but the sewer can still be visited by permission.

The work of the York Archaeological Trust has gone from strength to strength. From the public viewpoint at least, the culmination was the opening of a living museum of Viking York, complete with noises and smells.

The excavations *at York took place, over about 20 years, in a series of sites within that city and the finds included evidence which reflected several of the long-buried and disparate layers of this great city's past. Each site was exciting, and the nature of its finds unique, ranging from a sewer (above) that was a fine example of Roman engineering to a medieval cemetery (below).*

SELECTING THE SITE

WE HAVE ALREADY looked at some of the priorities in excavation, and at the advantages of well-planned rescue excavations. In a region where a number of sites are likely to be destroyed in the near future, further decisions have to be made about which are to be excavated. The choice may involve several factors, which sometimes conflict.

Ideally, whatever the immediate priorities in selecting sites in an area, in the long term an attempt should be made to balance the investigations between sites of all periods and types – from Palaeolithic to Medieval or later, and including cemeteries, settlements, industrial and religious locations and so forth. Another consideration is the relative scarcity of sites: cases can be made for selecting both the most common types, which should give a representative picture of everyday life, and the rare or unique ones, which may have held key positions in the societies to which they belonged. Both the peasant's hut and Stonehenge deserve investigation.

The excavator may also be called upon to decide whether to excavate a few sites thoroughly, small parts of many sites, or larger areas of fewer. Such decisions will vary according to factors such as the state of local research, convenience and practicability.

Initial Considerations

Unlike our antiquarian forefathers with their 'speed is of the essence' approach, modern excavators do not undertake their task lightly. The work apparently entailed in digging a site is only a fraction of that actually involved.

In addition to the obvious jobs of clearing, excavating, recording and backfilling a site, with all the attendant activities, there are many other things to do. All the material and information recovered has to be analyzed, often work for specialists in many fields. Site plans and sections need to be redrawn and labelled. The finds have to be drawn, and many of them conserved. A report must be written up on everything found and what it may mean. Estimates of the effort involved range from an optimistic assessment equal to that of the excavation itself, to a probably more realistic one of four or five times as much. Any excavator has to take this into consideration when he calculates the money he will require, the time entailed and any specialist assistance required. Planning for the report is essential, for unpublished sites are information lost and valuable funds wasted.

Funding for excavation may come from a variety of sources. Many countries have a state archaeological body that sponsors or organizes excavations. Frequently, local authorities also fund archaeological work, by employing fulltime archaeologists on their staff. *Ad hoc* teams may be assembed for specific projects, which may be funded either by public money or through some form of private sponsorship.

Developers often contribute generously to the cost of excavating sites in the areas they intend to develop. Other major sources of financial support are university archaeological departments, often in the form of training excavations for their students, and privately or publicly sponsored trusts and research bodies, including a number of overseas schools and missions. Museums also provide money for many excavations, as they have done in the past, though today their aims are rather more than the collection of exhibitable material.

Permission to dig

The prospective excavator must also obtain permission to undertake his excavation. Sometimes this involves negotiations only with the landowner and any tenants; in that case, approval will depend on agreements about compensation for the loss of crops, arrangements for access to the site, time limits for the excavation work and arrangements for restoring the site to its pre-excavation state. In many countries, however, all archaeological sites are regarded as the property of the nation, and official permission must be obtained from the government or other authorities.

The destination of material found during the excavation must also be agreed upon. In Britain, all finds, with the exception of gold and silver, automatically belong to the landowner, but he is often willing to present most to a museum, or at least to permit archaeologists to study them.

Laws vary considerably, and in many countries all archaeological finds are state property. This may mean that the archaeologist working abroad will have to make special arrangements to export material for a limited period for examination, or to import specialists to study it *in situ*.

Picking the Team

Once financial support and permission for excavation have been secured, the next priority is to choose the people to do the job. A small excavation presenting no special problems will

An archaeological *expedition from Chicago University's Oriental Institute prepares to excavate a site at Nippur in Iraq. The expedition director (at front) is supported by a team of specialists, which include a draughtsman, a*

The numbers involved in the average excavation will be somewhere in between these two extremes. The director will be supported by a number of experienced assistants or supervisors, who will watch the day-to-day running of different areas of the site and who will probably do all the planning, photography and surveying. Some of these supervisors may have specialist knowledge of particular categories of evidence, and they can advise on what material should be recovered, and how. By excavating certain areas themselves, they can often note details which might be missed by less-skilled diggers. A finds assistant is also likely to be included in the team, supervising the washing of pottery and other material, executing 'first aid' conservation and recording the finds.

On every site, however, the ordinary digger will be found. Despite his ubiquity, he is a very varied species. The most common varieties in America and Europe include the university student (not necessarily of archaeology), looking for an interesting and worthwhile holiday, or just addicted to digging. Another is the interested amateur, often available only at the weekends, but giving freely and generously of whatever time he has available.

In parts of Europe and increasingly in Asia and Africa, work may also be undertaken by paid labourers, often in large numbers. Generally these are local people who are interested in supplementing their income, but in some places, notably countries with a long archaeological tradition, such as Egypt and Iraq, these labourers usually possess the skill and expertise of hereditary craftsmen.

Finally, many western excavations include specimens of that curious sub-species, the itinerant digger. Bronzed and rheumatic, with clothes old and much mended, he or she has probably been digging since childhood. On leaving school or university, they have decided to spend some time on archaeological expeditions before embarking on a permanent career. When all the summer volunteers have gone home, they continue moving from dig to dig. Poorly paid, often surviving in conditions of extreme hardship, itinerant diggers provide the main labour force for winter excavations. Some will end up in full-time archaeological employment, with more comfortable winter work indoors; others will become disillusioned or physically wrecked and will turn to different work. As a rule, few itinerants last many years on the hard grind of 'the circuit'.

rveyor, a photographer, conservator and a finds sistant. Among the port team is a large mber of Iraqis – these e professional bourers, descendants of rkmen once employed the great pioneer chaeologists.

probably consist of the director and a handful of volunteers. At the opposite end of the scale, an excavation team may include a whole hierarchy of assistants and supervisors, as well as the diggers and a host of specialists, such as photographers, draughtsmen, conservators, finds assistants, surveyors, analysts of pollen, seeds, bones and soil, not to mention the cooks, camp commandants, night watchmen and servants, all of whom are necessary personnel.

WHAT KIND OF HOLE?

EXCAVATION LAYS BARE two dimensions of the past, the horizontal one and the vertical one. Horizontal excavation reveals the site as it was at a given time – the array of houses with their furnishings, rubbish pits, the defences of the settlement, the arrangements for keeping animals, the areas assigned to other activities, such as crafts and administration.

The vertical dimension shows the sequence of changes within the site and the relationship of one period to those before and after it, as revealed by the stratigraphy of the various vertical sections.

The Vertical Approach
During the earlier decades of the 20th century, when archaeology was very much concerned with chronology, excavation techniques concentrated on revealing the vertical dimension.

The best-known method was Sir Mortimer Wheeler's box, or grid, system. This involved dividing the site into squares of a given size which were excavated, leaving narrower unexcavated strips, termed 'baulks', between them, in which cross-sections were preserved.

Though this gives excellent vertical control, its modern opponents argue that the method largely forfeits an appreciation of the horizontal dimension of the site. To some extent, this is restored when the baulks are removed and the final plans of each layer or phase are studied. But because the evidence from each phase has never been viewed or photographed *in toto*, some understanding is inevitably lost, and may result in some aspects of the site being misunderstood.

The Horizontal Approach
Opponents of vertically-orientated methods advocate open area excavations - uncovering the site layer by layer. The technique has been particularly successful for shallow sites and for those where the horizontal picture is more important, for example Palaeolithic or Mesolithic sites, where structural remains are rare.

Modern recording techniques ensure that the vertical dimension is recorded on paper but it is never seen or photographed in actuality. This may be less of a disadvantage than the lack of total horizontal photographs in the rival methods, but it nevertheless may result in some aspects of the site being misunderstood.

Making the Choice
Clearly, no method can be said categorically to be the 'right' way to dig in every case. The merits of each must be assessed, according to the site and the circumstances.

Often, there may be a compromise; perhaps open area excavation in a number of large trenches, whose walls preserve a visible record of the overall stratigraphy.

The importance of the vertical record for dating purposes is demonstrated in this excavation of a posthole. The post stands in its hole (top), on packing stones, with the topsoil and subsoil around it mixed up by the original digging. The position of the coin dated AD 1520, amongst the packing stones, shows that it must have entered the hole before, or about, the time the post was erected. The presence of the potsherds which date from around 1300, could have been misleading if the exact vertical position of the coin had not been noted.

The position of a second coin (bottom) dating from 1600, in the new layer of soil which accumulated after the post had decayed, provides further evidence for dating.

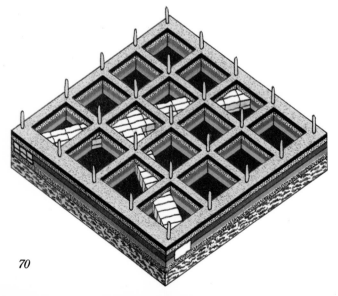

In a grid excavation, *square areas are first dug out of the site, leaving 'baulks' standing between them as a record of the vertical aspect. Wooden pegs at the corners of the boxes are reference points for surveying.*

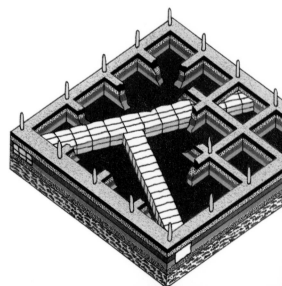

Later, the 'baulks' are *removed to reveal the deposits which lie below them, in this case part of a wall. The grid method of excavation is no longer commonly used.*

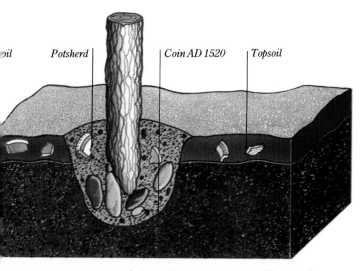

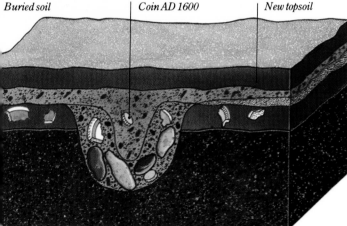

Potsherd | Coin AD 1520 | Topsoil

Buried soil | Coin AD 1600 | New topsoil

Laying out the Site

Once a site has been selected and an excavation strategy decided upon, the next step is usually to draw a contour survey (earthwork plan), to show in detail the topography before the first earth is removed. The height of the ground is measured at regular intervals across the site, using a level or a theodolite, and the readings are plotted on a plan which, like a map with contours above sea level, has lines joining the pieces of ground at the same heights.

The next stage is to establish a base line from which the site is divided up into squares or rectangles, or whatever subdivisions seem appropriate – the layout. That is superimposed on the plan of the site, and used in recording progress and finds. In the grid system of excavation, the baulks between each area dug become a physical reflection of the layout, but in open area excavation the boundaries between the subdivisions are hypothetical.

Whatever the excavation technique used, part of the layout must lie outside the excavation, to provide fixed reference points that cannot be disturbed. Markers on the site itself may be knocked and shifted during the digging, and it is vital to have some means of re-establishing their positions if that happens.

Finally, accuracy is all-important from the start of the layout, as any errors will be compounded as it proceeds.

rrow trench excavation *is particularly useful when it comes to* *avating defensive banks, ditches and walls. In such cases, the* *uence of construction is of particular interest.*

Open area excavation, *which involves uncovering the site layer by layer, is the method most commonly used today by archaeologists. Although the vertical picture is lost in the process, it can be recorded as the excavation proceeds.*

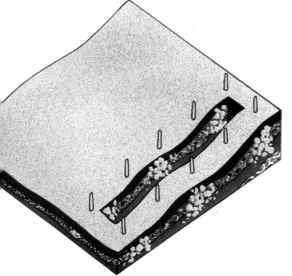

THE QUEST FOR CAMELOT

THE EXCAVATIONS at Cadbury Castle *(see page 58)* were primarily designed to test the possibility of early 6th century AD 'Arthurian' occupation, although evidence from other periods was also exposed and studied with equal care. The immense size of the interior, 7.5 hectares (18 acres), precluded its complete excavation. Therefore, in 1966, the first season, a contour survey was made to assess which parts of the interior might have been most suitable for building. Three trial trenches were excavated, in the three main zones in which settlement seemed possible.

Below the Ramparts

In 1967, the team began investigating the ramparts. The excavation of the steep outer banks was a major undertaking, but the results were disappointing. Although they had clearly been built in several phases, there was little associated material to date these phases.

The innermost rampart was likely to be the most complex, so work started with the cutting of a machine trench across it. This machine trench was followed by a parallel hand-dug trench, 10m (33ft) wide. The topmost, latest defence was the mortared wall of Ethelred, the third a late Iron Age bank rebuilt to defend the hill for the last stand against the Romans – the massacred bodies of the valiant defenders were discovered later, in the 1970 excavation of the south-west gateway. Between these two was a structure dubbed the 'Stony Bank'. Investigations between 1967 and 1970 showed this to belong to Arthurian times. A coin built into it indicated that the structure could date from no earlier than the 5th century AD. A cobbled

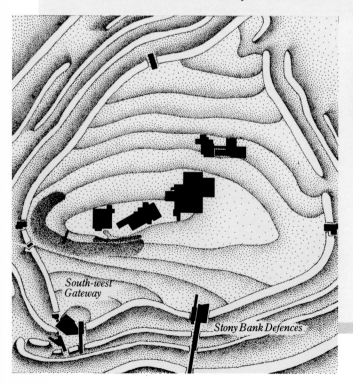

South-west Gateway

Stony Bank Defences

This plan *of the Cadbury site (left) shows excavations made between 1966 and 1970. First, three trial trenches were dug in the areas where settlement seemed most likely. Trenches were then cut across the ramparts, revealing the 'Stony Bank' defences and the south-west gateway. Several trenches were also dug in the interior.*

A machine-cut trench *(above) across the innermost rampart provided a useful picture of the stratigraphy, showing at least five main constructional phases. Althou[gh] this trench proved useful, late[r] machine trenches caused problems. It was concluded th[at] they did not justify the potentia[l] damage to physical remains.*

road leading into the south-west gateway incorporated a 6th century brooch, again providing a date for the Stony Bank defences.

Excavation uncovered the face of this rampart, which was a dry-stone wall with regular gaps where upright and horizontal cross timbers had once been placed. The gateway itself had also been of timber. Dark stains showed where the massive posts supporting this had decayed.

Inside the Walls

Several trenches were dug in the interior, mainly following indications of major structures from a preliminary geophysical survey *(see page 54)*. In one of these, the features uncovered included a narrow foundation trench containing a row of small postholes. Among the earth and gravel packed around these posts were two sherds of Tintagel ware, the distinctive late 5th/early 6th-century imported pottery that had served as major dating evidence on other Arthurian period sites. The unabraded condition of these sherds indicated that they could be used to date the construction of this building closely.

The trench containing the wall was selectively enlarged to include the predicted extent of the structure, without success. So it was decided to remove the plough-soil mechanically over a much wider area, a strip 5m (16ft) wide by 45m (150ft) long. Numerous features were exposed - postholes, pits, gullies and wall trenches of several periods. To pick out those that might belong to the Arthurian structure, the associated material from each had to be examined carefully and dated. After this the characteristics of the individual postholes, such as their depth and width, had to be examined to see which might belong together.

Eventually it was established that a line of postholes belonged to the 6th century building; they ran at right angles to the original wall, which turned out to be an internal partition. Extension of the area under excavation revealed the rest of the structure, a hall more than 18 by 9m (60 by 30ft).

Arthur's Seat?

Almost all defended hill settlements of the immediate post-Roman epoch were quite small, probably the strongholds of individual kings and their warbands. The topography of Cadbury Castle would have lent itself to building defences round a similarly small area. The fact that a much larger area was enclosed, with considerable effort, suggests Cadbury was intended to house a much larger group – an army rather than a warband.

Thus, though the connection with Arthur can never be proved, Cadbury's location and the nature of its defences make it a reasonable presumption that it could have served as the base for the British army that took the field against the Saxons and defeated them at nearby Mount Badon.

A sixth-century brooch *(above) found near the south-west gateway provided further evidence that Cadbury Castle dated from Arthurian times. The leg of a man (below) is among the remains of the massacred bodies of Cadbury's last defenders, discovered during excavations of the south-west gateway.*

SURVEYING TECHNIQUES

Taking levels *involves the use of a dumpy level, or a theodolite (right). Both instruments measure the height marked on a surveyor's staff at the point in an exact horizontal line from the instrument. If the height of one object – a datum point – is known, and the position of the surveying instrument remains constant, the staff can be moved to different objects, and their heights determined by a simple calculation.*

SURVEYING PLAYS an important role in excavation. After the initial contour survey, other similar studies (generally known as 'levelling') are made during the course of the dig to record height variations in major deposits or features – the slope of a road or the depth of a ditch, for instance. 'Spot heights' are also noted. These are heights of individual features, such as the top of a pit or a posthole, or the vertical position of a small find like a coin.

The pieces of equipment most commonly used in archaeological surveying are telescope-type levelling instruments, especially the dumpy level, and the theodolite. On archaeological sites, theodolites tend to be somewhat primitive, unlike the super-precision, self-adjusting modern instruments, which also measure distances.

The principle of taking levels relies on comparing the heights of the points to be measured with that of a fixed point of known height. Officially-fixed points are called bench marks. Their physical position is denoted by a symbol on a stone post, a plaque or similar object, and their precise height above sea-level is recorded on official maps.

Often, however, the nearest bench mark is inconveniently far from the excavation site. In that case, it is useful to create a temporary bench mark, or datum point, on an immovable feature close to the site, such as a building. Its height can be worked out from an official bench mark, using the technique described below.

Measuring Heights

Set the instrument up near a fixed point of known height. Get a helper to hold a surveyor's staff upright on the datum point; look through the instrument and read the height on the staff. The reading you obtain gives the vertical distance between the base of the staff and the level of the instrument's telescope. Let us say it is 1.35m (4ft 6in).

Now ask your assistant to move to the first point to be measured and to hold the staff on it. Rotate the movable telescope (*not* the whole instrument) until the staff is visible and take a second reading. Say it is 1.56m (5ft); you therefore know that the second point is lower than the first by 1.56-1.35 = 0.21m. As you know the height of the datum point, you can calculate that of the second point by subtracting 0.21m from it.

You can probably calculate several other spot heights in this way without having to move your

The difference *between the reading on this staff and the reading on the first staff, added to the height of the datum point, gives the height of this object.*

The first step *in taking levels is to read the height on a staff placed on the datum point.*

Other nearby *spot heights can be calculated in the same way, as long as the instrument is not moved from its original position.*

Dumpy level, or theodolite

TOWN PLANNERS OF IMPERIAL MEXICO

DURING THE 1960s, archaeologists mounted a full-scale investigation of the great Mexican city of Teotihuacan, which flourished some 2,000 years ago. A Mexican team excavated and restored much of the city centre, continuing work that had begun in the 1920s.

One team from the USA undertook an intensive survey of the surrounding countryside to provide a picture of rural settlement and local ecology, while a second American team prepared a detailed map of the entire city, in which there were several thousand structures. The mapping team also made small-scale excavations to supplement its surface findings.

Although it had already been discovered that the city centre was one of the world's finest examples of sophisticated early town planning, the mapping team was surprised to find that such planning had been carried out for the whole of Teotihuacan. The entire city was divided into residential blocks, generally squares of around 57m (185ft). These blocks presented a grim exterior of windowless walls, but were arranged internally in groups of rooms surrounding open courtyards, ensuring their inhabitants both privacy and fresh air.

All the blocks were set out along a precise grid, aligned parallel and at right angles to the principal avenue of the city, the so-called Street of the Dead. This ran from the Pyramid of the Moon, past the larger Pyramid of the Sun and between the Great Compound and the Citadel, and on for a further 3km (2 miles). The Citadel housed the Temple of Quetzalcoatl, the Plumed Serpent, an ornately decorated stepped pyramid. This temple and the pyramids of the Sun and Moon were the major religious structures in the city.

The Great Compound, on the other hand, seemed devoted to secular concerns. It includes what appear to be administrative buildings, while its enormous plaza was probably the city's main marketplace.

Teotihuacan was strategically placed to control trade between the Valley of Mexico and the adjacent Valley of Puebla and the Gulf Coast beyond, a factor in her ascendancy. Many blocks within the city seem to have been devoted to specialist crafts, such as obsidian working and pottery making.

The ancient city *of Teotihuacan dates from the 1st century B.C. It is one of the finest and most sophisticated examples of early town planning.*

The site was already a major settlement by the 1st century BC. It rose to be the main centre of the valley after the destruction of its main rival Cuicuilco by a volcanic eruption around 50 BC. By the 2nd century AD, more than 80 per cent of the valley's population was living within Teotihuacan, which came to rule an empire stretching over most of highland Mesoamerica and influencing even the lowland Maya civilization.

strument from its starting position. Eventually, owever, you may find that the next point to easure is too far away, or too high or low, and at the instrument must be shifted.

Get your assistant to 'freeze' at the last point easured, with the staff in place. Move the strument to its new position, and read the eight of the last point again from there. The evious reading was 2.01m and the new one is 65m (these two readings are known as resight' and 'backsight' respectively). So we

know that the new position of the instrument is 1.64m higher than it was before, because the point on which it was focused remained constant. The next set of readings must then be taken into account.

Though surveying is simple in principle, it must be very carefully performed, with strict checks to ensure accurate recording. Just one mistake will make a whole set of readings wrong, and that may often mean starting the whole job from the beginning.

Using Heavy Machinery

The use of *heavy earth-moving equipment (below) is sometimes a necessary preliminary step in an archaeological excavation, for instance where the site is buried under subsequent layers of construction or a hard surface. Here diggers are breaking up the ground surface at the site of the Billingsgate excavation in London (see pages 176-87). The actual site to be excavated lay some 3m (10ft) under a surfaced parking area and tons of post-War rubble.*

MANY MEMBERS OF the public and indeed some archaeologists are horrified at the idea of initiating excavations with earth-moving equipment. Certainly it is not a thing to be undertaken lightly. The main function of heavy earth-moving equipment on archaeological sites is to remove the soil that is of no archaeological interest and to put it back when the excavations are over. The second part is clear enough, and should arouse no strong feelings, but the first is a different matter.

The deposits removed by machinery are generally either ploughed soil or recent buildings and their cellars. They may also include natural layers that have accumulated on a long-abandoned site.

The archaeologist who directs the earth-mover's driver has a delicate task. His main job is to call a halt to the removal of soil at a level a little above that of the archaeological deposits. A margin is necessary because earth-moving equipment churns up and compacts soil to some depth below the level at which it is working. (Often, on sites stripped by machine, novices will excitedly discover 'pottery' immediately after the earth-mover has been at work. This is soil compacted so much that it becomes hard and shiny.)

On the other hand, having invested in the hire of a machine for a limited period, the director has to make sure he uses it to perform as much as possible of the initial stripping. If he stops too far short of the archaeological deposits, he could find his team of diggers tied up for days laboriously removing earth that the machine could have shifted in minutes.

Knowing the Depth

The Archaeologist who uses an earth-moving machine needs to have in advance a good idea of the depth at which archaeological material will start to be revealed. On cultivated land, consultation with the farmer will provide information about the depth to which ploughing takes place, and whether archaeological material is being turned up. A study of cuttings through the topsoil, such as streams and ditches, may also yield clues.

In towns, information may be gained by observing nearby construction sites. The records of previous excavations in the vicinity may also help.

In addition, augers and probes *(see page 56)* used at selected spots on the site will accurately indicate soil changes below ground, with minimal risk to archaeological remains. These changes, viewed in the light of what is known of local soils, are another pointer to the depth at which deposits of archaeological interest begin.

Armed with what is already known about the

Bronze Age Farm

IT IS OFTEN AN ACCIDENT which reveals unexpected evidence of some aspect of the past. Just such an accident occurred at Elp in the Drenthe province of the Netherlands. In 1960, an obvious Bronze Age barrow was being excavated and, while the site was being surveyed, the presence of what appeared to be some postholes was noticed nearby. Upon investigation, they proved to be the remains of several buildings which would have constituted a Bronze Age farm and, in 1962, these remains were investigated further.

The site was large and called for the use of heavy machinery. A bulldozer was called in and an area 90 by 70m (295 by 230ft) – thought to encompass the whole settlement – was laid out. The topsoil was removed in strips by the bulldozer and the area was then cleaned. On top of the ridge along which the settlement was built, some postholes had been removed by erosion, but elsewhere enough remained to indicate several buildings.

Radiocarbon dating showed that the site had been occupied for about 400 years, between the 13th and 14th centuries BC. During this period, the farmhouse and subsidiary buildings had been rebuilt five or six times, on each occasion shifting along the ridge.

The main building in each phase, on the crest of the ridge, was a large long-house, divided into two roughly equal portions. One half was the family dwelling. The other half – the eastern half – had a row of interior postholes that were the foundations of stall partitions: this part of the building must have housed the family's herd of cattle, numbering somewhere between 20 and 30 head.

In addition, in each phase there was a smaller house situated on the west of the ridge, this may have been the home of subordinate members of the community. There were also sheds and barns in which wheat and barley were probably stored.

depth of the uninteresting deposits, the archaeologist then watches closely as his machine driver carefully removes the soil. The instant the archaeologist notices something potentially interesting, such as a soil change or some possible archaeological material, he will call a halt and investigate. He can then decide whether the time has come to stop, or whether more soil should be mechanically removed.

Earth-moving equipment is expensive to hire and often absorbs a sizeable amount of the excavation budget. Where rescue work is taking place in advance of construction, it is sometimes possible to borrow one of the contractor's machines. But the archaeologist must be well-organized enough to know exactly what he wants done. A contractor who has looked sympathetically on one request for a few hours' machine time is likely to be less accommodating if the request is made repeatedly.

A Hard Slog

When the top layers of the site have been stripped by machine, some disturbed and compacted soil remains to be removed manually, using spades, shovels and picks. It is hard work, but it can be quite enjoyable, particularly as a way to warm up on cold days. The monotony is often relieved by a little competition in soil-shifting and barrow-filling.

Often the amount of topsoil to be removed does not justify the use of a machine, and then the whole task must be done by hand. The topsoil, and the turf if the site was grassed, is kept separate from lower layers cleared during the excavation proper, as it usually has to be put back afterwards.

Sometimes this surface skimming is done with shovels or hoes, but more often it is carried out with trowels, the archaeologist's multi-purpose tool. This is the stage at which volunteers begin to despair, as they trowel repeatedly over the same piece of ground and find nothing.

But at last something appears. The nature of the soil changes and 'features' begin to emerge – differences in soil that show up the presence of pits, postholes and ditches, spreads of stones or other surfaces that were once house floors, courtyards or roadways. The supervisor goes round labelling these. Probably, a pre-excavation plan is also made, showing the locations of the features that have been spotted. Such a plan is needed because, as the site dries out, subtle differences in soil tend to vanish and they could easily be missed later.

Using picks, shovels and spades *to remove rubble and topsoil from a site (left) can be hard work. However, as diggers draw near to where the archaeological deposits are thought to lie (above), their work slows down, becoming less strenuous and more precise. The remaining topsoil is then removed in thin layers, until archaeological features begin to emerge.*

DISSECTING THE SITE

AS WE HAVE SEEN, abandoned sites gradually change as a result of human activities and natural processes. The idea behind excavation is to take the site apart in the reverse order to that in which it was formed.

In some respects, the layers of an archaeological site resemble those of a sponge cake, and this analogy tells something about the technique of excavation. The top coating - the icing - is removed first, followed by the first layer of sponge, then the layer of cream. After that, the filling of, say, jam or black cherries is removed, exposing the cake's sponge base. If you were to pull out the cherries, the whole cake would collapse, while you cannot reach them anyway unless you dig holes down to them.

The features of an archaeological site, however, require more thought and pre-planning. They must be carefully examined to

work out the order in which they were created. That can often be determined on the basis of their relationships to one another. If, for example, there are two pits close together, the relationship of their outlines should show the order in which they were dug; the outline of the earlier one will be cut by that of the later. The later one's outline will be complete.

Assessing Relationships

Although the relationships between features are clear in many cases, in others the similarity between the deposits filling them makes them much harder to distinguish. In such cases, a variety of methods are employed to try to clarify the relationship.

The surface of the features may be carefully cleaned by trowelling off a tiny skim of soil, in the hope that the cleaned surface will be more revealing. During the process of trowelling, you may also detect some distinct textural differences between the various features.

If the site has become dry, spraying or splashing the features with water may help. One may dry out more rapidly than the other, or turn a slightly different colour when wet. This technique is also particularly useful in revealing mudbricks, which often blend completely with their surroundings when dry, but which frequently show up when wet.

The Art of Sectioning

In accordance with the idea that horizontal and vertical aspects of the site should be studied simultaneously wherever possible, many archaeologists advocate 'half-sectioning' features, or cutting sections across larger ones. In this technique, the layers in the selected portion are removed and recorded one by one, while the rest of the feature is temporarily left unexcavated.

Once the chosen portion has been completely excavated, its vertical aspect can be studied and recorded before the rest of the feature is removed. In this way, both the horizontal nature of the layers and their vertical relationships can be carefully studied.

Some archaeologists – particularly the exponents of open area excavation – prefer to excavate each layer within a feature completely horizontally, sacrificing the vertical view for the sake of a complete horizontal one. In both methods, plans (the horizontal aspect) and sections (the vertical aspect) are recorded on paper, but the methods differ in what is actually visible to the excavator as he goes along.

The debate about excavation of features is really a microcosm of the debate about excavation strategy in general, and the volunteer digger may find himself exposed to the advocates of both, to his confusion. Naturally, neither approach is wholly right or wrong, but one may be more appropriate than the other in particular circumstances.

Layer by Layer

Sometimes a feature is so deep or is so oddly shaped (undercut, for instance) that its complete excavation is impossible or dangerous. Then it must be excavated and recorded in stages, proceeding as the level of the surrounding deposits is lowered.

When all the features cutting or lying on the uppermost ground surface have been excavated

and recorded, the surface itself is removed to reveal the deposit below.

Let us take the example of early medieval ploughsoil cut by later medieval ditches, pits and house foundations. The later medieval features are excavated first. Only then is the ploughsoil itself removed, perhaps revealing a Roman road beneath. Remember that, while later holes cut down into a deposit, earlier structures will stick up. While removing the ploughsoil, therefore, the stubs of the walls of any Roman houses that bordered the road may well be encountered.

In principle, each deposit on a site should be removed stratigraphically, dealing with a complete layer at a time. In practice, however, a deposit may be too thick to clear all in one go, for instance if it has been mixed up by centuries of cultivation. In that case, excavation proceeds in arbitrary horizontal layers known as 'spits'. A spit of reasonable depth, perhaps 10cm (4in), is removed at one time and the process continues until the deposit is completely excavated and the next revealed.

The technique must be monitored carefully. The surface of the underlying deposits – the Roman road and houses in our example – and the depth of the deposit under excavation may both vary. Spit excavation must always be prepared to give way to stratigraphic excavation.

When studying an archaeological site, it is sometimes difficult to distinguish the relationship between different deposits. In this excavation, an area (middle background) has been sprayed with water to show its different features show up better. The results are about to be photographed.

Half-sectioning an area *means that the horizontal nature of the layers and their vertical relationships can both be assessed (below).*

The Tools of the Trade

Picks and shovels can be used to dig quickly through material which is of no archaeological interest. Ladders are also useful for reaching deeply dug features, such as cellars.

MOST ARCHAEOLOGICAL WORK, at least in Europe and America, relies on the trowel – not a garden trowel, but a forged mason's (pointing) trowel. There seems to be a general preference for starting with a 10cm (4in) trowel, but months of excavation on hard soils gradually reduce the size, so that the veteran archaeologist is often working with a blade very much shorter than it originally was. An array of trowels, in various stages of wear, is an archaeology status symbol.

The uses of the trowel are manifold. The main method of digging by trowel (trowelling) involves scraping off a layer of soil with the edge of the blade, and breaking up resistant soil with the point. Use of the trowel usually results in a clean surface in which features show up clearly, weather permitting. Experienced trowellers claim, with much justification, to be able to dig as fast with the trowel as with any of its rivals, such as a small pick, and the risk of damage is far less.

In addition, the trowel can chop through obstructive roots. It can also substitute as a scale in photographs of small finds (though it is more usual to use a calibrated scale).

Once the soil has been trowelled off, it has to be removed. Hand shovels are filled with earth using the trowel, or a brush if the material is dry. The earth (or 'spoil') is then taken in buckets or wheelbarrows to be dumped on the spoilheap at a safe, sensible distance from the excavation area. Before dumping, the soil may be sieved for any archaeological material that has previously been overlooked *(see page 88)*.

Supplements to the Trowel

The trowel is ubiquitous, but other digging tools are sometimes required. Picks and shovels (not spades) can be used to dig out rapidly those deposits that have been tested and found to be archaeologically uninformative.

Similarly speedy operations may be appropriate for removing an archaeological feature that has been examined in detail at some point and which seems uniform throughout, such as a road or a gravelled courtyard. Deeply dug modern features – Victorian cellars, in particular – merit this form of treatment.

At the opposite end of the scale, it may be necessary to use delicate tools to deal with fragile finds, though in many cases it is remarkable how delicately a trowel can be used with practice. The junction between soil and object is a natural plane of fracture and a carefully placed trowel point can ease the soil away and make it flake off, so long as the object is tougher than the soil surrounding it, which is not always the case.

Probes, and other dental tools, come in handy when excavating delicate material – fragile bones, disintegrating metal objects, crumbling pottery and so on. Toothbrushes and a penknife are also extremely useful. Various sizes of spoons are suitable for removing the soil from small stake holes.

In warm, dry climates, daily care of archaeological tools may not be necessary. But in wetter environments, a regular routine is observed. At rest breaks during the day, all loose soil is cleared up, the tools are neatly stacked near where each digger has been working, and covered with upturned buckets or wheelbarrows. The instruction for this process to begin – 'clear up your loose' – is a welcome signal to the hungry, thirsty digger that the break is only a few minutes away. At the end of the day, the tools are thoroughly cleaned of mud that has accumulated on or in them.

Coping with the Weather

A dream excavation is conducted in moderately sunny conditions, with light evening showers to keep the site moist and workable. In practice, the weather is seldom so obliging.

In hot climates, the site is likely to dry up, making digging difficult and obscuring archaeological features. Splashing with water, spraying with a watering can or plant spray, is useful in such conditions, as we have seen. The digger can protect himself or herself from the

The ever-present *archaeologist's trowel is often used for scraping loose soil (or 'spoil') into a hand shovel (top left). The spoil is then taken by bucket to be dumped on the spoil heap.*

in by wearing wide-brimmed hats and loose, ngsleeved shirts.

Wet weather, on the other hand, is harder to al with. Where heavy rain is expected, some nd of moveable shelter is usually provided. It is aced over the part of the site being dug, to otect both that and the diggers.

Although light showers may help the cavators, excessive rainfall will reduce the ound to a quagmire in which excavation is not ly physically impossible for the diggers, but so damaging to the site. For this reason, if wet eather is expected, it is a good idea to cover e exposed areas of the site with polythene eeting to protect the surface until it comes to excavated.

If the soil *is very dry, it is often removed with a small brush, rather like a hearth brush, instead of with a trowel (below left).*

ESTABLISHING A RECORD

TWO SETS OF data are accumulated as a result of excavation. One is tangible and can be examined even when the dig is over – artefacts, human, animal and plant remains and so on. The other is destroyed as the excavation progresses, and must therefore be recorded immediately it appears. This set of data is structural and contextual – the remains of buildings and other deposits, layers and features.

Archaeological surveying *(see pages 54-57)*, used continually during excavation, is one technique for recording structural and contextual information. There are several others used in conjunction with it to build up an accurate account of the excavation in progress, including photography and sketching.

The Role of Planning

Planning is the term used to define the recording of the horizontal aspect of the site – the distribution of layers and features and their horizontal relationships. The scale at which plans are made depends on the size of the features and their density. A site with a road, a couple of ditches and a few large pits will show up nicely on a plan at a scale of 1:20 or possibly 1:50, whereas a site covered with the stakeholes of

The drawing frame *is set horizontally over the area to be drawn, using skewers to keep it in place. The image is then transferred from the little boxes on the ground to the tiny boxes on the drawing board, working to a scale of one tenth or one twentieth of the original size.*

numerous wattle-and-daub houses needs to be planned at 1:10, or even 1:5.

Plans should be made on good-quality transparent film such as Permatrace, which will not expand or contract in any normal weather conditions. The film is stretched over a drawing board of manageable proportions and fixed down with masking tape or bulldog clips. Beneath this, fastened to the surface of the board, is a large sheet of metric graph paper. The planner begins by marking on the drawing paper all the relevant details – the scale at which the plan is drawn, who is doing it, the date, and the name of the site and area. Then the relevant fixed points of the grid are marked in the correct position, along with an approximate indication of north (if the gridpoints are correctly marked, the true position of north can be ascertained later).

Few draughtsmen are sufficiently confident to make their initial drawings in ink (it runs in the rain, anyway). Most planning is done with ordinary lead pencil, which is traced over in ink indoors later.

The methods used by the planner depend largely on the scale and on the prevalence of the features being plotted. On a site where there are many features, most of them small and close together, a drawing frame is essential. Where many of the features are large and the site is not very complex planning by triangulation is quicker and easier. Let us look at the frame first.

The Drawing Frame

The drawing frame is a rigid square of wood, whose *internal* dimensions are usually 1m by 1m, divided by (preferably) nylon strings into 10cm units. If the plan is being made at the scale 1:10, each box of the drawing frame will correspond to a 1cm box on the graph paper beneath the drawing film, making planning relatively easy. At 1:20, each 1cm box represents 20cm on the ground.

The drawing frame is set over the area to be drawn, using its accompanying skewers to hold in place. If the surface is bumpy, a spirit level should be placed on two adjacent sides to check that the frame is horizontal. It is also vital to know where you have placed the grid on the plan; this can be done by triangulating the corners of the frame *(see opposite)* permanent markers of the site grid.

Planning with a drawing frame requires some contortion to get a completely vertical view over what is being drawn. Yet it is a relatively easy task to transfer the image seen in the little boxes

the ground with tolerable accuracy to the tiny
boxes on the drawing board, one tenth or one
twentieth of original size.

Techniques of Triangulation

A well-developed visual sense helps in
triangulation. There is no drawing frame to
provide a grid over the feature being drawn.
Instead, you draw by joining up, by eye, a series
of dots plotted on the site plan.

The equipment you need consists of two 30m
measuring tapes and a plumb bob, a weighted
line that hangs exactly vertically when
suspended. For the plotting, you need a ruler
and a drawing compass. The actual technique is
difficult for one person to carry out; it is usual for
someone to do the mechanical side of the work
while another does the plotting.

Before triangulation starts, choose a series of
points on the feature to be drawn that seem to
you to delineate its salient horizontal
characteristics, perhaps marking them with pegs
or in some other way. You can add others if
necessary as you go along. The next step is to
mark each point accurately on the site plan.
Hook the top end of one measuring tape over
one of the grid pegs inserted when the site was
laid out, so that the tape passes over the point
you are plotting. Hook the top end of the other
tape over another grid peg, chosen so that the
two tapes cross each other at as narrow an angle
and as near to the point being plotted as
possible. Get your helper to take the unattached
end of each tape and to adjust them so that they
intersect exactly over the point, testing that
they do so by using the plumb bob. Read off the
distance of the point of intersection from each
grid peg on the tape attached to it.

With that information, you can now mark the
point accurately on the site plan. Suppose tape A
is 1.35m from its grid peg to the intersection,
and tape B is 2.65m. Reduce those distances to
the scale of the site plan – at 1:10, they become
13.5cm and 26.5cm respectively. With the
compass, lightly draw an arc with a radius of
13.5cm from the appropriate grid peg symbol on
the site plan. Then draw another arc with a
radius of 26.5cm from the second grid peg
symbol. The point where the two arcs cross is
the position of the selected point on the site plan.

Follow the same procedure for plotting all the
points you have chosen around the feature on
the site itself. Once they have been recorded on
the plan, join them up with freehand lines to
obtain a horizontal representation of the feature.

Triangulation is *a
method used to record the
exact locations of features
within a given area so that
they can be plotted on a
scale-plan, thus providing
a detailed 'map' of the site.
The site will already have
been staked out with pegs.
One person carries out the
function of pinpointing the
feature on the site, while
someone else does the
actual plotting, as shown
above. A tape measure is
attached to each of two pegs
most closely positioned to
the feature (1) and a plumb
line is dropped directly over
the point to be marked. It is
important that the tapes be
as taut and as close to the
ground as possible, to
minimize any distortion.
The lengths of both tapes
are now measured.
Meanwhile, the second
person positions the point
of his compass (2) at the
spot on the graph paper
corresponding (in scale) to
the exact position of one of
the pegs and, setting
the compass at a measure
equal to the length of the
tape (again, in scale),
draws an arc. This is
repeated at the second peg
placement. Where these
arcs intersect is the point to
be plotted.*

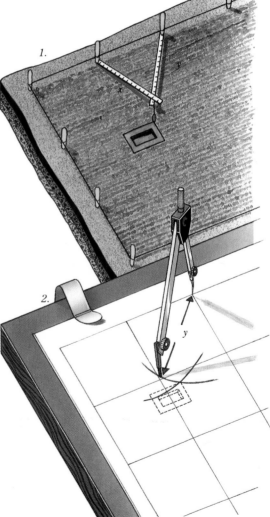

SECTION DRAWINGS

SECTION DRAWINGS record the vertical aspect of the site and that of the features within it – in other words, the site's stratigraphy. As with plans, the scale of section drawings depends on what needs to be drawn.

A section containing a few thick deposits can adequately be drawn at 1:20, while one consisting of numerous thin layers should be recorded at 1:10. Like plans, sections can be drawn on plastic film, but they are frequently drawn directly on to graph paper, perhaps in a site notebook.

To draw a short section, you need paper, pencils and erasers, two nails or surveyor's arrows, string, two tapes, a couple of clothes pegs and a line level. The last-named is a small spirit level with two hooks that allow it to be suspended from a horizontal piece of string.

Set a nail at one end of the section that is to be drawn and attach the string to the nail. Hang the line level at one end of the string. You can then fix the unattached end of the string with the second nail at the other end of the section, checking from the line level that the string is absolutely horizontal. (The line level must be hung at one end of the string; if it is hung in the centre, its weight will cause the string to sag and give a false impression of horizontality.)

When the string is level, one tape is attached to the nails with the clothes pegs, to provide a horizontal scale. Vertical readings are taken with the second tape at regular or appropriate intervals; adjusted for scale, they provide a series of reference points that are then marked as dots on the drawing.

The dots are then joined up, looking closely at the section to make sure the drawing resembles it. The height or depth of the section string is also measured in relation to a fixed point of known height, and the information recorded on the drawing.

Large sections, such as the side of an excavation trench, can be plotted in much the same way. But because the section string is long, the line level is not accurate enough to ensure the string is horizontal. Instead, the surveying instrument is used to insert a precisely horizontal line of steel pins or

To make a sectional drawing *of a vertical aspect of a site (below), two tape measures are used. The first tape is set horizontally, with vertical readings being taken with the second tape at regular intervals along it.*

A line level *is a small spirit level with two hooks that allow it to be suspended from a horizontal piece of string (above). The line level must be hung at one end of the string; if it is hung in the centre, its weight will cause the string to sag and give an inaccurate reading.*

rveyors' arrows, and the section string will
en be attached to these.

In open area excavations, where layers are
tally removed one at a time, there is no section
sible from which a drawing can be made. To
ot the thickness of the layers and their
terrelationships, measurements are made of
e height of the top of each deposit as it is
posed, along a predetermined line. This is
own as a 'running' section.

he Use of Photography

otographs taken at excavations have both
vantages and drawbacks. The camera
ptures everything it sees, which means that
otographs may be harder to understand than
awings, in which only the relevant details have
en selected and recorded. On the other hand,
cause photographs are complete, they can
ovide a crosscheck on drawings and extra
formation if, in retrospect, a drawing proves
adequate or even inaccurate.

Shots for the purpose of record are usually
ken in both black-and-white and colour.
enerally, several exposures are taken on
fferent settings. Every shot must also contain
scale – usually a wooden or metal staff
librated into units.

Ranging rods or other staffs are used for
otographs of large things, such as major
ctions or long views of the site, while small
ales calibrated into units of 10cm or less are
ed when photographing small finds and
atures. The scale is placed parallel to the
order of the photograph (horizontally for
orizontal shots and vertically for sections).

In addition to ground-level photographs,
noramic views and shots comparable to low-
vel aerial pictures can be taken from a suitable
intage point – a hill or tall building directly
erlooking the site, the roof of a vehicle, or
om a specially built photographic tower.

Before record shots are taken, the area or
oject to be photographed is carefully cleaned,
o that it will show up to best advantage.
leaning is even more meticulous before
otographs for publication; this may involve
dious activities like cutting the grass around
e edge of the excavated area – and removing
very blade of grass that has fallen on to it. Some
te directors like their publication photographs
be completely free of extraneous items such
buckets, wheelbarrows and volunteer
ggers, but others find these enhance the shot,
neatly distributed. It is a good idea to include a

When photographing
*a site (left), ranging rods
of known length are
placed in the picture to
show the scale. A person is
also often included, as
this gives a more
immediate sense of scale
than a rod. Smaller
measuring sticks (below)
are used when
photographing small finds
and features.*

person in a photograph, if possible, as this gives
a much more immediate sense of scale than does
a ranging rod.

Planning by Photo

A further use of photography, practised on only a
few land excavations, but in general use in
underwater archaeology, is photogrammetry –
planning the site by photographs. Frequent
vertical record shots are taken of all the areas
being excavated, from which accurate plans can
then be made.

While vertical photographs can easily be taken
underwater, on land it is more difficult as some
means must be found of suspending a camera
vertically above the area to be photographed.
The framework used to support the camera
must be stable, but it must also be such that it
will not damage the site. Various arrangements
to achieve this have been devised, but despite its
usefulness photogrammetry still remains an
unusual recording technique.

ADDING TO THE RECORD

PLANS, SECTIONS and photographs give a picture of the features of a site and their interrelationships, but the nature of the deposits and the material found in them must obviously be recorded, too. There are many different recording systems in use. On some sites, daily entries are made in a notebook, giving details of what is being excavated, the progress being made and other relevant information, such as the weather, who is in charge of the area and which volunteers are working in it.

Site notebooks allow considerable flexibility in the amount of information recorded, but on balance pre-printed recording sheets are probably preferable. On a recording sheet, information is neatly presented in one place (in a site notebook, it may be necessary to hunt through many pages to glean all the information about a particular context). A further advantage of the recording sheet is that, because the presentation is standardised, information can readily be transferred to a computer. Many long-term excavation teams now use a computer for rapid sorting and retrieval of data. Not only is this extremely helpful on site, but it also eases the task of preparing the final report. Its disadvantage is that there is little provision for expressing changes of opinion as excavation proceeds.

The Vital Details
Whatever method is used, the information that is recorded will be much the same. First of all, there is a record of the nature of the deposit – generally, details of the colour, degree of compaction, texture and particle size of the soil. The last two are usually commented upon by eye and feel.

Compaction can be measured using a penetrometer, a small device that is pushed into the soil, while colour is often determined with a Munsell soil colour chart. This is a book in which pages show soil colours, each with a little window that is placed over a sample of the soil for comparison. Once the colour has been identified, its Munsell code number can be recorded. Details of any inclusions in the deposit, such as small stones or fragments of brick, are also noted.

Next, information about the interrelationship between the deposit under consideration and the others around it is entered. On the recording sheet, there is usually a set of boxes labelled 'lies above…', 'lies below…', 'cuts…' and 'is cut by…' for the purpose. If the deposit forms a

layer within a feature, that is also noted. So are the plans and section drawings on which this deposit appears.

All such information is quite concise. By contrast, information about the excavation of the deposit and what it reveals can be lengthy. It may include some details of the material being recovered, though this is also recorded elsewhere. It is likely to contain the first germs of the archaeological interpretation. Detailed recording of impressions during excavation can be highly rewarding and so it is always useful to note all relevant thoughts, even if they are later disproved. Once excavated, any information not recorded will be lost; it is far better to be able to discard redundant information during the later writing-up stage than to find oneself without that little detail that could have made all the difference.

Artefacts and other Remains
The detail in which findspots are recorded depends on the abundance of the material recovered and the importance attached to its precise context. On Roman sites, vast quantities of potsherds are likely, while on some Bronze Age sites a single sherd might be an unusual occurrence. The Roman pottery will be recorded simply as deriving from a particular layer, or, if it is a large one, from a grid square or spit within it. The Bronze Age sherd, on the other hand, may well be treated as what is termed a 'small find' (an object of relative rarity and importance) and its three-dimensional position recorded, usually by triangulation and spot height. On a Palaeolithic site, flint tools and the debris from their manufacture may be just as abundant as the pottery on Roman sites, but the laborious three-dimensional recording of every single chip of stone may reveal important details about the distribution of activities on the site.

While excavation is taking place, the volunteers are provided with finds trays in which to deposit the material they recover. Each layer will have a separate finds tray; if it is a widespread layer, a finds tray may be provided for each subdivision of it. Finds trays are always carefully labelled.

The digger fills the tray with everything he finds whose position does not have to be recorded three-dimensionally. Fragile objects, such as crumbly pottery or delicate bones are kept separate from heavy objects that are likely to crush them.

Small finds, such as coins, pieces of pottery

A preprinted *site recording sheet (right) n only allows information be neatly presented; its r means that details can b assigned to appropriate categories right from the start. The system reduce the risk of human error. Its use also means that information contained c the sheet can be readily transferred to a compute for detailed analysis.*

The site recording sheet, with annotations:

Description of context *includes details of the type of material found on the site.*

Site grid references, *altitude, and the order in which the various layers were deposited, are noted.*

This section *provides a basis for a statistical analysis of the finds. Different categories of finds are recorded by ticking the appropriate box. The amount of the find recovered is noted by entering A (ALL), S (SOME), or N (NONE).*

When a sample *is taken, the appropriate category is ticked and the number of large polythene bags used is recorded in the box below.*

Interpretative *notes are made after all the details above have been completed and checked. Fuller notes are made at a later stage.*

---

nd bronze objects, are often photographed *in itu* before they are removed. Their three-imensional position is calculated and, usually, arked on the site plan. Human remains and ssociated material are also recorded in detail.

he Finds Assistant

.esponsibility for the archaeological material hat has been excavated then passes to the finds ssistant, who supervizes its cleaning nd marking. Each category of material from ach deposit is separately packed in well-labelled ags and boxes, ready for further treatment and nalysis. A record is made of what material has een found in which archaeological contexts, the umber of bags or boxes it is stored in, and any ther relevant details. Small finds are entered

individually in the finds register, with their three-dimensional positions.

In addition to the artefacts discovered during excavation, a number of samples of other material will probaby be taken. Any large amount of charcoal, for instance, may be useful for radiocarbon dating. Soil samples provide reference material if there are any later doubts about the nature of a deposit, and can help to answer specific dating questions *(see page 130)*. Samples are also taken to obtain such organic material as pollen, seeds, and insect remains.

In general, routine samples are taken from every deposit, and larger ones from deposits that are expected to be particularly productive. Such samples are usually processed on site to extract the relevant material.

SIEVING ON SITE

THE VOLUNTEER DIGGER, after an initial period of having to ask 'is this something archaeological?' every time he finds anything at all, soon learns to identify and recover most of the finds from the patch he is digging. Even the most careful and sharp-eyed digger, however, is likely to miss a few things, so it is useful to sieve the excavated soil to check for further remains. Sieving is usually undertaken on or beside the spoil heap.

The simplest method of sieving is carried out with a handsieve of the kind used in grading ordinary garden soil. A more thorough method is to use a set of nested sieves in a metal-framed shaker – frequently a nest of three sieves is used – to separate objects into different sizes.

Besides objects missed due to temporary loss of concentration, sieving can also recover things too small to be noticed while digging, such as beads and tiny bones.

Where there is a convenient water source on or near the site, the process of recovery can be improved still further by wet sieving. The sieve is immersed slightly in water and gently agitated. The soil dissolves and falls through, leaving behind any objects. These show up easily among the remaining stones because they have been washed clean.

Wet sieving *(below) is usually done in a tank with an outlet through which the accumulated soil can drain.*

Sieving the contents *of the spoil heap (above) can turn up many objects which would otherwise be lost. A seed machine (below) is used to recover seeds and plant material.*

TERRA AMATA

CONSTRUCTION WORK late in 1965 near the shipyard area of Nice in France uncovered an extensive deposit containing early Palaeolithic tools. The importance of the find was immediately appreciated, construction was suspended and emergency excavations were carried out in the first half of 1966.

The excavators discovered the remains of 21 'living floors', the bases of ancient and primitive dwellings. All required very careful excavation, using only trowels and brushes, and extremely detailed recording, which included making casts of the floors. The reward was a detailed picture of a few days in the life of our ancestor *Homo erectus.*

A group of these hominids built a series of oval huts on this site, known as Terra Amata, 300,000 years ago. The huts, outlined by stakes and supported by stout posts, each contained a central hearth protected from draughts by a wall of stones. Analysis of pollen from fossilized faeces found around the huts showed that the visitors came here in the late spring or early summer.

They hunted large mammals, including elephant and rhinoceros, gathered shellfish, and occasionally also caught fish. After a short stay, they moved on elsewhere, but they returned in successive years and rebuilt their huts on the same spots.

Among the things they left behind were the debris from making stone tools, and lumps of red ochre, which they may have used for body painting. A round depression in the ground, filled with white material, may be the remains of a wooden bowl.

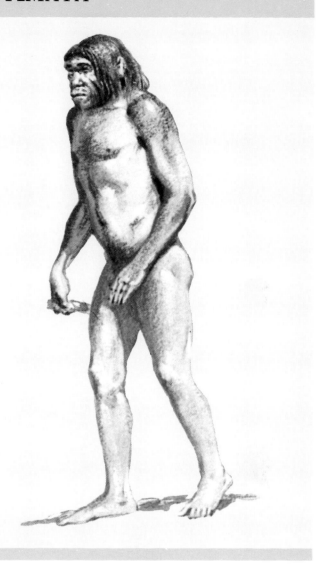

The inhabitants of Terra Amata, *in the south of France, lived about 300,000 years ago. They were hunter-gatherers who used flint tools and built oval wooden huts which are the earliest known man-made structures.*

ed Machines

mples collected to recover plant material are ually bulky, so it is best if the material can be tracted from them on site, rather than nsporting them elsewhere for processing. veral machines have been designed to cope th the task of extraction.

One uses a process called 'froth flotation' rrowed from the mining industry, where it is ed to obtain metal from low-grade ore. The chine consists of a small tank supported on a nd, with a narrow conical valved outlet at the ttom through which the soil can be discarded. notor blows air through a set of nozzles in a e set in the bottom of the tank, which is filled with water during the operation. A frothing agent and a 'collector', such as kerosene, are added to the water. When small quantities of coarsely sieved sample soil are poured into the tank, seeds and other tiny organic particles attach themselves to the rising air bubbles, a tendency that is enhanced by the 'collector'.

The froth holds the seeds in the surface water, which overflows gently through a spout into a small sieve. Any material that has been deposited is then wrapped in moistened paper towelling and left for some time until it is completely dry.

Other 'seed machines' operate slightly differently, but the results are much the same.

A Saxon Ship Burial

The Sutton Hoo ship *has left only its imprint in the sand, so extreme care was needed during the site's excavation.*

THE IMPORTANCE OF correct conservation is extremely well demonstrated by one of the classic archaeological discoveries of the present century – the ship burial at Sutton Hoo in Suffolk, Britain. Investigations leading to the discovery began in 1938, when one of three barrows opened on the site that year yielded traces of a small ship. It was also established that the barrows held pagan Saxon burials.

The following year, excavation of the largest barrow began, revealing the first traces of a much larger ship. It had been set in a burial trench dug into sand which, since it had remained moist, had to some extent preserved organic materials, though in a generally disintegrating state. A few fragments of wood remained in places.

Of the ship's timbers, however, the only traces were a series of discolorations in the sand where they had rotted, and the rusted nails that had once held them together. To reveal these and to uncover the burial chamber, the sand was carefully removed in thin horizontal slices. The chamber lay in the centre of the ship. Stains and fragments of the original wood showed that it was rectangular and had once had a pitched roof, made of two layers of planks set at right angles to each other.

Although the uncovering of the ship demanded great care, this was nothing to the problems that the excavators faced when they came to remove the contents of the burial chamber. The dampness of the sand had partly preserved several objects of leather and wood, but all the metal objects, with the exception of the goldwork, were in a sorry state. Many pieces had also been damaged when the roof of the chamber had collapsed centuries before.

The relatively stable pieces had to be carefully exposed using paint brushes and needles, their position recorded and photographs taken. This was a key process, as it was often not clear which fragments came from which objects.

In the case of the leatherwork and the fabrics, it was imperative to keep them moist, while a number of other pieces were too fragile to stand excavation. These were lifted in their sandy matrix, carefully packed (the waterlogged ones with wet moss), and sent to a laboratory for appropriate treatment.

Saxon Treasures

In addition to the difficulties of the excavation itself, the nature of the finds posed a problem. The jewellery and metalwork that were meticulously revealed included many pieces of gold and silver that were literally priceless. Although the discovery was kept as secret as possible, it was thought sensible to bring in police to guard the site at night until work was completed.

The treasures recovered from the grave are today some of the best-known in the world. They include a number of silver bowls and dishes imported from the Eastern Roman Empire.

Some of the military equipment, such as an iron helmet with gilded bronze decoration and a shield, were of Swedish origin. Other pieces were probably of native Saxon craftsmanship – gold and bejewelled buckles, strap mounts and a scabbard, and items of personal jewellery.

The most significant finds included an iron standard bearing a bronze stag and a stone object that may have been a sceptre. These support the notion that the grave was that of a king. Two silver spoons carrying the names Saul and Paul were a christening gift, indicating that this king had been converted to Christianity.

Finally, a collection of gold coins in a beautifully decorated purse provided a date for the burial of around AD 625-630. On present evidence, it seems most probable that this tomb was erected for Raedwald, King of East Anglia and High King of England.

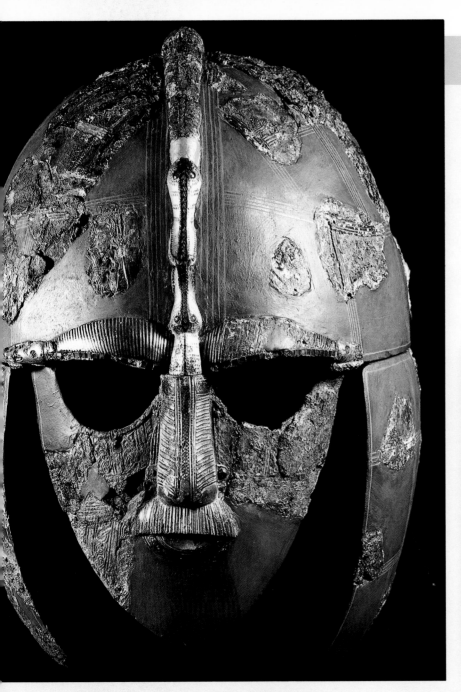

Original fragments *of the decorated iron helmet (left) found at Sutton Hoo have been used in this reconstruction. The gilt bronze nosepiece sweeps up over the top of the helmet in a form representing a dragon.*

Made of solid gold, *the great gold buckle (above) 127mm (5in) long, weighs more than 395 grams (14 ounces). It is covered with an interlaced design of snakes and other animals.*

...he winged dragon *(right) is ...rt of the decoration on the ...tton Hoo shield. The dragon, ...cm (11in) long, is made of ...t bronze studded with garnet.*

CONSERVATION IN THE FIELD

THE DEGREE TO which archaeological materials are preserved depends on the conditions in which they have survived. Decay by physical action affects only those items exposed to the elements – extremes of hot and cold, wind, rain, snow, water or ice, and seismic activity. The weathering of ruined buildings is an example of decay as a result of physical action. But it can also affect, for instance, long-buried ancient stone tools exposed to the air by erosion or earth movements.

The process of chemical and biological decay depends upon the presence of moisture, warmth and oxygen, and upon the acidity or alkalinity of the environment. These types of decay are generally most rapid in humid tropical conditions, but are usually negligible in desert or frozen areas. In acid soils, bone and glass will be poorly preserved, but in highly acid conditions some organic remains may survive. This is particularly so in acid bogs, from which seeds and insect remains have been recovered. In such bogs, oxidization of metal is prevented, resulting in good preservation.

In alkaline soils, organic remains decay rapidly, though bone is preserved and may become semi-fossilized. Glass rapidly degenerates. Insoluble salts form an encrustation on pottery, bone, stone and metals which may cause damage. In alkaline water-logged conditions, wood may be preserved, though weakened. Wood also survives well in sea water; so may other materials, but their chemical composition may be changed.

Storage in Safety

Whatever the effects of the environment, material eventually reaches an equilibrium with it, in which further decay will not take place. In general, wet objects should be stored in water, or in damp tissue paper or some similar suitable material. Dry objects should be stored dry, with a desiccating agent such as silica gel crystals if complete dryness is needed. Organic materials should be treated with a reversible fungicide to prevent moulds.

Plastic bags and rigid plastic boxes are suitable for storing most materials; fragile objects must be packed with enough padding to remove the risk of damage. In the case of unstable materials it is essential to send them to a laboratory conservator as soon as possible. Before removing a fragile object from the ground a photograph should be taken of it in case it disintegrates.

On-the-spot Treatment

Various treatments may be necessary or desirable before an object leaves the excavation site. It is generally possible to clean stable artefacts, such as most pottery and many stone objects, without damaging them, making the task of the conservator easier.

In some cases, it may be necessary to arrest any decay that exposure to the air has initiated or reactivated, for example the so-called 'bronze disease' (cupric chloride). Similarly, soluble and insoluble salts in the material should be removed if they are likely to cause damage. In other cases, the object may be too fragile to be removed from the ground or to survive the journey to the conservation laboratory and so must be consolidated *in situ*.

The golden rules when treating archaeological material in the field are: do not apply any treatment unless it is absolutely necessary; make sure that any treatment given is reversible; and *do not do anything* (not even washing) to material destined for radiocarbon or other forms of dating or chemical, physical or biological analysis, as that may complicate such analyses or make them impossible.

Four stages in *the process of preserving a mosaic: first, a backing cloth is covered with a latex adhesive, ready to receive the pieces of the mosaic, face downwards. The mosaic, stuck to the cloth, is removed to the laboratory where the area between the tesserae is carefully cleaned before the object is set in plaster. Finally, the backing cloth is removed .*

PRESERVING TOLLUND MAN

IN 1950, a well-preserved Iron Age corpse was discovered by two peat cutters in a bog at Tollund, in Denmark. This was not the first such body to be uncovered in Europe, but it is certainly one of the best-preserved.

A curious feature of most of the corpses is the presence of the remains of a noose around the neck, pulled tight and choking, which indicates death by hanging. Most of the bodies were also virtually naked; Tollund Man wore only a skin cap and a leather belt. It is generally held that such hangings were a form of ritual sacrifice.

Tollund Man was removed from the bog and taken to the National Museum in Copenhagen for thorough study in a specially constructed box that was packed with peat. However, practical considerations made it possible to conserve only the head and not the whole body. This was soaked for over a year, first in formalin and acetic acid, then in alcohol, toluol and finally wax.

The remains of Tollund Man are now permanently on display in Denmark. He looks as if he were merely asleep – it is astonishing to think that he died 2000 years ago.

The head of Tollund Man, *some 2000 years old, is a striking testimony to the remarkable preservative powers of peat. Even the eyebrows, eyelashes and stubble on the chin are clearly visible, as is the rope with which he was garrotted.*

Consolidants and Adhesives

In general, the consolidants and adhesives used in field conservation are soluble in water, alcohol, toluene or acetone. These include soluble nylon (particularly useful as it allows penetration of water, so it can be used to consolidate material before it is washed to remove salts), PVA (polyvinyl acetate), PEG (polyethylene glycol wax), polyvinyl butyral and polymethacrylate.

Benzotriazole is used to stabilize 'bronze disease' until laboratory treatment is possible (silver oxide is an acceptable substitute). Cellulose nitrate (HMG) is a useful all-purpose adhesive; alternatives are PVA adhesive or rubber/resin compounds.

If an object is particularly fragile or very large, some form of structural support may be necessary. Bandages can provide simple reinforcement, while plaster of Paris is widely used. It is relatively cheap, easy to apply and usually easy to remove when the object reaches the laboratory. Fibreglass sheets applied with a resin such as PV butyral are more versatile than plaster, but rather harder to remove.

Other suitable supports include latex rubber jackets, which peel off easily, and polyurethane foam, applied over a separating barrier, preferably of aluminium foil. However, such foam is expensive and emits toxic fumes.

Before setting an object in plaster, it is essential to protect it by covering it with a layer of damp paper, or polythene or rubber sheeting. The surface of the object may be further protected by coating it with a synthetic resin before it is wrapped in the separating material. The plaster of Paris jacket should be reinforced with bandages or scrim.

Those Vital Labels

Material sent from the site for conservation or analysis should, like all other finds, be clearly labelled and recorded. The labels should carry all the relevant information, including details of any treatment given, to save the conservator's time. A copy of the full record of the find should be sent with it, too.

If possible, one label should be placed with the material inside its container and another on the outside. As a further precaution against confusion, it is helpful to put an identifying code mark on the material itself.

Use a marking pen, and put the mark in an unobtrusive place. If the surface is not suitable for marking, put on a small patch of PVA. paor lacquer, which can be marked when dry.

AS IT WAS

AS THE LAST days of an excavation approach, the pace of activities increases dramatically. Every member of the team is suddenly aware of all that remains to be done, and inevitably something unexpected will turn up, usually on the last day in the last half-hour, that requires time that is not available.

At last, however, it is all over. It remains only to fill in the site and to pack up the tools. Backfilling and returning the site to its former state are a general requirement. Even if the site is to be redeveloped, it is dangerous to leave an open hole, so it will be filled in unless the redevelopment is actually in progress. On rural sites, the subsoil, topsoil and turf are replaced in the correct order. Ideally, backfilling is done by machine; it is a tedious and lengthy task replacing soil by hand, and virtually impossible to compress it sufficiently to replace it.

Knossos Palace, *on the island of Crete, has been extensively reconstructed to reflect the original as closely as possible. The colonaded staircase shown below is one of the most striking of the reconstructed features. The palace was the centre of the Minoan empire in the 2nd century BC.*

The Case for Preservation

Sometimes, the structural remains excavated are impressive and interesting enough to justify the expense and effort of opening them to the public. In such a case, they must be consolidated to prevent them from collapsing.

After an excavation, *if structural remains are not* *be preserved, the site is backfilled and returned as close as possible to its original state.*

The remains need to be made sufficiently strong to survive both the elements and the visitors that are expected to view the site. But the consolidation must be unobtrusive, so that the visitor is able to see the structures, so far as possible, in something like their original state.

The degree to which restoration (as opposed to consolidation) should be undertaken is a much-disputed matter. For example, when Sir Arthur Evans restored the Minoan palace of Knossos, he rebuilt and repainted much of the crumbling masonry in an effort to recreate the original appearance of the palace as closely as possible.

He has been both praised and severely criticised for this approach. The issue really is whether or not reconstruction should occur on site, where it may perhaps obscure or destroy evidence that might later be vital in reinterpreting it.

A viable alternative is presentation of a reconstruction in a museum on site. This allows data and interpretation to be kept separate and academically more acceptable. However, it is unlikely to equal the immediacy of the impression gained by actually walking round a reconstructed original site.

Obviously, there is no 'correct' answer; but whatever is done – for instance, artefact restoration – should be carried out as accurately as possible and should also make it obvious which portions are original and which have been restored.

At the Fringe of the Empire

LOCAL POLITICS in south-east England took on an international dimension after Julius Caesar invaded the country in 55 and 54 BC. When, in AD 43, the Romans began their final full-scale conquest, they did so ostensibly in defence of the pro-Roman king of the Atrebates who had fled across the channel to seek their protection. The Atrebatic territory around Chichester provided the Romans with a friendly supply base from which to subdue the west of England; and Cogidubnus, the king of the Atrebates in Roman Britain, enjoyed considerable Roman patronage and prosperity as a result.

In 1960, a chance find by a workman of a substantial quantity of Roman tiles led to the discovery of a large complex of buildings at Fishbourne, near Chichester. Excavations revealed several phases of construction: a substantial wooden house built in the AD 40s, replaced in the late 60s by a series of masonry buildings. These in turn were demolished around AD 75 to make way for what can only be described as a palace, a vast four-winged building arranged around a central ornamental garden. The geographical location of the palace and the political history of the region make it probable that these were the successive residences of King Cogidubnus.

The magnificent palace was lavishly provided with marble wall panels and mouldings, colourful wall paintings and fine mosaics. The south wing, probably the private rooms of the king and his family, housed the bath suite, while the other wings contained administrative chambers, guest rooms and reception areas.

In later days the palace was modified; the addition of further bath suites suggests it may have been divided between several families. A number of new multi-coloured mosaics were created, as the craft of mosaic-making became established in Britain. A hypocaust, the Roman system of underfloor central heating, was installed for several rooms. While the heating was being extended to a room in the north wing, the palace was entirely destroyed by fire.

Recognition of the importance of Fishbourne – the only palace of its size outside the heartlands of the Roman Empire – led to a concentrated effort to preserve the site. Much of the north wing is now incorporated into a museum. The building is carefully designed to give an impression of the size of the wing in Roman times, but it is deliberately constructed of metal and glass to distinguish it clearly from the original Roman remains.

Traces of the garden *at Fishbourne have been excavated (below), revealing trenches where box hedges once grew, planted in a rich loam which is clearly distinguishable from the surrounding poor, stony soil.*

Fishborne Roman palace, *as it was in AD 75, is displayed in a model (left) in the Fishbourne museum. The palace was the largest and most lavish Roman residence built in Britain; probably the home of Cogidubnus, the local king. Superb mosaic floors (above) are perhaps the most impressive feature of the Fishbourne remains which are now on display in the museum.*

EXCAVATING UNUSUAL SITES

THE TECHNIQUES that have been discussed so far assume the site to be, more or less 'normal', with some structural remains and a number of reasonably preserved finds requiring little special attention. A number of sites, however, present special problems – either because of the nature of the preserved material, or because of the circumstances in which it has been preserved.

Two aspects of waterlogged sites, for example, particularly affect their excavation. First, they are likely to contain a great deal of well-preserved organic material – wooden structures or artefacts, leatherwork or basketry, and plant and animal matter that can provide information on diet and on the local environment.

Many of these items, especially wooden ones, will start to deteriorate soon after exposure to the air, so care must be taken to protect them during excavation and recovery. Arrangements must also be made for their immediate treatment, on or near the site, to conserve them. In dry weather, the exposed waterlogged material that cannot immediately be lifted and taken to safety must be kept constantly wet. Drying can also be inhibited by wrapping exposed material in polythene.

Secondly, wooden structural remains on waterlogged sites, such as posts, stakes and trackway, are usually three-dimensional and fragile. Measures must be taken to prevent them from being compressed or otherwise physically damaged in the course of excavation.

In the early stages, before the actual remains are exposed, the weight of individual excavators is spread over a wider area by using toe-boards for standing or kneeling. Later, when the remains begin to be revealed, it may be necessary to make complicated networks of planks laid across boxes set on firm ground, on which the excavators sit or lie flat to dig.

The tools employed in excavating waterlogged materials must generally be more delicate than the customary trowel. Plastic spatulas and flat wooden ice-cream sticks can be used to peel off firm deposits, such as peat. Loose-textured deposits may be sprayed off with a low-pressure jet of water.

Other examples of unusual sites include tombs in Siberia which contain organic material preserved in frozen layers. In order to excavate such sites, the frozen layers must be thawed. the 19th century, fires were lit on top of the tombs. More recently, they have been thawed by pouring boiling water over them.

The Camp beside the Lake

As the ice sheets began to melt and withdraw northwards around 12,000 years ago, the lifestyle of the inhabitants of western Europe changed. Until then, reindeer had played a major part in their economy. Now, in the warming climate, a broader range of resources became available. More significantly for archaeologists, these early Europeans moved from the caves and rock-shelters thay had occupied in Palaeolithic times – sites easy for modern investigators to identify – to open localities, where their camps are much harder to locate.

Between the 1920s and the 1940s, many of the tools of stone, and sometimes bone or antler, used by these Mesolithic hunter-gatherers came to light. To understand more about such people, however, a well-preserved example of one of their settlements had still to be discovered and excavated. In 1949, Professor Grahame Clark of Cambridge University examined an area in the Vale of Pickering in north-east England, where Mesolithic tools had been found. The study revealed just such a site at Star Carr. It had once stood beside a lake that subsequently became choked with peat deposits. Clark expected that the boggy soil would yield waterlogged organic remains, greatly increasing our knowledge of Mesolithic man and his environment.

Antler harpoons (below), used by mesolithic hunter-gatherers, were discovered at Star Carr in Yorkshire earlier this century. The harpoons, and many other artefacts made from flint, stone and bone, were preserved in peat beside a lake.

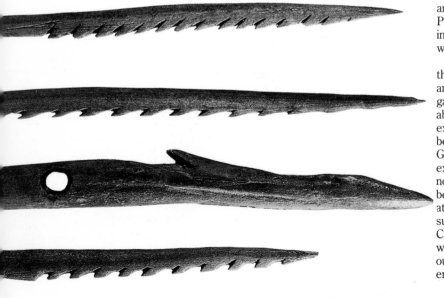

FROZEN HORSEMEN OF SIBERIA

AT PAZYRYK in the cold Siberian steppes, richly furnished burials were made by tribes of nomadic horsemen in around 400 BC, but shortly afterwards, these graves were robbed of all their gold. The holes dug by the thieves filled with rain water which froze, preserving all the remaining grave goods, as well as the bodies of the dead and their horses, which had been ritually killed and buried with them.

The graves at Pazyryk were rediscovered in 1924. One was excavated in 1929, and four more between 1947 and 1949. To penetrate the frozen ground, buckets of boiling water were poured over it. The resulting slush made it necessary to shore up the site to ensure the safety of the excavators.

What was revealed, however, entirely compensated for the difficult excavating conditions. Each burial had been made in a wooden chamber at the bottom of a shaft, above which a cairn of earth and stones had been erected. Several bodies had been remarkably preserved in the ice. One of them was elaborately tattooed with motifs of fabulous monsters like griffins, as well as animals such as deer and mountain goats. These animal designs were echoed on the colourful textiles and carpets which were discovered – tigers killing their prey were particularly popular. Other fabrics bore geometric designs.

The excavators also found articles of wood, metal and horn, fur and leather. Among them were items of saddlery, all-important to these mounted tribesmen – bridles similar to those of today and simple saddles consisting of two cushions.

The mummified *head of a tribal chief (above), preserved in ice for more than 2000 years, was among several frozen bodies discovered in burial mounds at Pazyryk in the Siberian steppes. The skull has been damaged by a blow from a battle axe.*

Brightly coloured *textiles, such as this felt wall-hanging showing a nomadic horseman, were among the finds at Pazyryk.*

Hunters of the Swamp

Excavations of Star Carr took place over three seasons from 1949 to 1951, entirely uncovering what proved to be a Mesolithic camp. The lake's bank had been swampy, so the camp-dwellers had made a firm platform by covering part of it with branches and twigs of birch, as well as with other debris that lay to hand. Large lumps of moss were placed on top of the platform, probably so that it would be more comfortable.

The distribution of flints and other tools on the platform was carefully recorded by the excavators. The information helped to define the area that had been settled; outside it the number of tools found dropped sharply. Clark estimated that the camp could accommodate three or four families, at most around twenty people.

Clearly, toolmaking was one of the main activities at Star Carr. Tools were made from flint and deer antlers but, surprisingly, not from animal bones, although there were plenty of those – mostly red deer, with roe deer, elk, ox and pig.

Deer Skull Masks

Many of the antlers and attached skull frontal portions seem to have been modified for human wear. The most likely explanation is that they were masks worn as primitve camouflage when stalking deer.

Other remains recovered from the site included rolls of birch bark – the bark was perhaps a source of resin with which to fix spear and arrow heads to their shafts – and pieces of bracket fungus, possibly for tinder. A wooden paddle suggests the camp-dwellers had boats. Pollen studies of the lake deposits and radiocarbon dating suggest that the camp was in use in about 7500 BC. There were also indications that the site had been occupied more than once.

The excavation of Star Carr is now regarded as a landmark in of modern archaeology. Clark and his team conducted a pioneering study of economic man within his environment – a far cry from the artefact-orientated approach prevalent in the mid-20th century.

UNDERWATER ARCHAEOLOGY

THE PRINCIPLES APPLIED to underwater archaeology are, in theory, exactly the same as those applied on land. But the environment imposes obvious restrictions. With standard equipment and in the most favourable conditions, a diver can stay under water for only about four hours in the day, a period of time that decreases rapidly with cold and depth. The need to stay alert to the hazards inherent in diving reduces concentration on the archaeological task in hand, and powers of memory reportedly weaken too. So detailed and meticulous recording is normally carried out on-the-spot, rather than being left until the return to the surface.

Underwater surveying is difficult. Instruments employed on land are of little use, because visibility is much lower under water. Expensive items of equipment, such as sonic rangeometers – sonar-type scanners – are useful, but few archaeological projects can afford them. So the survey has to rely largely on measuring rods, and on tapes that, annoyingly, are often shifted by currents.

Poor visibility also limits the scope of photography. Single-photograph views of the whole site are often impossible to obtain, although an overall picture can be built up with a mosaic of photos of individual areas. On the other hand, photogrammetric planning is far easier under water than on land, and saves the valuable diving time conventional planning would require.

Some underwater archaeologists do make conventional plans, however, with the same pencils and plastic drawing film that their land-based counterparts use.

Not all Drawbacks

Despite the difficulties, there are some advantages in working under water. Excavation is often easy, involving no tools, but just a gentle fanning movement of the hand. The sediments displaced in this way can be removed with a low-power dredge or a large-bore air lift. The latter also helps keep the excavation area free of silt, while the dredge can be used as an excavation tool, comparable to the pickaxe on land. Stones can be carried away with the aid of airlifting bags.

Underwater sites have the added attraction of preserving many materials that would have perished at most land-based excavations. The warship *Mary Rose (see page 105)*, for instance, was substantially preserved herself and in addition contained a whole range of fascinating objects.

When surveying underwater, archaeologists rely heavily on tapes and measuring rods (left), since the poor visibility rules out the use of levelling instruments. As many details as possible are recorded during the dive (below), using the same pencils and plastic drawing film that are used on land.

Settlements Below the Surface

The remains of a massive wall (left) at Amnisos, a Minoan town in northern Crete, extend several miles into the sea. It was probably some sort of jetty, but its function has never been properly explained. The village of Achziv (below), in northern Israel, is built on the site of a Bronze Age hill fortress which was surrounded by a moat. The remains of the moat can be seen to the right of the village.

MANY SETTLEMENTS in Neolithic Europe were built by the shores of lakes, usually on platforms supported by piles. Often, the water-level of the lake has subsequently risen, submerging the buildings and protecting them from biological decay.

Charavines, in Lake Paladru in France, is one such village. It first appeared above the surface of the lake in 1921, during a particularly dry spell; normally it lies in 2-4m (6-12ft) of water. The investigation involved a number of amateur divers whose first task was to map the forest of piles still standing.

Next, the site was divided into a grid of triangles, instead of the more usual squares or rectangles. Measurements were then recorded from three points, improving their accuracy in the poor visibility. The excavators cleared the site with their bare hands, and soil and artefacts were removed in buckets and boxes.

The lake's water had preserved a remarkable range of material undisturbed, giving a fascinating insight into the life of this little village. Tree-ring studies of timbers revealed that they had been left to season for a year before the first house was built. A second house was added a year later.

Two Periods of Occupation

Pollen cores from Charavines show that the site had two short periods of occupation. Settlers arrived and cleared the forest nearby to plant crops. After 20-30 years, they left and the forest regenerated. The village was reoccupied some 30-40 years later, when the forest was

cleared again and wheat, barley and flax were cultivated. The inhabitants also made use of many of the wild fruits, berries and nuts that were locally available.

After another 20-30 years, the rising lake levels forced the villagers to again abandon the settlement. Behind them they left many traces of their daily activities. Many of these, such as butchering animals and weaving flax and wool, took place outside their houses.

Basketry and pottery were abundant and on occasion contained the remains of food. Other finds included dugout canoes in which the villagers ventured out on the lake, and bows and arrows, as well as wooden spoons and weaving combs, and even a half-eaten apple.

INDUSTRIAL ARCHAEOLOGY

THE ECONOMIES OF many countries of the world have been transformed within the last four or five generations from predominantly rural to predominantly industrial. What is termed industrial archaeology applies itself to the study of these transformations, not only in terms of technology, but in human terms, too.

The pursuit of industrial archaeology is still sufficiently new for its aims and methods not to be clearly defined. Like conventional archaeology, however, it encompasses much more than just excavation.

At present, its main concern is the detailed recording, preferably *in situ*, and understanding of the physical remains of our recent past. These include factories, mills and mines, communications systems such as canals, roads and railways, domestic and public architecture, and machinery and equipment.

Beyond this, however, there is a deeper intention – to make us aware of the immediate past, of which we are the direct heirs, to which our grandparents belonged, and which has shaped our present. To build a complete picture of this past, the industrial archaeologist may dip

The Hay inclined plane *at Coalport, England, built in 1792, was used to raise and lower canal boats over a steep incline on the Shropshire Canal. The boats were winched on cradles which ran on rails; a pair of 5-ton boats could be passed in four minutes, compared with about three hours using a conventional lock system. The incline was closed in 1907 and quickly became overgrown. In the 1970s it was partially restored and is now part of the Ironbridge Gorge museum.*

deeply into many other fields: geography, social and economic history, sociology and anthropology.

One of the sources such investigators can tap is the memory of survivors who can recall recently vanished ways of life, and this ability to communicate directly is the one thing that divides industrial archaeology sharply from other branches of the discipline. In other respects, however, the division is more felt than real; the methods of historical archaeology, including the study of documentary sources and of details of the urban and rural landscape as well as excavation, are equally applicable to industrial archaeology, despite the immense technological differences in the physical remains being studied.

The Rogers locomotive, *built 1882 for the Long Is Railroad, was a pro the Rogers Locomot Works in Great Fal New Jersey, USA. works, founded by t great pioneering en Thomas Rogers, we among the most imp in America in the la 19th century; they h now been converted an industrial muse where some of the machinery used to b locomotives is on dis*

ROGERS LOCOMOTIVE

IN THE EARLY 1970s, plans for construction work in the historic Great Falls area of Paterson, New Jersey, USA, led to a large-scale industrial archaeological investigation. Paterson was America's first planned industrial city, in the early 19th century.

By the 1830s iron and machinery were the city's chief products; shortly afterwards the manufacture of railway locomotives became predominant. The locomotive works established in the Great Falls area by the pioneer and innovative engineer Thomas Rogers were among the most important in America.

Initial investigations in 1973-75 established that a considerable number of historic buildings, representative of all periods in Paterson's industrial history, remained, many of them in good repair and some still in use. As a result of this preliminary study, the city's Department of Community Development decided to rehabilitate them, and to encourage modern companies to use them.

An Industrial Museum

The surviving buildings of the Rogers Locomotive Works, many of them dating from the 1870s, were deemed to be of particular historic importance. It was agreed that part of the works should be converted into an industrial museum.

During 1978 and 1979, these buildings were thoroughly investigated by archaeologists. Their job was to assess the potential damage that reconstruction would inflict and, where possible, to recommend alternative locations. When the work began, the archaeologists watched, and if necessary halted the operations to examine features of particular interest. Their investigations supplemented the picture already created from historical records.

Because the area had been swampy before the first buildings were put up in the 1830s, the ground-level had been raised with layers of yellow clay, silt, rubble, and any debris that came to hand. Over the next 40 or so years, the factories and workshops occupied a relatively small area. But in the 1870s they were demolished and replaced by a much larger complex. Locomotive production ceased around 1915. Some buildings were knocked down, while others were turned over to light manufacturing.

The excavations uncovered a large portion of an 1870s' blacksmith's shop, with the foundations of a number of powerful steam hammers and the brick bases of several gantry cranes. Animal bones were also found which were probably the remains of meals; recorded memories of workers of the era indicated that they often ate while they toiled, because no meal breaks were allowed.

PART 4

PROCESSING THE FINDS

Opposite: *This coin – a brass* sestertius *– bearing the image of the Emperor Trajan (AD 104-111), was unearthed during excavations at Lime Street, London, and is evidence of the city's Roman occupation.*

CONSERVATION AND ANALYSIS

THE EXCAVATION HAS been completed and all
the volunteer diggers have gone home. The
director and his team are left surrounded by
boxes and plastic bags full of soil samples, animal
bones, potsherds or pieces of stone, and heaps
of notebooks, drawings and photographs. How
will all this be miraculously transformed into a
detailed, informative report of the team's
findings?

Three groups of people are likely to be
involved in this task. First there are the
conservators, whose task is two-fold. They
must ensure that all the material that has been
recovered is preserved in as near a pristine state
as possible. They must also treat the material in
such a way as to make it suitable for further
study. The first task is of key importance, since,
although some conservation 'first aid' may have
been done on site, it is more likely than not that
many of the finds will require specialized
laboratory treatment.

The material that has been collected from the
excavation will, it is hoped, yield the answers to
a whole series of questions, such as when was
the site occupied, what did the people eat, what
did their dwellings and environment look like,
where did they obtain their raw materials and
how did they manufacture things from them?

The job of extracting many of the answers falls
to the scientific researchers. Among their
number are biologists who study human, animal
and plant remains, and specialists in the analysis
of stone, pottery, metal and other artefacts. An
important group of researchers, who may
devote their time entirely to archaeological
work, perform the analyses that establish the
age of some of the finds.

Finally, there is the archaeological director
and his team, which also often includes various
specialists, such as pottery analysts. Using
typology (see page 118), they sort the mass of
sherds, stone and metal tools and other material
into a logical order. The director draws together
all the strands of evidence provided by the
specialist analyses in his project report. This
summarizes the discoveries made in the survey
or excavation and sets out the site's place in the
archaeology of the region in which it lies, or the
period into which it falls.

Conservation in the Laboratory

Conservation is as vital a part of modern
archaeology as is the careful and patient
excavation of the site itself. The archaeological
conservator has a number of important tasks. In
many archaeological sites, particular conditions
exist which have allowed objects to be
preserved; these conditions must be stablized
and consolidated by the conservator to prevent
deterioration. Waterlogged wood, for example,
shrinks and warps as it dries out, so the water
must be replaced with wax to preserve the
original shape and size. Other objects may
require only skilful cleaning, so that the
archaeologist will be able to study them in detail.
In addition, the conservator may be asked to
repair and restore artefacts, particularly for
museum display.

Obviously, any conservator's aim is to do the
best job possible with the tools and techniques at
his disposal. Since, however, the pace of
technical development means that new and more
effective methods are constantly being devised,
the conservator aims to use only treatments that
can be reversed, choosing, for instance,
adhesives and consolidants that can be removed
with appropriate solvents. Sometimes, though,
this principle and the need to preserve
effectively are in conflict, as happened in the
case of the *Mary Rose* cannons.

Artefacts can best be appreciated if restored
as closely as possible to their original
appearance. Yet it must always be possible to
distinguish between the original parts of the
object and the restored portions. What the
conservator must do is to strike a balance
between these conflicting requirements – and,
here, of course, much depends on individual
viewpoints. Some conservators completely
restore objects so that their work can be
detected only when the object is examined
closely. Others make it easy to distinguish
between original and restoration by using
deliberately different materials.

Cleaning the Finds

Most well-preserved specimens of pottery,
bone, leather, wood, glass, textiles and stone
can be gently washed in clean soft water.
Though gold can also be washed, other metals
generally must be mechanically cleaned using
dental tools and fine blades. So, too, must ivory,
tortoise-shell, antler, horn and objects made
from unfired clay.

Most materials can be left to dry naturally in
the air, but some, such as glass, could be
damaged. In such cases, the water is removed
by soaking in alcohol and then ether before
drying. Alternatively, objects can be dried and
consolidated – a process which involves

*Conservators have to
examine every fragment
they receive in great detail.
Before analysis,
this piece of corroded iron
(below) was
unrecognizable. X-ray
analysis (bottom) revealed
the shape and size of an
object which, after
cleaning, was found to be
a 14th-century barrel
padlock (right).*

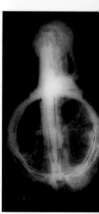

CONSERVING THE MARY ROSE

ONE OF THE GREATEST problems posed by the raising of the Tudor warship *Mary Rose* has been the sheer number of fragile wood and leather objects it has produced, especially as many of them, like the bundles of arrows and chests of long-bows, are unique. Like so many finds, removal of these from their stable underwater environment meant that deterioration would begin.

To combat this problem, a special laboratory was established, with two main aims – to conserve as much as possible of the material recovered, and to experiment with various ways of treating the material to find out which gave the best results. Wood and leather were first washed to remove soluble sea-salts, and then soaked in a chemical bath to get rid of insoluble iron salts from the disintegrated iron fittings of the ship. Wood was then consolidated by soaking in successively more concentrated baths of PEG, while the leather was soaked in a Bavon solution. These objects were then freeze-dried.

The conservation of the ship's wrought and cast iron cannons presented a major challenge. Various techniques were tried, but only one proved to be reliable. It involved heating the iron in a specially constructed hydrogen furnace – which converted the oxidized iron to metallic iron. As the process is irreversible once it is underway, its use has come under heavy criticism by some conservators. But when faced with the risk of the finds themselves

actually deteriorating, the *Mary Rose* team was forced to adopt this less-than-satisfactory approach. To meet the anticipated criticism, some samples of iron which had not been conserved were set aside for any future analyses that might be required.

Members of the Mary Rose team *use electrical engravers to restore fine detail to the ship's cannons.*

removing the water and simultaneously replacing it with wax or polyethylene glycol (PEG).

Removing Salts from Non-metals

Potentially damaging soluble salts are generally removed from pottery, bone or stone by repeated soaking in clean water. If the surface of the specimen is flaking or decorated, it is consolidated first with permeable soluble nylon. Ivory requires extremely delicate treatment. It can be soaked only for a few seconds, and must be dried immediately in alcohol and ether.

Encrusted insoluble salts should be removed by hand if possible. They can be softened first with drops of near-concentrated acid but this must be washed off immediately after application.

Treating Metals

Before treating any metal object, it must be examined carefully to assess the thickness of the corroded layer and the strength of the metal under it, as well as ascertaining whether it is decorated. This initial examination is often done with X-rays, but it can be carried out by physical probing with needles. If there is decoration, preserving it is a priority, especially if it is thin

and easily damaged. A variety of acids are used to remove corrosion from silver, copper and bronze, while some commercial rust solvents can be employed on iron.

Occasionally, the shape of a cast iron object in seawater may be preserved inside a coating of calcerous matter – even though the object itself has rusted away completely. The coating can be cut into pieces, cleaned, and used as a mould to produce a replica of the original.

Mending and Restoration

Most materials can be mended with various adhesives. Epoxy and polyester resins and soluble nylon are particularly suitable, as they do not shrink appreciably when dry. Small uncorroded metal objects may also be soldered.

When reconstructing pottery, a sand tray is used to hold the pieces together while the adhesive sets. Missing pieces of the pot are restored using plaster of Paris appropriately coloured with paint, or a dough made up from a mixture of alvar, jute and kaolin. A lump of plasticine moulded to the correct shape is placed behind the hole, on the inside of the vessel. The edges of the hole are coated with PVA and the gap carefully filled.

PROCESSING ORGANIC REMAINS

THE STUDY OF organic remains can give archaeologists two broad types of information. The first enables scholars to construct a picture of the prehistoric environment and man's impact on it, while the second shows the workings of primitive economies.

Examination of plant and animal material, including fish and molluscs, helps to determine what our forebears ate, while insect, parasite and other micro-organic remains are valuable aids in determining details of such things as the storage of grain and crop and animal pathology. In addition, archaeologists look for evidence of seasonal exploitation of particular resources – an important facet of prehistoric economies.

In addition, organic remains may have had interesting secondary economic functions. Shells and feathers, for example, were sometimes used for personal ornaments, while bones and antlers were carved into tools.

Speed of Decay

All organic material is subject to decay, but the speed at which that takes place depends on the nature of the material itself and on its environment. In some circumstances, ancient organic matter can remain remarkably well-preserved. For example, prehistoric grain is often found carbonized – turned to charcoal accidentally or deliberately by fire, but readily identifiable.

14,000 years *after it was shaped by a Stone Age craftsman in Dordogne, France, a bison carved from reindeer antler is still remarkably well preserved.*

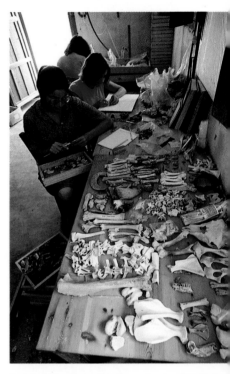

A rich collection *of human and animal fossils has been recovered from the Aegean volcanic island of Santorini (Thera) which erupted about 1400 BC, kil thousands and sealing the fate of the Minoan empire*

Bone and shell survive well in alkaline or neutral soils; acid soil destroys them, althoug also inhibits or prevents the activity of the organisms responsible for biological decay. Therefore, acid soils are likely to yield pollen grains and other plant material occasionally. T same characteristic is shared by heavy clay so which may inhibit decay by excluding air.

Climatic extremes deter the processes of biological decay. In dry, hot regions, in freezin conditions and in completely waterlogged marshlands preservation may be virtually tota All parts and types of plants, from pollen to trees, soft tissue of animals and humans, inse and even micro-organisms can survive, althou acid bogs totally destroy both bone and shell. because of this that bodies which are recovere from bogs are sometimes found without any bones at all, but with skin that is, in fact, in a hi state of preservation.

Arid sites, particularly in America, frequen yield preserved or fossilized faeces, called coprolites. They have also been recovered fr

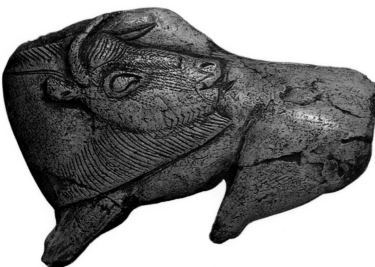

aterlogged deposits, especially cesspits, and rovide extremely valuable information on diet.

Analyzing the Material

Analysis of organic remains begins with the identification of the family, genus or species of the material in each category. Sometimes that can be relatively easy, but often it is difficult.

Mammal bones are generally identifiable to species or genus. Fish, on the other hand, are much harder to identify, partly because the range of species likely to be present on a site is greater than that of mammals.

Although identification keys, drawings, photographs and descriptions can be helpful, for most types of material a reference collection of specimens is virtually essential. Ideally, reference collections should include varying specimens of each species.

Seeking the Source

Organic remains found on an archaeological site may be evidence of what the local environment was like in the past, or of the ecological influence of man. For that reason, it is essential to distinguish between their possible sources. Wood used in building or in making tools, for example, is usually chosen carefully, and may have been brought to the area from a considerable distance away. Firewood, on the other hand, is normally gathered nearby, so it can be more relevant to the reconstruction of the local ecology.

The presence of large animals on a site is generally due to man, and provides only a broad indication of climate or environment. Small creatures such as rodents are much less wide-ranging, and can suggest quite specific ecological conditions.

The evidence from mollusc and insect remains is particularly useful. Most species of land and freshwater snails have distinct preferences in their habitats, so those recovered should give a good picture of the local environment. Insects – particularly beetles, whose harder portions survive well in the absence of oxygen – are even more specific, as many of them are restricted to a single type of host plant.

Animal fossils *found in the La Brea tar pits, in what is now downtown Los Angeles, have provided archaeologists with a wealth of information about animal life during the late Pleistocene era (500,000-10,000 years ago). The animals, including sabre-toothed tigers, mammoths and bison, as well as birds and insects, died after becoming trapped in the tar.*

POLLEN ANALYSIS

THE MICROSCOPIC GRAINS of pollen produced by flowering plants and dispersed by insects, birds, the wind and other agencies come in a wide variety of shapes and sizes. Most can be identified to their genus, and a few to their species (though grass is an exception – its pollen is identical throughout the whole family of grasses). The spores of non-flowering plants can be similarly identified.

Different trees and plants produce different amounts of pollen, and not all types preserve well. However, to a large extent, the pollen spectrum – the range of pollen types that settle in a deposit – reflects the general vegetation of the region. Studies of modern pollen spectra and their comparison with modern regional vegetation form the basis for interpreting pollen spectra of the past.

Cores are taken through ancient lake sediments and peat bogs, and the types and amounts of the different pollens present in each layer within this core are counted. Usually 200-500 grains are counted from each sample. The results of this are depicted in a pollen diagram, showing the changing proportions of the pollen of different plants (the pollen profile).

Pollen analysis was first developed as a dating technique in northern Europe. Changes in

vegetation, particularly of the forests, owing to climatic shifts, were reflected in the changing nature of the pollen spectra. By establishing the sequence of vegetational periods (pollen zones), a relative chronology for much of northern and western Europe could be produced. Following this, absolute dates for the pollen zones were established using varve (layer of glacial sediment deposited yearly in lakes and fjords) chronology (*see page 135*).

Landscape Changes

Since the development of radiocarbon dating, pollen zone dating has become less important, but pollen analysis is a major source of information about the environment, and about human activities. As investigations continue, it becomes increasingly apparent that many changes in vegetation were due to man.

One of the first examples of this to be recognized was what is known as the 'landnam' (or land-taking) phase in early Neolithic Europe. A substantial decrease in tree pollen associated with an increase in the pollen of cereals, weeds of cultivation and other light-loving species marked the beginning of forest clearance and cultivation. Pollen analyses also suggest that Mesolithic man was using fire to make clearings

Pollen diagrams sh*o*
the types and amounts *o*
pollens present in an ar
during different period
This diagram of
vegetation in Jutland,
Denmark, covers more
than 12,000 years (tim
periods are shown on th
vertical scales at the
sides). For each
individual species, the
thickness of the line
indicates the amount of
pollen – and thus the
amount of vegetation –
present.

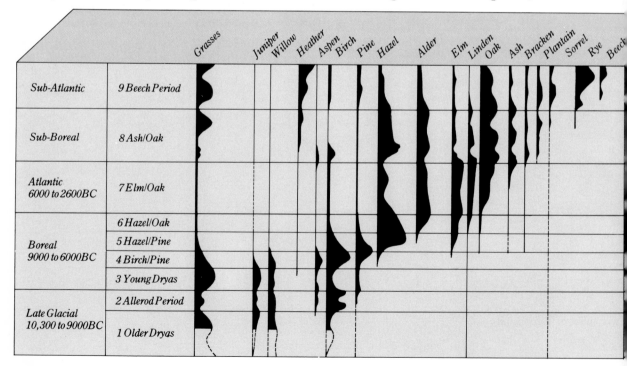

CLIMATE CHANGES OF THE STONE AGE

SINCE THE EARLY 19TH CENTURY, archaeologists have been observing and investigating the abundant Palaeolithic deposits in the caves and rock-shelters of south-western France. In the 1950s and 1960s, Francois Bordes, France's leading Palaeolithic authority, excavated Pech de l'Aze, a cave occupied by Neanderthal Man. Bordes's team included specialists from many disciplines, such as soil scientists.

Pech de l'Aze consists of two caves connected by a low tunnel. Pech II was first occupied in very cold, dry conditions during the Riss Glaciation (the third major ice age of the Pleistocene era), when the local vegetation was grassy steppe with a few pine trees, inhabited by such animals as red and roe deer, horses, Merck's rhinoceros and elephants.

Later in the Riss period the climate became warmer and wetter, with more trees, but although it subsequently reverted to cold and dry the cave was no longer inhabited.

Traces of any habitation of the caves during the warm, damp interglacial period that followed the Riss have been obliterated. But in any case, in such conditions, man may have preferred to live in open air camps.

At the beginning of the Wurm Glaciation, the most recent ice age, a large section of the cave roof collapsed and it was only somewhat later that Neanderthal Man reoccupied Pech II, from which he hunted rabbits and red deer. Pech I was also occupied at this time. But due to the extremely wet climate in the main interstadial during Wurm, when the ice sheets temporarily retreated, deposits in that cave were washed out, leaving only traces. Subsequently, Pech I was preferred to Pech II and considerable deposits accumulated, full of stone tools and the bones of animals which, together with the pollen and sedimentary evidence, indicate continuing fluctuations between cold dry steppe and somewhat warmer and wetter parkland environments.

he forest, encouraging the growth of species table for human food.

While lake and bog pollen spectra reflect gional vegetation as a whole, soil samples give ore localized picture, and so may be used to onstruct local ecology. Buried land surfaces eath earthworks may indicate details of local d use. As pollen in the soil is concentrated r the surface, the analysis of its distribution hin earthworks, such as banks and barrows, y help to determine details of construction.

udying the Soil

alysis of the soil can tell archaeologists about conditions in which it was formed, the inges that have taken place since then and, netimes, about the activities of early man.
ls consist of an inorganic matrix of particles of k and minerals and organic material (humus) ived from the decay of plants growing on it.
e detailed study of humus itself will give some ormation about local vegetation patterns in the st; this is a useful supplement to any ormation which has already been obtained m pollen analysis.

The presence of humus can be detected by ling a small sample of soil in caustic soda. If it here, the liquid will appear a deep brown our when decanted. Uncarbonized organic terial will burn if a soil sample is heated, and ating will also reveal the presence and quantity carbon and of iron compounds.

Examination of the soil under a microscope y reveal organic and inorganic inclusions that icate the original function of archaeological

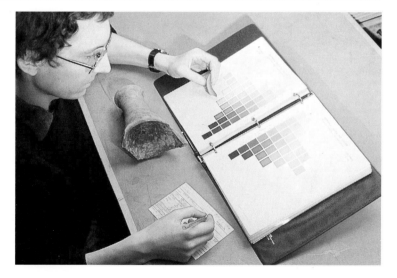

structures or deposits. Minute pieces of charcoal, for instance, suggest ancient fires.

Chemical tests are also used to detect important elements. Sulphates in soils in temperate climates may indicate that wood ash was at one time present. Concentrations of phosphate are usually a sign of human occupation. Localized high concentrations of manganese, visible as 'soil silhouettes', are sometimes found in graves, showing the former presence of a now-vanished body.

Routine analysis of soils includes the determination of its colour using what is called a Munsell chart. The grain size and structure are also noted.

A Munsell chart is used to determine the colour of a sample by comparing it with the coloured chips on the chart. A notation is used to describe the colour; this may be translated into a verbal description.

PRESERVING POWERS OF PEAT

WATERLOGGED GROUND, as noted earlier, is capable of preserving a wide range of organic remains, although if it is acid, as in peat bogs, it rapidly destroys shell and bone. At two sites in England, widely separated by both time and distance, archaeologists are obtaining fresh pictures of earlier epochs thanks to the preservative powers of boggy soil past and present.

Tracks across the Marshes

The Somerset Levels in south-western England became a freshwater swamp during the 5th millennium BC. Gradually this developed into peat and fen woodland. Good agricultural land and rich grazing, and the wide variety of natural resources available in the marsh, lagoons and neighbouring wooded slopes, attracted farmers, who settled there around 4500 BC and remained until Roman times. The extensive peat deposits are today being rapidly removed for fertilizer, exposing many excellently preserved prehistoric remains.

Among the most remarkable finds has been a trackway, the Sweet Track, built 6000 years ago. Throughout their occupation of the area, the prehistoric peoples constructed such wooden paths to connect the sand islands in the Levels with the surrounding hills.

The Sweet Track was substantial. It was built of wooden planks, laid lengthways, supported by peat, on a foundation of wooden poles held in place by pairs of cross-pegs driven into the ground. A later track, the Abbot's Way, was made of planks laid crossways, secured by pegs.

The variety of timber and brush in the tracks gives a good picture of the nearby woodlands in prehistoric times, and reveals that they were being managed from the days of the first farmers. Studies of hazel and other woods employed show that the trees were being coppiced – regularly pruned down to near ground level to provide a crop of vigorous young stems. Their foliage would have supplemented the diet of grazing animals, while the stems themselves made rods to be used in the tracks.

The evidence from the timber is richly supplemented by information from pollen, plant fragments and beetle remains. They show local vegetation patterns, the stages in the transformation of the Levels from open water to swamp or raised bog, and various periods of clearance and regeneration in the surrounding woodland.

Early settlers in the area were not only knowledgeable about forest management. The tracks provide a fascinating glimpse of their remarkable skill in working wood with only stone axes and flint knives. The careful selection of the timber demonstrates that they were well aware, too, of the various properties of different woods.

The Sweet Track – *a wooden trackway built by prehistoric inhabitants of England some 6000 years ago across swampy ground in Somerset – has been well preserved beneath a peat bog.*

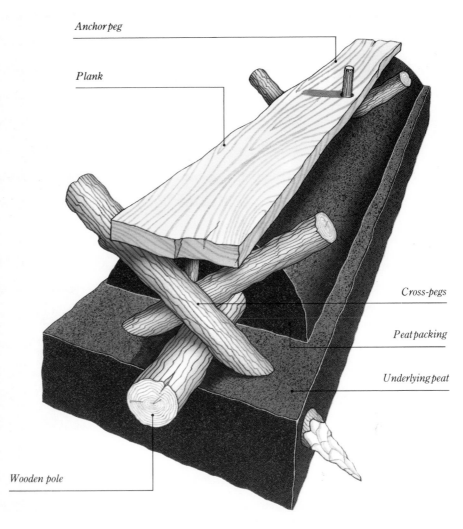

Anchor peg

Plank

Cross-pegs

Peat packing

Underlying peat

Wooden pole

This schematic reconstruction *of a section of the Sweet Track shows the main elements of its construction. Long wooden poles laid end to end across the swamp were held in place by pairs of cross-pegs driven into the ground. They supported a surface of planks, wedged in place by peat and anchored with pegs.*

Prehistoric Diet and Economy

ANIMAL BONES are the source of information about man's diet most commonly recovered from archaeological sites, because, except in acid conditions, they are usually preserved and are easily noticed and recognized. The first stage after recovery is to identify the animal they came from, and its age and sex. Other details noted include size, pathology, butchery marks and whether the bone has been adapted as a tool.

The age of young animals can be worked out by studying the number of teeth which have appeared, and the age of older animals by the extent to which the teeth are worn. Some analysts also calculate the minimum number of individual (MNI) animals of each species from the bones found, but that is not always considered a useful exercise.

Analysis by age, sex and the relative proportions of each species within each period of an excavated site provides details of hunting strategies and animal husbandry methods, and their evolution. For example, where domestic stock was kept mainly for meat, most of the animals will have been killed in adolescence when body growth slows down, and only a few adults kept for breeding. If milk and milk products played an important role in the diet, a greater proportion of females will have been maintained into adulthood, while the majority of animals would be slaughtered in early infancy to stop them competing for the milk.

The relative proportions of different species also reflects the environment and man's exploitation of it, as some species are better adapted to woodland grazing while others prefer grassland. Changes in the composition of domestic stock or hunted animals may therefore reflect ecological changes, such as forest clearance or the deterioration of poor arable land into rough pasture.

Even after stock-farming began, wild animals remained an important element of many economies of the past – as a supplementary source of food, or because they provided necessary materials for clothing, tools or even fuel. In some regions, wild animals continued as the main source of meat. In North and Central America, for instance, few creatures were suitable for domestication, although domestic dogs and turkeys were kept. Most meat eaten by prehistoric farmers there came from wild animals such as deer, rabbits and birds.

Bones can also indicate the time of year at which a particular site was occupied. Those of migratory birds are particularly helpful. In cool or dry climates, most mammals have a regular birth season, so a concentration of remains of animals at a particular age is a further pointer.

Plants as Food

Little is known about the part played in man's diet by plants before the end of the most recent ice age. With the development of settled farming, however, the chances of survival of plant material greatly increased.

Occasionally, whole caches of grain are discovered, while carbonized seeds and fruits are relatively common finds. Nevertheless, the generally poor preservation of plant material and difficulties in recovering it from sites means that plants are almost always under-represented.

As with animals, the advent of agriculture did not mean that the exploitation of undomesticated resources ceased. On a number of Neolithic sites by lakes in Western Europe, aquatic and other wild plants made up the bulk of the vegetable diet. Weeds associated with cultivation, such as *Chenopodium* (fat hen), were probably harvested with the crops.

Most of the information we have on the development of agriculture relates to the cultivation of cereals and legumes. Many other important food staples, tubers like manioc, for instance, and yams, decay completely so the archaeological evidence for their exploitation is generally only indirect, from equipment used in their preparation or traces of appropriate cultivation systems. Occasionally, however, parts of these plants are preserved in coprolites.

Harvests from the Waters

Fish remains recovered from archaeological sites may include jaws, vertebrae, otoliths (ear-stones) and scales. Sometimes the particular species or genus can be identified, but the large number of possible species, and the similarities between many of them, make this a hard task.

Otoliths, vertebrae and scales grow in annual rings, which means that the ages of the fish may sometimes be determined. The size of the otoliths also give some indication of the weight.

In addition to yielding information about the local aquatic environment, discarded fish bones often help archaeologists to determine the seasons at which the site was occupied, particularly on coasts, where certain species shoal at known times of year. The remains can give a clue to local fishing methods, and sometimes provide indirect evidence that those who caught them possessed considerable

The remains *of a neolithic village – more than 4500 years old – discovered at Skara Br[...] on the Orkney Islands, provide an excellent example of a shell midd[...] (foreground). The heap[...] discarded shells indica[...] that the inhabitants of t[...] village included shellfis[...] in their diet. Shell middens usually also contain other food debr[...] giving further clues to t[...] kind of food eaten.*

SHELL MIDDENS OF DENMARK

DENMARK IN THE 6TH MILLENNIUM BC was an archipelago of far more islands than it is today, separated by a deeper sea. Around the islands dwelt hunter/gatherers of what is now called the Ertebolle culture, after an archaeological site in northern Jutland.

Most of the known sites of these people are shell middens, and the larger ones, such as Ertebolle itself, seem to have been occupied year-round. Despite the fact that the shell middens are composed largely of discarded shells, shellfish were in fact eaten only in fairly small quantities. The large number of shells is explained by the fact that the edible part of shellfish is fairly small compared with the shells which are discarded. Pigs and red deer provided the bulk of the diet, supplemented by fish, oysters and migratory birds. Smaller middens were probably seasonal camps, occupied to exploit resources available at particular times of the year in localities away from the main camp. These resources included sea mammals such as stranded whales, fish such as cod and mackerel, swans and other birds. Ringkloster, in central Jutland, is such a seasonal site. From the bones found there, it appears to have been occupied during winter and spring to obtain red deer antlers and to hunt pine marten for furs and baby deer for skins.

The coastal middens were composed largely of the shells of oysters, which were a critical resource during the spring. When the sea level fell, the oysters disappeared and the local people took to agriculture, abandoning the larger sites, but still camping in the smaller ones to obtain seasonally available food.

seafaring skills. For example, it is known that some prehistoric groups hunted whales and other marine mammals whose remains provide similar information. On coasts and estuaries all over the world, shell middens are prominent archaeological sites. They are huge heaps of the discarded shells of aquatic molluscs, a nutritious supplement to prehistoric man's diet, though rarely a major part of it. The middens generally incorporate other food debris. Analysis of that and the shells can tell archaeologists about the general diet of the shellfish-eaters, and the season at which the midden was occupied. It may also be possible to estimate from the remains the rough size of the group that visited.

Telltale Traces

Coprolites – preserved faeces – are an unusual but extremely valuable source of dietary information. They are sometimes found in waterlogged latrines in Europe, but most examples come from arid cave sites in the Americas.

For analysis, coprolites are reconstituted, using a suitable liquid such as a solution of trisodium phosphate. Their components can be surprisingly varied and give a very detailed picture of diet and food preparation.

Typical material recovered from coprolites includes tiny fragments of fish and animal bone, various plant parts, particularly seeds and pollen, and bits of edible insects and molluscs, as well as material accidentally ingested such as hair, feathers and insects (like fruit fly larvae).

Tapeworms and other parasites may also be discovered in coprolites and in cesspits – a reminder of the high levels of parasitic infestation which people of the past endured.

HUMAN REMAINS:1

THE OBJECT OF the first analysis made of human remains found on archaeological sites is similar to that for animals – to determine age, sex and numbers. When, as usually happens, the remains are bones, the techniques are basically the same, too. However, when studying human remains, details about individual people are usually of interest, and establishing the minimum number of individuals present (MNI) has higher priority than in the case of animals.

The MNI is calculated by counting the total presence of bones occurring once only in an individual body, such as skulls, or occurring twice, such as thigh bones. When no other evidence is available, marked differences in the size or development of bones may imply more than one individual.

Determining the age of children and teenagers depends mainly on which teeth are present in the jaw. In adolescents and young adults, the degree of fusion between the heads and shafts of the long bones is a reliable indicator. The age of fully adult, mature and senile individuals can be determined, though less precisely, from tooth wear and structural changes, such as those associated with osteoarthritis, in some bones.

The rate of development and skeletal change varies to some extent between races. It is also influenced by diet, health and environment – a diet of coarse, gritty plant foods causes teeth to wear rapidly, while malnutrition will retard children's growth. Nevertheless, it is generally possible to age a child's skeleton to within a year and an adult's to within ten years.

Measurements and bone structures are the two key factors in determining a skeleton's sex.

The average man is larger overall than his fem: counterpart. His bones tend to be bigger and heavier and his muscle attachments to be mor strongly developed. The most marked differe is in the pelvis, the only part of the body whose function differs between the sexes.

Diseases of Antiquity

Palaeopathologists, the experts who study diseases in ancient times, obtain most of their information from skeletal remains. Valuable additional data comes from soft tissues preserved in mummies and bog bodies, and fro representations in ancient art.

Diseases such as syphilis, yaws, tuberculos and leprosy cause marked deformation and destruction of the bones of the head, spine and limbs. Tumours are sometimes present on bones. Osteoarthritis, too, produces characteristic skeletal changes and is found ev in dinosaur skeletons.

Dental caries was less common among prehistoric peoples than it is today, but eviden of it occurs, along with gum disease and abscesses. Congenital disabilities such as club foot are also known. The high incidence of a congenital condition or of genetically determin anomalies, such as minor variations in the bon of the skull, among individuals in a tomb or cemetery may imply a blood relationship between them. Such evidence is rare, howeve

Lesions and deformities of bones can be informative. Abnormal wear of a particular bon or bones may suggest what the human they belonged to did during life. Similarly, certain types of injury are associated with the hazards specific activities.

Sometimes, injuries form a pattern that implies details of the environment or society. The arm and leg fractures common among Saxons probably come from frequent stumblin on rough ground; the leg was damaged by twisting and the arm was injured as the owner instinctively threw it out in falling. In ancient Egyptian skeletons, broken forearms are very common, particularly among women. Such fractures were often caused when an arm was raised to ward off a blow

Injuries from weapons also leave characteristic traces in the skeleton. Swords cuts are narrow, while spears and other piercir weapons produce well-defined holes. Club blo produce dents with cracks radiating from them

During childhood, while the body is still developing, periods of illness and malnutrition

Differences *between the male and female pelvis are sufficiently marked to be a reliable means of determining the sex of a skeleton. The female pelvis (left) has a wider sciatic notch than the male pelvis; it also has a groove – or sulcus – in the pre-auricular surface (at the base of the spine).*

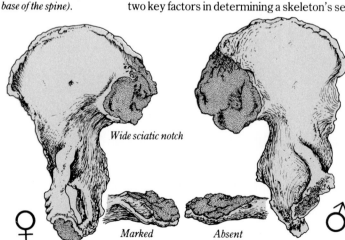

Wide sciatic notch

Marked   *Absent*

Pre-auricular sulcus

HUNTERS OF PERIGORD

The anxious *backward glance of a hunted reindeer is captured vividly in this Stone Age engraving, on a reindeer's antler, found in southern France. Such engravings give important clues to the diet of early man. Fish can be seen leaping between the reindeer's feet.*

THE CAVES OF PERIGORD in France are a rich source of information about life in the late Upper Palaeolithic (Magdalenian) period. Reindeer were the major source of food – their bones make up more than 90 percent of the animal remains from this period recovered in the Perigord region.

The reindeer grazed around Perigord in the winter and almost certainly migrated elsewhere in summer in search of pasture – most probably to the Atlantic or Mediterranean coastal plains which at that time were more extensive than they are today. The inhabitants of Perigord may well have followed the herds, as the presence of sea shells in their caves suggests. These caves also contain vivid paintings, including representations of fish and seals.

Remains of migratory birds and fish, especially salmon, suggest that, in the spring, the inhabitants of Perigord exploited these food sources as well. At the same time they developed new weapons and other implements – harpoons for spearing fish and, perhaps, bows and arrows to shoot the birds.

ay be reflected permanently by lines of rested growth in bones and bands of arrested amel development on teeth. Rickets, a ildhood ailment that is a result of vitamin D ficiency, leaves marked changes in the eleton, including bow legs, pigeon chest and ht and brittle bones.

Not all morphological changes are natural or cidental. Deliberate deformation was practised ong many groups as an aid to beauty. Teeth re knocked out or modified by filing, chipping even inlaying. Some societies moulded babies' ads by binding or flattening them against a adle board to produce a shape that they ught was attractive. Trepanning, a dangerous eration involving the removal of a disc of bone m the skull, has been widely practised since olithic times. Its purpose is uncertain, but in ny cases it may have been intended to relieve essure on the cranium due to a brain tumour or acture. Despite the risks involved, many dividuals survived the operation, some having many as eight or more healed or healing les.

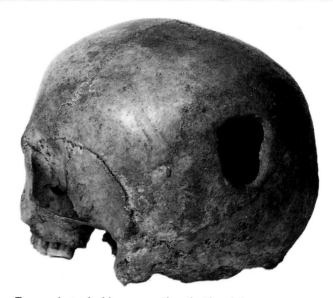

Trepanning – the bizarre practice *of cutting a hole in the skull – was carried out by primitive people apparently as a cure for insanity.*

HUMAN REMAINS: 2

Cremated Remains

At first sight, cremated remains may not seem to be a potential source of information, but in fact they can tell us a lot. Bones are rarely reduced completely to ash, and they can usually be recognized even when they have cracked in the fire and subsequently been broken so that they fit into a funerary urn.

The minimum number of individuals involved, and their ages and sex, can be established using the same criteria as those for uncremated skeletons. However, in cremations it is even more difficult to be precise about the ages of adults and children.

In addition, some of the circumstances of the cremation can often be reconstructed. Charred pieces of wood may be recovered, showing what type was used for the pyre. Fragments of cremated animal bone may provide details of funerary food offerings. Other such fragments, together with charred pieces of metal and ornaments, may give clues to the furs or other garments in which the body was wrapped.

The condition of the bones themselves can can also be revealing. They may be able to indicate the position of the body on the pyre, the degree of burning and whether the cremation was of a fresh body, or of collected bones.

Preserved Bodies

Corpses preserved accidentally, such as bog bodies, or deliberately, such as embalmed mummies, obviously yield far more informatic than can be obtained from bones alone. The so tissue retains evidence of diseases and the ac cause of death can often be established.

Other interesting details, such as hairstyles and body decoration, may also be discovered: fascinating example is the elaborate tattooing the bodies of the frozen horsemen of Pazyryk Siberia *(see page 97)*. An examination of the stomach contents of a preserved body can rev what was the last meal to be eaten. Tollund Man, for instance, ate gruel containing the se of many plants, possibly a ritual concoction designed to ensure fertility; Lady Li of the Chinese Han dynasty died of a heart attack shortly after eating a musk melon.

Early Egyptians buried in the hot sand have been remarkably well preserved by desiccatic Later, mummification was developed to contir this tradition of preservation. Before a mumm elaborate bandaging is unwrapped, it is often rayed to check its condition and its potential interest. After it is unwrapped, the mummy, c parts of it, may be rehydrated by soaking in flu and an autopsy can then be performed.

Astonishingly *well-preserved tattooing on the body of a nomadic chieftain – nearly 2,500 years old – demonstrates how freak conditions can result in the extraordinary preservation of human remains. The chieftain was among several horsemen who were discovered frozen in their graves at Pazyryk in the Siberian steppes. The tattoos depict wild animals – some of them imaginary monsters. Part of the tattooing on his arm is enlarged at right.*

SHANIDAR RITES

Excavations of *the Shanidar cave, Iraq, in 1957, provided archaeologists with fresh evidence about early civilised man. Seven Neanderthal skeletons were found in the cave (left), victims of a rock fall 46,000 years ago. One had a withered arm, amputated at the elbow – an example of primitive surgery. When the skull was examined (below), the incisors were found to be badly worn, suggesting that the individual used his teeth to supplement his good arm.*

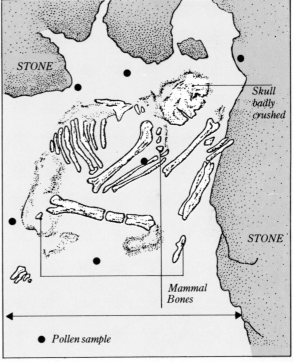

MORE THAN 40,000 YEARS AGO, the Neanderthal peoples began burying their dead, providing us with the first glimpse of the development of human emotions. Red ochre was often scattered over the graves, and offerings such as joints of meat and stone tools often accompanied the burial.

One individual in the Shanidar cave in northern Iraq was covered with flower heads, indicated by the pollen that remained above the skeleton. He was part of a group of seven, some of whom had died when part of the cave roof collapsed.

Another of this group was a cripple, with a withered and useless arm. He would have been unable to hunt or provide for himself, so the community must have taken care of him. His survival into old age demonstrates how strongly developed were the humanitarian instincts of the Neanderthals.

Specimens of pollen *found in one of the Neanderthal burials at Shanidar indicate that the body was interred in a flower-lined grave. Hyacinths, hollyhocks and groundsel – which were believed to have medicinal properties – had been worked into the branches of a pine-like shrub.*

STONE

Skull badly crushed

STONE

Mammal Bones

● *Pollen sample*

Death of an Archer

s the Tudor warship *Mary Rose* suddenly began o sink *(see page 105)*, two young men on the ain gundeck started up the companionway to e open deck, but were thrown back. The lder, a man in his mid-20s, fell across his omrade, and their bones lay in that position for ore than 400 years, to be revealed when the hip was excavated.

Examination of the older man showed that years of archery practice had produced unnatural wear in many parts of his skeleton. Some of his vertebrae showed signs of the stresses caused by the deliberate twisting of the spine, while his left ulna (lower arm bone) was thickened and worn. In the days of the *Mary Rose*, all Englishmen were required by law to be practised in archery from early childhood onwards.

TECHNIQUES OF TYPOLOGY

Constructing *a typology of the artefacts recovered from a site is the first stage in the process of analysing finds. This typology is of objects from an Iron Age site in south India – beads, shell discs and chisels.*

AFTER THE ARTEFACTS recovered in field surveys or excavations have been cleaned and, if necessary, conserved, they are ready for the archaeologist to use them to obtain information about the past. His first task is to impose some order on the finds by dividing them into groups, or types, that have some meaning to him – constructing what is called typology.

Many criteria may be employed in this classification. First, there are obvious broad general classes into which the material can be grouped: pottery, stone tools, metal tools and weapons, jewellery and so on.

Having made these divisions, the archaeologist then looks at the contents of each class in more detail. Let us take pottery as an example, as this is the most common and informative material on many sites. The pottery will probably be divided into groups on the basis of different fabrics.

Pottery fabrics depend on the degree to which the clay was worked before the vessel was formed and the kind of temper that was used. The conditions of firing and the methods used to shape the vessel are also important.

At the end of this stage, the archaeologist is likely to have divided the pottery into groups o hand-made or wheel-made wares, fine, mediu and coarse wares, wares tempered with shell, sand, straw or grog (ground-up pottery), and poorly-fired and well-fired wares. He will also have grouped together sherds into pieces of individual vessels.

Sorted by Shape

Within each type of ware, the pots are again subdivided, this time according to shape, into jars, bowls, dishes, vases, cups and so on. Distinguishing between different shapes is ofte a matter of intuition, and therefore of potential disagreement. For that reason, some archaeologists now try to describe the shapes l using mathematical terms, either ratios or geometrical figures.

As well as overall shape, more specific detail may be included in the classification process, such as the form of the base or rim, the addition of a spout or handle, the curve of the neck or body. For instance, an important Mesopotamia pottery type is known as the bevelled rim bowl: it was used to measure the standard daily ratior of a temple employee in the early days of Mesopotamian civilization.

The size of the pots may also be taken into account. Differences in size frequently relate to the actual function the pot served– itself a further criterion that the archaeologist may use in constructing a pottery typology.

Finally, decoration usually gives plenty of scope for classification. Pottery is decorated in variety of ways. Its colour can be determined by the clay selected, and by the firing conditions. The surface treatment that is used will also produce different colours or textures: a vessel may be slipped by applying a wash of dissolved clay, or glazed.

At various stages before firing, the surface can also be smoothed, polished or decorated. Paint, in a contrasting colour or colours, is the most common form of decoration. Others include the application of clay blobs or strips; the creation of patterns on the surface by impressio or incision using objects such as shells, combs, bird bones or pieces of cord; and deliberate roughening called rustification.

Piecing Together

Many of the artefacts found on a site are likely to be incomplete; pottery in particular is susceptible to breakage, leaving sherds rather

A piece of Sumer pottery, found at Nippur in Iran, which has been pieced together as completely as possible, is now being measured and drawn (above).

than whole vessels. A single sherd, however, is enough to show the type of ware from which the vessel was made.

The shape of the vessel from which the sherd came is harder to determine, unless the sherd involved is a characteristic portion of a standardised vessel type. If the fragment is a rim sherd, the analyst can work out the diameter of the whole vessel by gauging the sherd on a chart of concentric rings of different diameters. Once pottery – or any other material – has been sorted into types, it can be compared with that known from other sites.

One of the most important facts to ascertain from the material is the date of the site, or of features within it. Another may be to establish the function of various parts of the site. Pieces of storage jar, for instance, may suggest that a granary, or storage area has been unearthed.

Pottery used by a particular group may imply that members of that group occupied the site, or traded with its inhabitants. For example, surface finds of Roman Arretine ware at Arikamedu in southern India first suggested that the Romans had been there. Excavations by Sir Mortimer Wheeler in 1945 uncovered a major Roman trading settlement, beneath which the remains of a small Indian fishing village were discovered.

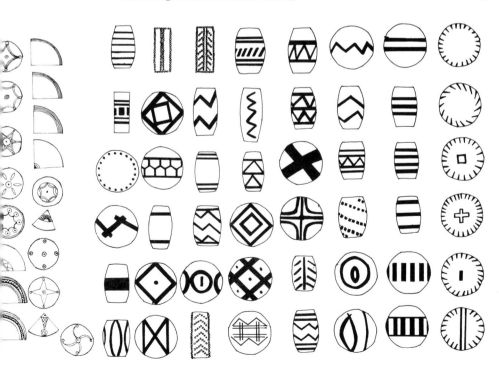

Typology is *an important stage in the recording of finds at an archaeological site. Shown left is an assemblage of designs on artefacts found at an Iron Age megalithic site in south India. They are clearly drawn and in as much detail as possible. The archaeologist has broken them into two major groupings: the first two vertical rows of fine-line designs to the far left (including the spiral design by itself at the bottom) are designs typically found on shell discs; the remaining eight rows of coarser, broad-line designs are those found on beads. This chart will form an invaluable reference for subsequent analyses.*

PHYSICAL EXAMINATION

BY SIMPLY LOOKING at ancient artefacts and the context in which they were found, we can learn a considerable amount about the culture that produced them. But often modern archaeologists want to know more – for example, about the raw materials used in making the artefacts, the sources of those materials, and the methods of manufacture.

Today, there are many scientific techniques of physical analysis that archaeologists can call upon for help. Unfortunately, they often require elaborate and expensive equipment not normally found outside laboratories. However, the optical microscope, generally used in the first stage of analyzing ancient artefacts, is not beyond the means of most people.

Microscopic examination can reveal details of an object's structure, and much more. Study of thin sections of stone objects and pottery may suggest the source of the raw materials used to make them. Minute abrasions, called microwear, on the surface of stone tools give clues to the purpose for which they were used (microwear on teeth, by the same token, may provide data about diet). Examination of samples from metal objects indicates the metallurgical processes employed in making them.

Optical microscopes are adequate for examining most types of remains, both organic and inorganic. But more expensive scanning electron microscopes are valuable for studying rough surfaces of material such as bone.

Radiography
Various X-ray techniques are used to determine the chemical composition of ancient objects, although not all of their components can be

A scanning electron microscope *can provide valuable information about the materials used in ancient artefacts. The object to be examined is placed in the specimen chamber (behind the technician's head).*

detected by this means. In X-ray fluorescent spectrometry, the item to be studied is bombarded with X-rays, causing it to emit secondary (fluorescent) X-rays whose wavelengths are characteristic of the elements present. These can be identified and their concentration determined.

However, as the X-rays cannot penetrate deeply, this technique is limited to surface examination and therefore gives an inaccurate picture of the composition of corroded or unhomogeneous metal objects. The problem can be alleviated by using an X-ray milliprobe or an electron probe microanalyser. Both devices concentrate the X-rays into a minute area which may be cleaned of corrosion without visibly altering the appearance of the object.

X-rays directed at a small sample of the object under study are diffracted in directions determined by its crystal structure. The technique, X-ray diffraction analysis, provides information on the structure of the object and the mechanical and thermal treatment it has undergone during manufacture.

Information can also be obtained by infra-red absorption spectrometry. Infra-red rays are focused on a small sample and the degree to which rays of different wavelengths are absorbed allows the identification of chemical compounds present.

Other Techniques
Optical emission spectroscopy is used particularly to detect trace elements. A small sample from the specimen is electrically excited, releasing light of different wavelengths characteristic of the elements present, which allows their identity and concentration to be determined.

Small objects can be examined by neutron activation analysis. They are placed in a nuclear reactor and bombarded with neutrons, which excite the atomic nuclei to form radioactive isotopes. When these decay, they produce characteristic gamma rays that indicate the elements present and their concentration.

The concentration of individual elements can be determined by atomic absorption spectrometry. This measures the extent to which light of a wavelength characteristic of a particular element is absorbed by an atomized sample. Other techniques, including such things as measurement of specific gravity, isotopic analysis and beta-ray back-scattering, are also sometimes employed.

THE MOULSFORD TORC

UNDER BRITISH LAW, most objects found are the property of the landowner. Objects of gold or silver, however, are treated differently. Those which were simply abandoned or lost remain the property of the landowner (or occasionally the finder). But if the original owner hid the objects with the intention of recovering them and the owner cannot be found, obviously the case with newly discovered ancient artefacts, then they become the property of the Crown, Treasure Trove. An inquest is therefore held to determine whether the objects were lost or hidden. If the Crown decides to retain nominal ownership, it is usual practice for the finder of the object to be paid the value as a reward.

An inquest into a Bronze Age gold torc (neck band) found at Moulsford, Berkshire, in 1960 required the melted-down value of the object to be established. Several methods of physical analysis were used.

Measurement of the torc's specific gravity gave a rough indication of its gold content, but showed variations between the four bars of which it was composed. Neutron activation analysis posed problems: the torc's bulk required irradiation in an unusually large atomic pile, but irradiation had to be kept to a minimum to protect the public when the torc eventually went on display.

The torc had also suffered what is called surface enrichment – that is, the silver and copper on the surface had been depleted by leaching, while the gold had not. X-ray fluorescence spectrometry, which only penetrates the surface, indicated an artificially high gold content.

Neutron activation analysis yielded the best results. Variations in the chemical composition of sections of the torc indicated that it had been made of pieces of natural electrum (gold and silver alloy) from different sources.

The Moulsford Torc (above) was analyzed by various spectrometric techniques to determine its value. It was found that the twisted bars were not made of solid gold but of a natural alloy of gold and silver called electrum. Copper had been added to enhance its colour. The end-caps of each terminal (below) were found to contain large quantities of lead.

ANALYZING STONE TOOLS

THE MINERAL CONTENT of some types of stone varies according to the conditions under which the rock from which each came was geologically formed. So it is often possible to match the stone used in ancient artefacts to its original source.

In thin-section examination, a small slice, approximately 4mm by 15mm, is cut from the artefact to be studied, ground down to a thickness of 0.03mm and mounted between glass slides for scrutiny under the microscope. The minerals present are identified and their shape, size, relative proportions and textural interrelationships are noted and compared with material from known sources.

Using such methods, British Neolithic stone axes have been divided into more than 20 groups, some subdivided, and the probable sources of most identified by comparison with known geology. Investigation of these sources has in many cases revealed Neolithic "factory" sites, such as Great Langdale in the Lake District, where the stone was shaped into 'rough-outs' that were finished somewhere else later.

Axes of greenstone probably come from a source in Cornwall, but the factory itself has not been identified and it may have been drowned by a rise in sea level since Neolithic times. Surprisingly, the products of different factories were widely distributed throughout large areas of Britain; axes from several sources are often found on the same site.

Focus on Flint
Flint lacks mineralogical variation and is therefore not amenable to thin-section examination. But it does contain trace elements, and analysis of the overall pattern of those can allow different sources to be distinguished. The trace elements are identified using neutron activation analysis and atomic absorption spectrometry.

Although flint was widely available locally to toolmakers in Neolithic Europe, they clearly prized particularly attractive or high-quality grades. Flint from the Grand Pressigny quarries in France, for example, has been found up to 800km (500 miles) away, in areas which had good flint sources themselves.

One of the most impressive mines in Neolithic Europe is at Spiennes in Belgium. Initially, the flint was extracted by driving horizontal galleries into the flint-bearing chalk, while later more than 50 deep vertical shafts were sunk. These have yielded flint and antler picks used in the quarrying. Similar antler tools were found in the flint mines at Grimes Graves in England, also being extensively worked at that time.

From the Volcano
Obsidian, a dark, glassy rock formed when volcanic lava solidifies very rapidly, was, like good flint, highly valued in Neolithic times. But obsidian suitable for making tools is relatively rare and forms homogeneous deposits, so identifying its source is much easier and more reliable than with flint.

Trace element analysis by optical emission spectroscopy, X-ray fluorescence spectrometry and neutron activation analysis (*see pages 120-1*) have all proved effective in locating the origins of obsidian used for artefacts. Sources can also be distinguished by their date of formation, using fission track dating (*see page 144*).

Uses of Artefacts
As we have already seen, microscopic examination of the edges of stone tools may reveal microwear, polish and tiny striations resulting from use. A body of experimental data has been built up to show the wear patterns associated with specific uses, and from interaction with other materials such as bone, wood or plants. By comparing that with the microwear of a particular artefact, it is possible to say what the artefact was used for.

Tools for cutting plant stems, for example, often bear a silica gloss from contact with the silica present in plants and this can be seen with the naked eye. Phytoliths, minute silica bodies from plant material, may identify the plants more specifically.

Experiments with replicas enabled archaeologists to identify quite precisely the uses of various tools found at Pincevent in the Seine valley near Paris, a site briefly occupied in the late Magdalenian period, which ended about 10,000 years ago. The distribution of finds from the site marks out the floor area of three tents, each with a central hearth, where people sat to make stone tools, butcher animals and eat them, tossing the bones over their shoulders.

The replicas were tested on a variety of appropriate materials, and the wear patterns compared with the originals. The comparisons revealed backed bladelet knives used for cutting up meat, blades for butchering, piercers for making holes in hides and for cutting grooves in antlers, a scraper for cleaning hides and, probably, the point from a projectile.

On the scree slopes *below Stickle Pike in the English Lake District (above) lies the site of a Neolithic axe factory. The tools were cut from the hard, grey-green rock and roughly-fashioned on site before being transported elsewhere for finishing.*

TRADE IN OBSIDIAN

FINDS OF TOOLS and other artefacts of obsidian provide a fascinating glimpse of the exchange networks of some ancient peoples. In the Near East, for example, obsidian sources were exploited from at least the 9th millennium BC until around 4000 BC, when the development of metallurgy led to a decline in demand.

Analysis by optical emission spectroscopy reveals an interesting pattern of distribution. In sites within a radius of 240-320km (150 to 200 miles) from the sources in Turkey and Armenia, 80 per cent or more of stone tools were made of obsidian. Villages near to the sources, such as the remarkable settlement at Catal Huyuk, developed considerable expertise in manufacturing a wide range of obsidian objects, including mirrors. Further away, the proportion of obsidian tools falls quite rapidly, but obsidian still reached some sites which were more than 960km (600 miles) from its source.

Obsidian occurs widely in the Americas and was extensively traded in antiquity, for use in tools, weapons, mirrors and elaborate ornaments. A major outcrop lies at El Chayal, on the outskirts of the present Guatemala City. More than 1000 years ago, the site was the Maya city of Kaminaljuyu. The highland Mexican Teotihuacan empire at its height colonized or took over Kaminaljuyu, probably to control trade in El Chayal obsidian.

Another important source was at Ixtepeque on the Salvadorian border. Studies of the distribution in lowland Yucatan of the products from both Ixtepeque and El Chayal, using neutron activation analysis, have provided information on the trade routes used, both overland and by canoe along rivers and round the coast. The research also gives an indication of the movement of invisible exports and imports. These included such things as cacao, salt, cotton textiles and feathers.

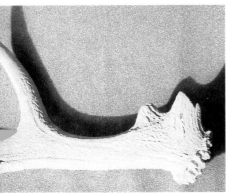

pick axe *fashioned from reindeer bone, found at _vebury, England, is typical of tools used in the Stone _e throughout Europe to quarry flint.*

At Grimes Graves, *Norfolk, England, a Stone Age flint mine was intensively worked for 300 years, around 2000 BC. Miners sunk shafts up to 12m (40ft) deep through sand, clay and chalk; they worked by the light of lamps containing animal fat and wicks of moss, to reach the high quality flint known as floorstone, much coveted for making axe heads.*

STUDYING POTTERY

POTTERY WAS INVENTED more than 10,000 years ago and is one of the most common categories of finds on archaeological sites, because it was a relatively cheap, everyday commodity and is a material that preserves well in most conditions. On most sites there are usually plenty of fragments (sherds) that can be spared for destructive analysis.

Much information can be gained about pottery just by examining it with the naked eye. Surface details, outside and in, and the cross-section of the vessel can indicate the degree to which the clay was worked, and the nature, size and quantity of temper added. They may also reveal the techniques used in manufacture and decoration, whether the vessel's surface was wet-smoothed (self-slipped) or coated in a slip or glaze, and something about the firing conditions.

Pottery, like stone, may be studied in thin section under a microscope. However, in the sedimentary deposits from which clays come the distribution of minerals is not homogeneous; so the proportions and distribution of minerals, vital clues in the analysis of stone, are not so important with pottery. Furthermore, some minerals that were originally present may be removed when the clay is worked.

Nevertheless, characteristic mineral inclusions may still allow a clay source to be pinpointed. A fine example of this has been the analysis of Hembury F ware, a pottery type widely distributed in south and south-west Britain in the Neolithic period, often associated with stone axes of the Cornish group. The clay from which Hembury F was made closely matches gabbro clays found on the Lizard peninsula in Cornwall and it is likely that the pottery was manufactured there.

Heavy mineral analysis relies on the fact that sands of different geological origins contain different heavy minerals (those with a specific gravity of more than 2.9). A sample of pottery is crushed and floated in a suitable liquid, to extract the heavy minerals present. The identity of these may allow the clay source to be determined. The manufacture of Romano-British black burnished ware type 1, which contains the heavy mineral tourmaline, has been traced to the Wareham-Poole harbour area of southern England using this technique for analysis.

Chemical Composition

The sources of clay in ceramics may also be determined by assessing their chemical composition, using optical emission spectroscopy, X-ray fluorescence spectrometry or neutron activation analysis (*see pages 120-1*). These are particularly useful for studying fine-textured pottery or wares which have been tempered with quartz sand, which are not amenable to petrological analysis.

X-ray fluorescence spectrometry is also used in determining the constituents of glazes. Lead and alkali-silicate glazes can be distinguished by beta ray backscattering. Isotopic analysis may reveal the source of lead used in the glazes.

Details of the firing conditions of pottery, particularly temperature, can be established by a technique known as Mossbauer spectroscopy and by various thermal analyses. By observing how much weight is lost when the pottery is reheated, the firing temperature can be determined. The same information can be recovered by observing the temperature at which shrinkage of the pottery begins.

A prehistoric potsherd found near Peterborough, England bears a pattern of diagonal markings which is very commonly found on Neolithic pottery. The sherd was probably part a cooking pot.

Neolithic pots dating from about 3500 BC, from the Lot region of France, were shaped without the benefit of a potter's wheel; they were hand-made by coiling a roll of clay into the desired shape. A fine liquid clay was used to give a smooth finish and the pots were fired in primitive kilns.

PUEBLO SURPRISE

PECOS, A LARGE INDIAN PUEBLO in the Rio Grande area of the south-western USA, was selected for investigation by the pioneer American archaeologist, Alfred Kidder, in the early 20th century because of its long occupation. As he was preparing the final report on the excavation, in the 1930s, he was approached by Anna Shepard, later to become one of the world's leading authorities on archaeological ceramics, but then a young researcher interested in testing the recently developed petrological analysis of pottery on an assemblage of archaeological pots.

Not much was expected of the study, as it was assumed that all the pottery would be locally made, but Kidder was very willing for her to try. The results were surprising.

Most of the pots were indeed locally made, as was shown by their content of local sand or sandstone temper. However, some, notably among the distinctive Rio Grande glaze paint pottery, were not. They contained rock temper not available in the immediate vicinity of Pecos.

Further investigations established the history of the pottery in Pecos. Glaze paint ware, decorated with a paint that used lead ores available in the Ortiz mountains, was probably first made in the Albuquerque district and was traded to settlements in the Galisteo valley, where its highly unusual appearance made it popular.

Later, Galisteo settlements began producing glaze paint ware themselves and traded it to Pecos. All the glaze paint ware of the earliest type, glaze I, at Pecos was rock-tempered. However, the people of Pecos eventually obtained the secret of producing glaze paint ware and started their own experiments, initially producing a rather degenerate version of glaze I, which had previously puzzled Kidder, and was now explained.

They soon got the hang of the technique, producing local versions of the later styles II, III and IV, distinguishable from other regional products only by their sand temper. Glaze V was an entirely local style, very flamboyant in character, and was not adopted elsewhere in the Rio Grande area. The arrival of the Spaniards in the region, in the 16th century, disrupted the supply of lead and ended the local industry; the few examples at Pecos of the latest style, glaze VI, were all rock-tempered imports.

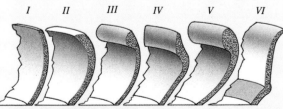

Thin-sectioning of pottery *enables minerals present in the clay to be identified, giving a clue to the origin of the vessel. At Pecos, glaze paint pottery of styles I and VI was found to be imported, while styles II to V were made of local materials.*

METHODS WITH METALS

An optical microscope *is often useful for examining metal artefacts to determine how they were made. The objects are first polished with emery paper of increasing fineness and then etched with a mild acid.*

A NAKED-EYE examination or inspection under a microscope usually reveals how a metal artefact was made. For microscopic study, part of the object is first polished carefully with a metal polish until a mirror finish is achieved. At this stage, any flaws and inclusions will be apparent.

Next, the polished surface is etched with a suitable reagent (such as 10 percent ferric chloride solution with 2 percent hydrochloric acid for most metals, or 20 percent citric acid in alcohol for iron). Such etching helps to reveal the structure of the metal. The shape and pattern of the grains in the metal are modified by heating and working, so their appearance indicates what processes were used in manufacture.

Ancient non-ferrous artefacts may show details of casting from molten metal, cold-working and annealing (reheating to reduce brittleness). Different techniques of minting coins, such as casting or striking from a larger metal sheet, can be distinguished by variations in grain structure. Iron and steel objects similarly reveal details of manufacture, including heating, hammering, carburization (combination with carbon, to form steel) and quenching (plunging when hot into cold water to increase hardness).

Chemical Composition

Information about the composition of metal objects, such as whether they are alloys or what impurities the metal contains, can be obtained only by physical analysis. Optical emission spectroscopy and atomic absorption spectrometry are suitable in most cases.

Ancient metals, particularly iron, are frequently corroded, while burial may cause surface enrichment of gold and silver. Their composition is studied by using an X-ray milliprobe or an electron probe microanalyzer

A planing axe *dating from the 11th century, found at Milk Street, London, has now been cleaned and restored with up-to-the-minute conservation techniques. It was double-sided and probably used for boatbuilding.*

on a minute area of the object, from which the surface has been removed. This is particularly useful with coins, which are generally too small and too valuable for a sample to be removed for destructive analysis.

X-ray photography can show the original form of corroded metal objects, especially those of iron, and whether they are sufficiently well-preserved to justify cleaning.

Measurement of specific gravity is a simple but limited technique enabling the relative proportions of two major components in an alloy to be calculated. It does not, however, work if there are more than two such components.

Sources of Metal

The methods of physical examination used in establishing the chemical composition of metals are also used in attempting to identify the source from which the metal ore came. Source identification of metals, however, is complicated and subject to several limitations.

One is the problem of determining where the potential sources are. Many of those exploited in antiquity were worked out long ago and forgotten. Others may remain, but are not economically viable today, and can therefore be hard to trace.

Secondly, ore deposits are not chemically homogeneous in vertical section. Usually the upper layers have been leached and the bottom ones enriched, so the deposit itself is hard to characterize in terms of the ore body it contains. Even where some matching is possible between archaeological ores and their sources, the processes of extraction and manufacture are likely to alter the concentrations of chemical impurities. The problem is reduced if a metal object contains lead, as different sources contain the lead isotopes in different proportions, and those are not altered in manufacture. The proportions are obtained by lead isotope analysis using a mass spectrometer.

In addition, many metal artefacts are made from ores from different sources, mixed together in variable proportions. This was probably rare when metallurgy began, but as metal objects became common and widespread, scrap items were often melted down for reuse. Nevertheless, despite all the difficulties, exhaustive studies have been carried out of early metal artefacts and of ore sources known to have been worked in antiquity. They have yielded at least general information on the sources exploited by particular ancient cultures.

DAWN OF EUROPE'S BRONZE AGE

THE EARLIER KNOWN copper artefacts in Europe, apart from a few isolated items made by cold-hammering from the naturally-occurring pure metal, come from sites in the Balkans and date from before 4000 BC. At Rudna Glava in Yugoslavia, impressive copper mines were already being worked at that date. The copper was smelted and cast in simple one-piece moulds.

Many copper objects of this period have a high content of arsenic or, sometimes, antimony. These have the effect of lessening the softness of the pure metal, and it is probable that the ores containing them were deliberately chosen for that reason. Chemical analyses show that this early metallurgy was based on easily worked oxide and carbonate ores, virtually free from other impurities, except silver. Evidence shows that similar methods of copper working developed during the 4th millenium in the Aegean, Italy and southern Spain.

By the later 3rd millennium BC, the easily worked ores of the Balkans were in short supply, ironically just as innovations in metallurgy, particularly the two-piece mould for casting more complex objects, were introduced from the Caucasian region further east. However, in central Europe, exploitation of the less easily worked sulphide ores was beginning. Physical analysis shows two main groups of metal artefacts at this time, one probably derived from sources including the Harz mountains in Germany, the other coming from Slovakia or the Alpine regions. Local tin was added to produce a harder and stronger metal – bronze. Significantly, the development of pastoralism, involving seasonal movement of people and their herds into the High Alpine pastures, goes hand in hand with the first exploitation of Alpine ore sources.

By the later 2nd millennium, this area had come to dominate European metallurgy. Bronze was now widely

The remains of a copper smelting hearth *dating from about 1400 BC have been uncovered at Timna, in Israel, the area of King Solomon's mines. Copper was smelted here for 1500 years.*

used for everyday tools and weapons, and sophisticated technology allowed the production of elaborate forms. The replacement of bronze by iron tools during the 1st millennium BC released bronze for luxury items and even finer bronze jewellery and vessels were created in the centuries that followed.

ther Materials

one, pottery and other metals account for any of the artefacts that archaeologists require be analyzed, but there are others too. They clude amber (fossilized resin), glass and ence (glazed earthenware made from quartz, ne and soda which is particularly associated th ancient Egypt).

Gas chromatography, a purely chemical ethod of analysis, and infra-red absorption ectrometry are used in studying amber. fferences in the botanical origins of amber and he degree of fossilization enable a distinction be made between sources in the Baltic, mania and Sicily.

Infra-red absorption spectrometry, X-ray fraction and X-ray fluorescence spectrometry widely used in the analysis of pigments. rly pigments were generally made from

naturally occurring minerals such as red ochre, or from chemical compounds. The use of red ochre in Neanderthal burials has been interpreted as possibly symbolizing blood.

Glass has proved difficult to analyze, as it is often poorly preserved. Even so, variations in manufacturing methods and colouring techniques have been detected using such techniques as optical emission spectroscopy, neutron activation analysis and X-ray fluorescence spectrometry.

The same techniques have also been applied to faience, whose blue-glazed core is generally made of quartz, lime and soda. However, they have not conclusively established whether segmented faience beads found in Bronze Age graves in southern England are of local or Egyptian origin. Current opinion holds that the beads were locally made.

The ancient Egyptians *created elaborate bead necklaces from faience – a glazed earthenware made of quartz, lime and soda.*

FAKES AND FORGERIES

For over a century *scientists have been hoping to find some evidence of a link between Man and his presumed ancestor, the Great Ape. In 1912, just such a link appeared to have been found near Pilt Down Common in southern England. Above is an artist's impression from a* London Illustrated News *of that year showing what Piltdown Man would have looked like, based on the skull fragments that had been put forward. In fact, Piltdown Man was one of the greatest – and potentially most successful – frauds ever perpetrated on the scientific community. It was not exposed for some decades, no doubt much to the scornful amusement of the person behind it all, whose identity we shall probably never know.*

ARCHAEOLOGICAL FORGERIES were, until recently, comparatively rare. Those that were perpetrated tended to stem from some personal grievance against the scientific community (*see 'Piltdown Man Exposed', page 133*), personal fame or national prestige (*see 'Surprises at Glozel', page 143*). Today, however, the explosion in the value of even minor antiquities has turned archaeological fakes into big business.

As the demand for antiquities has grown, so has the wanton looting and consequent destruction of archaeological sites to provide them. The frequent willingness of both private individuals and public institutions to purchase material of uncertain provenance has greatly encouraged this illicit traffic.

Ironically, the increasing skills of the forgers have proved of value to archaeologists. An awareness that an item may be a forgery has stimulated a demand for an unassailable pedigree of genuine antiquity and legal acquisition. That is making the sale of looted objects less easy.

Scientific Tests

Many of the scientific techniques applied to the analysis of ancient materials are used for authentication. So are some dating methods – dendrochronology (on wooden artefacts), radiocarbon (on organic materials) and thermoluminescence (on pottery, terracotta and some bronzes). Forgeries can be detected by being shown to be of the wrong date, though skilful re-use of ancient materials may fool the investigator.

Another major authentication technique involves testing for anachronistic constituents or manufacturing processes. X-ray fluorescence spectrometry and neutron activation analysis are both used for this purpose, and so are various forms of chemical analysis.

Common anachronisms in metal objects include the inappropriate use of casting techniques such as piece-mould and *cire perdue* (lost wax) casting, the inclusion of inappropriate alloys such as those containing zinc, or the presence of impurities which denote ore from a mine not worked at the period from which the object is supposed to date. Some forgeries are revealed by being too pure; one forger, for instance, used high-quality gold to produce 'Roman' coins – unfortunately he chose to imitate coins from a time when the Roman currency was actually debased.

Other forgeries convert genuine antiquities of low value into ones of higher value, usually by coating a base metal object with gold or silver. X-ray fluorescence spectrometry is valuable in detecting such fakes.

TL – THE ART SLEUTH

THERMOLUMINESCENCE DATING, or TL for short, is of great value in authenticating antiquities. One important application has been in establishing the age of terracotta figures which were purported to date from the Renaissance period in Europe.

In the middle of the 15th century, terracotta became a popular and cheap substitute for stone as a medium in the making of sculptures. In addition, when sculptors worked in stone or bronze, they often made trial models from terracotta. A revival in the popularity of Renaissance work during the 19th century promoted a flourishing trade in forgeries. TL has been used to great effect in distinguishing these pseudo-Renaissance pieces from the genuine items.

Antique bronzes can also often be authenticated by TL dating. In the *cire perdue* and piece-moulding techniques of casting bronze, a clay casting core is used and either fired before casting or in the casting process. Although this clay core is usually removed later, small pieces of fired material from it are often left in awkward angles of the finished bronze piece itself, and TL can be applied to these bits of clay for dating.

The most intriguing art forgery case in which TL has been used originated in China. In the early 1940s, terracotta figurines said to come from the small town of Hui Hsien appeared on the market, rapidly followed by numerous forgeries. The originals were unlike any known before, but were attributed to the 'Warring States' period (c. 350 BC). TL investigations in 1972 revealed that the originals themselves were also modern.

Excavations in China *have unearthed a great number of clay horses, such as this exceptionally fine one, which were used as burial pieces during the T'ang Dynasty (618-906 AD). Their desirability has resulted in widespread forgery and the only way to determine the true age of a specific piece is by subjecting it to thermoluminescence dating techniques.*

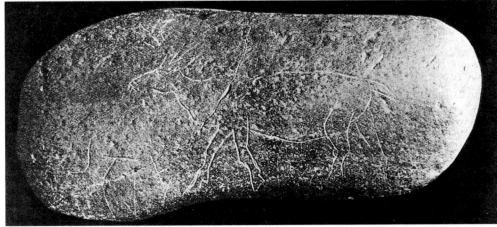

In 1924, a so-called Paleolithic find *was made at Glozel, in France, by a young villager. With the help of a doctor from nearby Vichy, M. Morlet (shown left), artefacts continued to be unearthed for 3 years. These included bones, stonemason's tools, and stones bearing carvings of reindeer-like creatures (above); the carvings were not typical of the period and aroused suspicion. Most puzzling of all were clay bricks inscribed with an alphabet bearing a great resemblance to ancient Phoenician, pointing to a Mediterranean link. Although a few French archaeologists say the site should be re-examined, it is widely held to be a fraud.*

129

THE IMPORTANCE OF DATING: 1

Stratigraphy can be used to date finds according to the depth at which they were discovered. This section drawing from an excavation by Sir John Mortimer Wheeler at Brahmagiri in south India, shows an example of how finds are dated by this method. The burial urn at the bottom of the picture, for instance, is reckoned to belong to the earlier Stone Age, or Neolithic, culture.

THE ARCHAEOLOGIST today is concerned with establishing the reasons behind developments in man's past. Why did men adopt agriculture? Who built the megaliths and what is their significance? What lies behind the extensive movement of goods and materials in prehistory?

Before such questions can be tackled at all, it is imperative to know *when* developments occurred – and the rate at which changes took place. As we saw in Part I, it was not until the advent of radiocarbon dating that it became possible to establish a firm timescale for prehistory, and to place each archaeological site on it. The only exceptions were areas such as Egypt and Mesopotamia, where early historical dates are known, or those with an unusual basis for absolute dating, such as that provided by dendrochronology in the American south-west.

The ever-increasing armoury of scientific dating techniques available to modern archaeologists largely frees them from the preoccupation with chronology that characterized their predecessors. But the absolute (chronometric) dates these techniques provide define only the skeleton shape of the past. The flesh in which that is clothed is supplied by relative dating methods, some of them in use since the 19th century. For absolute dates are expensive to obtain, and the budget of an excavation will not usually stretch to more than a few. So absolute dating is generally confined to carefully selected items from significant deposits, to relate the site chronologically to others and perhaps to answer questions such as how long it was occupied.

Stratigraphy and Typology

Stratigraphy, based on the principle that the most recent archaeological deposits lie nearest to ground level and deposits grow progressively earlier the deeper one digs, is one method of relative dating. But although it is helpful in many instances, there are some in which it cannot provide the information the archaeologist needs.

Deposits may not have a stratigraphic relationship. Where, for example, two pits have obviously been separately dug from the same ground surface, there is nothing in the stratigraphy to suggest which is the earlier. Similarly, excavations are often divided into trenches or squares, raising questions about the relationships between the layers exposed in different parts of the site.

In such cases, the relative dating is generally established by using typology *(see page 118)* – the classification of artefacts into types on the basis of similarities in such variables as form, fabric and decoration. Pottery is most frequently used for typological dating, as it has enormous potential for variation. The relative dates of different artefact types are known from the stratigraphy of numerous excavations.

However, care is needed when single artefacts form a basis for dating. It is impossible to determine precisely how long an artefact was in circulation. For instance, grave offerings may well include both treasured heirlooms and objects made only shortly before the burial took place. Datable material (particularly small artefacts) may also appear in contexts to which it is not related at all, as a result of natural disturbances such as the burrowing of animals or the action of tree roots, or man's activities,

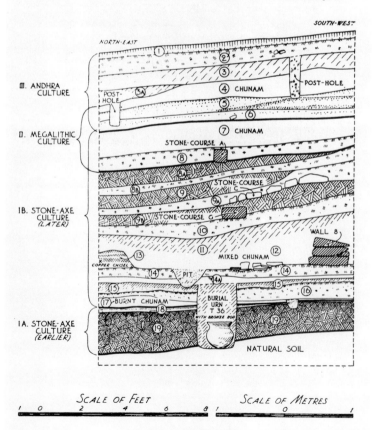

BRAHMAGIRI, 1947: SECTION Br. 21
SHOWING INTERRELATIONSHIP OF CULTURES

rticularly ploughing. The archaeologist must
 careful to establish whether dated material is
nuinely associated with the context in which it
is found.

ssemblages

oups of artefacts found together, known as
semblages, are much more useful for dating
an single items are. Recurring assemblages
e often called 'cultures' by the archaeologist
d spoken of at times as if there was a direct
uation between assemblages and human
oups – the so-called 'culture-people'
pothesis. It is a convenient (though potentially
sleading) way of dealing with a past known
most exclusively from material remains. What
semblages or 'cultures' actually signify in
man terms is an issue discussed in Part 4.
The value of assemblages over individual
ms for dating can be seen from the example of
Roman coin. On its own, it might suggest we
e dealing with a Roman deposit. But closer
amination of the associated material might
ow that the deposit is of post-Roman date and
at the coin, lost years previously, had been
rned up by post-Roman ploughing.

riation

ratigraphy and typology go hand in hand in
ting material. Sometimes, however, there are
w or no clues from stratigraphy: a cemetery
ere no graves intersect, or a region in which
es were never occupied long enough to build
 any depth of deposit. Nowadays, we may
tain a few absolute dates – radiocarbon for
me of the skeletons, TL for a few of the pots –
t we cannot afford to date every grave or
ery vessel in that way. How do we establish
e sequence of burials or of occupation of these
ort-lived sites?
In many cases, the answers may be provided
 seriation – a method which relies on the fact
at, over a period of time, the composition of
chaeological assemblages gradually changes,
d certain types of artefact found in them are
placed by others. Using mathematical
chniques, it is possible to put a series of
semblages into chronological order on the
sis of their similarities. Some forms of
riation rely simply on the presence or absence
key artefact types, while others are
ncerned with the changing proportions of
ferent types within one class of artefact.
 Unfortunately, seriation has several
awbacks. First, there is the problem that the

A collection *of cooking
objects (right) found at
Kalavasos in Cyprus can
be dated to the Bronze Age
because of its similarity to
other collections of
artefacts from the same
period. This process of
dating, called 'seriation',
was first used by Sir
Flinders Petrie (below) in
1899, to date prehistoric
Egyptian remains.*

material recovered by excavation may not be
fully representative of that once present. The
element of chance in deposition, preservation
and discovery may mean that changes observed
in the assemblages are purely fortuitous,
invalidating the seriation based on them.
　　Then, the presence, absence or varying
proportions of key artefacts in the assemblages
may signify something other than the passage of
time. For example, variations in grave goods
could reflect the personal wealth or social status
of the occupant of the grave, rather than changes
in artefacts current at the time of burial.
　　Finally, it must be remembered that the
trial-and-error arrangement of any large number
of assemblages, grouping them in order of their
apparent similarities, is a long and laborious
process. Modern computer-aided mathematical
techniques have reduced elements of the work
that is involved to some extent, but it is still time-
consuming by its very nature.

THE IMPORTANCE OF DATING: 2

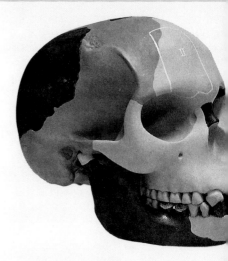

F-U-N Dating

Three scientific techniques, often used in conjunction with one another, have proved particularly valuable in establishing relative dates for bones, teeth, antlers and ivory when items of any of those materials are found together, but when it is not clear whether they are contemporaneous and absolute dating is not possible. Such problems frequently arise in cave deposits where fossilized human material occurs with the bones of extinct fauna. The three techniques measure fluorine, uranium and nitrogen levels, and are collectively known as F-U-N.

Unlike many scientific techniques – for instance radiocarbon dating *(see page 138)* – in which a constant rate of change, dependent only on the passing of time, allows absolute dates to be obtained, changes in the level of fluorine, nitrogen and uranium depend also on other variables, such as temperature and humidity. This means that they can be used to establish the relative ages of materials found together, since within the environment of a given locality the rate of change of F-U-N levels should be the same for all contemporary material.

Fluorine dating relies on the incorporation into bone mineral of fluorine ions dissolved in ground water – an irreversible process. Uranium dating is closely related to fluorine dating. Uranium dissolved in ground water permeates bone and probably replaces calcium ions in bone mineral. The rate of uptake is more rapid in gravels and sands than in limestone formations and clays.

Changes in fluorine and uranium concentrations occur so slowly that they generally cannot confidently be measured in material younger than about 10,000 years. The opposite is true of nitrogen, which has virtually vanished in material of Pleistocene date. Nitrogen dating depends upon the gradual reduction of this element in skeletal material, due to the breakdown of collagen (bone protein) into amino acids, which are leached away. In freezing conditions, impermeable soils such as clays, or situations where bacteria have been excluded, the loss of nitrogen is greatly reduced.

By using the F-U-N techniques together, archaeologists reduce the risk of errors that could arise from anomalous levels of one of the three elements in certain specimens, such as occurred in the Piltdown Hoax. High nitrogen and low fluorine and uranium levels suggest material of recent date, while the converse usually denotes very ancient material.

Original fragments *of Piltdown Man are represented by the black areas in this reconstruction of his skull. The jaw was later found to belong to a modern orang-utan.*

PILTDOWN MAN HOAX EXPOSED

THE SKULL AND JAWBONE of a supposed ancestor of *Homo sapiens* were sent to the British Museum in 1912 by a lawyer, Charles Dawson, who claimed to have found them in a gravel pit at Piltdown in Sussex. Dawson's discovery caused a great stir in scientific circles, coming as it did at the height of the worldwide quest for the 'missing link' between mankind and the apes.

Piltdown Man fitted then-held notions of how the missing link would look, with his man-like skull and ape-like jaw. Moreover, he was British and therefore highly acceptable to a nation that for decades had been casting envious glances at the abundant traces of early man in France.

By 1915, Dawson, working with Sir Arthur Smith Woodward, keeper of Geology at the British Museum, had unearthed further fragments of Piltdown Man, as well as the remains of two groups of fossil animals. However, accumulating evidence about the course of human evolution increasingly made Piltdown Man seem an anomaly. When, in 1949, fluorine tests on the Piltdown bones by Dr Kenneth Oakley of the British Museum showed these to be younger than the associated Early Pleistocene fauna, the anomaly became much greater.

These puzzling results drew the attention of Professor J.S. Weiner of the Department of Anatomy at Oxford University who began to suspect the authenticity of Piltdown Man. Together with his colleague, Professor Wilfrid Le Gros Clark, and Dr Oakley, he conducted an exhaustive examination of the Piltdown bones.

The investigators discovered that the teeth had been deliberately filed down to resemble those of humans, and that both the skull and the jaw had been stained to make them appear ancient. Oakley applied an improved fluorine test to the Piltdown collection; later, nitrogen and uranium tests were also carried out. The bones of Piltdown Man contained so little fluorine and uranium and so much nitrogen that they were clearly of relatively recent date, at most a few hundred years old. Careful examination revealed that the skull had belonged to a modern man, while the jaw came from a young orang-utan.

Tests of relative age carried out on the animal bones associated with Piltdown Man showed that they, too, were a hoax – a jumble of ancient material from various sources. Among them was the molar of an early Pleistocene elephant, *Archidiskodon africanavus*, which had an unusually high uranium content for its date. That linked it to a site in Tunisia where material, including teeth with similarly high uranium levels, had been found.

No one knows for certain who was responsible for the Piltdown fakes. Dawson, now known to have been guilty of other deceptions, seems the prime suspect and it is difficult to imagine how anyone but Dawson could have arranged the discoveries. However, it could be argued that he was not sufficiently knowledgable to have executed such a skilled forgery and that he could not have laid hands on the genuine fossil animal bones which were placed with Piltdown Man. This points to someone within the scientific establishment who disliked and wished to discredit Sir Arthur Smith Woodward and his colleagues. Sir Grafton Elliot Smith, the eminent physical anthropologist, and William Sollas, professor of Geology at Oxford have been suggested as possible perpetrators. If this were the case, however, it is difficult to see why the hoax was not exposed earlier, to ensure the desired discomfiture of Piltdown Man's supporters. The mystery still remains.

Charles Dawson and Dr A. Smith Woodward *(left) discovered relics of 'Piltdown Man' in a gravel pit at Pilt Down, Sussex between 1912 and 1915. The claimed 'missing link' was finally proved to be a hoax in 1949.*

ABSOLUTE DATING TECHNIQUES

Thomas Jefferson
(right), 'the father of American Archaeology' and president of the American Philosophical Society, was one of the first people to suggest the study of tree rings as a means of dating burial mounds of the American Indians.

SINCE THE PRINCIPLES of radiocarbon dating (*see page 138*), the first universally valid dating technique, were developed in the 1940s and 1950s, science has produced numerous other absolute dating methods, and more are being added. The latest weapons in the armoury are amino-acid racemization and uranium series disequilibrium dating (USDD). Recent developments have also revolutionized radiocarbon dating.

Radiocarbon remains the absolute dating method most widely applied today, because it can be used on a wide range of materials, and because decades of research have constantly refined its accuracy and efficiency. However, thermoluminescence (TL), applied to dating ceramics and therefore of use almost universally on sites of the last 10,000 years, may well challenge the supremacy of radiocarbon in the future.

The range of radiocarbon dating is limited – at most 100,000 years even using the most modern techniques. The early stages of man's evolution, which can be traced back several million years, are therefore dated by a number of other methods, applicable mainly to geological material and often used in combination with each other.

In addition to the major techniques, there are several of more limited scope. Though most can be used only to date certain materials, such as wood or obsidian, in suitable situations they can give excellent results.

Dendrochronology

Tree-ring dating, or dendrochronology, was the first method of absolute dating applied in archaeology, and it is still of great value in environments where wood remains well-preserved, such as arid or waterlogged sites. Over the last 15 years it has also made a significant contribution as the basis for calibrating radiocarbon dates.

As early as the 18th century, it has been known that trees develop by growing a ring of tissue each year, so that their ages can be determined by counting the number of rings in their trunks. The future US president Thomas Jefferson suggested using that fact to determine the minimum ages of ancient Amerindian earthworks from the trees on them.

Modern dendrochronology was pioneered in the early 20th century by the astronomer A. E. Douglass. While exploring the possible use of tree-rings in his investigation of sun-spot cycles, he became aware of their potential for dating wooden archaeological structures, in particular those in the pueblos of the American south-west. A ten-year investigation of Pueblo Bonito culminated in 1929 when Douglass linked a floating chronology – a series of tree-rings of unknown date – to a tree-ring sequence running up to the present day. As a result of this work it was possible to date many of the major Pueblo ruins.

Complacent or Sensitive

Trees, for dating purposes, fall into two categories – called complacent and sensitive. Complacent trees have annual rings of uniform width and are therefore of no use for dendrochronology. In sensitive trees, however, environmental conditions influence the width of the annual rings. Rainfall is the critical factor in arid areas, while in more humid regions, temperature is also important. Conditions such as soil depth and drainage in the immediate locality play a part, too.

Within broad limits, sensitive trees in any geographical region all exhibit the same pattern in their growth rings over the same period. By matching parts of the sequence of growth rings from living trees with those discernible in older timbers, a continuous dated regional sequence can be built up. At present, the longest such sequence – 8200 years – is based on the bristlecone pine, *Pinus aristata*, which grows in the arid White Mountains of California. A number of floating chronologies of considerable length have also been established. Although they have not been tied at any point to a precise calendar year, their approximate dates are frequently known.

eed for Caution

endrochronology provides a precise date for
itable pieces of wood in archaeological
ntexts, but it must be used cautiously. Above
, care must be taken to establish how the piece
wood being dated relates to the structure
om which it derives. For example, timber may
ve been freshly cut to repair a centuries-old
ilding; conversely, a new structure may
corporate old timbers.

Tree-ring data is best obtained from cross-
ctions of timber, but in the case of living trees
ndrochronologists have to be content with
illing out cores. The samples are sanded and
lished or scraped, so the rings can be
curately measured and counted, allowing for
ogressive changes in width with age. The
quences of rings from different trees or
chaeological timbers are matched in groups of
umber of years, to avoid fortuitous similarities
d to overcome occasional aberrations such as
issing or false rings, which may be due to
traneous factors such as frost damage.

arves

the period immediately after the most recent
e age, the annual summer melting of the
rthern glaciers fed the lakes of Scandinavia
th melt water carrying sand and clay particles.
ver the years, these particles gradually settled
the lake beds; at first the coarse particles
rmed a light layer and, later, progressively
er particles produced a dark layer.

The thickness of these annual layers, or
arves' as they are called, was determined by
e amount of glacial melting that occurred that
ar. A sequence of distinctive annual varves
om a number of deposits was built up by Baron
erard de Geer, an eminent Swedish geologist,
rly this century. He linked this sequence of
rves to a more-recently laid-down series of
tuary varves, to produce a combined dated
quence going back to about 10,000 BC.

Pollen, which is preserved within the varves,
ovided the means of dating the pollen zones
d also of dating the sequence of post-glacial
getational and climatic periods known from
llen analysis (see page 108). Archaeological
aterial belonging to a particular pollen zone
uld therefore be assigned an approximate
te. Though varve dating has been superseded
techniques like radiocarbon, it is now proving
eful in checking the tree-ring calibration of
diocarbon dating.

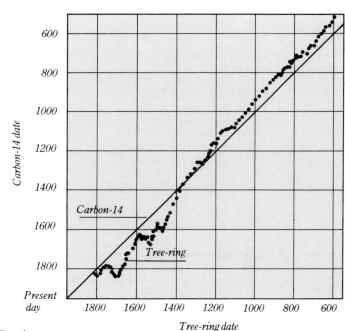

A calibration curve
(above) compares the
absolute accuracy of tree
ring dating (in this case
based on the bristlecone
pines of California) with
the less reliable carbon-14
dating method.

Tree rings from
different trees in the same
area can sometimes be
recognized as dating from
the same period because of
a recognizable pattern.
The rings can then be
overlapped to make a
master pattern extending
into the past. Each ring
represents one year.

OBSIDIAN HYDRATION

OBSIDIAN HYDRATION DATING, unlike many scientific techniques, is cheap, quick and easy. It is widely used in the Americas, where many prehistoric artefacts were manufactured from this glassy volcanic rock.

When a piece of obsidian is chipped to make a tool, the freshly exposed surface begins to absorb water at a rate that depends both upon the source of the obsidian and the temperature, but not, surprisingly, on relative humidity. By examining a thin section of the tool under a microscope and measuring the thickness of the hydration layer, the date of manufacture of the artefact can be calculated.

Amino Acid Racemization

Amino acids, often surviving in ancient bone, exist in two forms – the L (laevo), which is synthesized in living organisms, and the D (dextro), into which the L form gradually changes. Sophisticated equipment for studying amino acids has been developed by medical and biological scientists, allowing measurement of the degree of this change in archaeological material.

The process of change, called racemization, occurs at different rates in different amino acids. Aspartic acid, which racemizes rapidly, can be used to date post-Pleistocene bone, while isoleucine and alanine, which change much more

slowly, can date material probably up to 1 million years old. However, the rate of racemization also depends very much on temperature, so material can be dated by racemization only if it comes from an environment whose past temperature can confidently be determined. Older material must be from stable environments that have undergone little temperature variation, such as deep-sea sediments and the deepest recesses of caves. With more recent material, the contribution of temperature can be assessed by measuring the degree of racemization in a sample of radiocarbon dated bone. That provides a local temperature standard for calculating the age of other bones by racemization dating. Further research is being done into this technique.

Archaeomagnetism

The direction and the intensity of the earth's magnetic field are both constantly changing, due to variations in electrical currents in the earth's molten core. Records kept in London, Paris and Rome over the past four centuries have been used in conjunction with fired clay structures of known date to build up a partial picture of any changes which take place. However, because these changes will also be affected by latitude, the significance of the information is limited since it is only of regional applicability.

The position of magnetic north, which constantly changing, is shown on the graphs be as measured from Brit and the SW United States. Such knowledge can be used to date pottery, which preserve: replica of the earth's magnetism at the time o place the pottery was fir

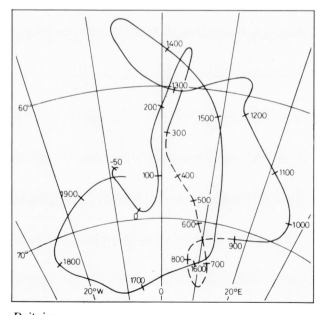

Britain

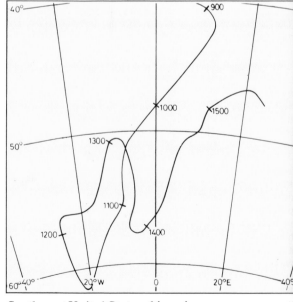

South-west United States of America

Clays used in pottery commonly contain the magnetic oxides haematite and magnetite. When, as happens during firing, the oxides are heated above a critical temperature (it is called the Curie point, and it is different for different oxides) they lose all ability to retain magnetism. But as they cool to slightly below their Curie points, the oxides become susceptible to the surrounding magnetic field, usually that of the earth, and acquire its magnetism. At what is termed the blocking temperature, which is slightly lower again, this acquired, or thermo-remanent, magnetism becomes fixed. In effect, the pottery preserves a replica of the earth's magnetism at the time and place of firing.

By comparing the remanent magnetism of archaeological material with regional records, it can be dated. A magnetometer is used to measure both intensity and direction.

Intensity may be ascertained from any fired clay for which the source (and hence the latitude) is known. Direction is composed of two elements: declination (compass direction) and inclination (angle of dip). Inclination can be ascertained in archaeological material for which the source and the position during firing can be determined – for instance, bricks stacked horizontally in the kiln. Declination can be obtained only from material still in the position in which it was fired – kilns, hearths and brick or daub structures that suffered fire damage.

Uranium Series Disequilibrium

The soluble radioactive element uranium decays into a series of insoluble daughter products that under certain circumstances become separated from their parent. The proportions of these daughter products relative to each other and to the parent uranium, constitute the basis of a series of techniques; collectively these techniques form what is known as uranium series disequilibrium dating (USDD).

The decay of uranium is the basis of thorium/protactinium ratio dating, already established for determining the ages of deep-sea cores. Recently, similar principles have been applied elsewhere. For instance, uranium is present in cave drip waters which form stalagmites and travertine layers, but its daughter products are not. Their subsequent production in the cave deposits allows the date of a deposit's formation to be determined – invaluable in dating Palaeolithic caves. A similar process in open air aquatic deposits and in fossil soils may also provide dating evidence.

Obsidian hydration *dating was used to establish the age of hundreds of artefacts, recovered by divers (above) from the seabed off the small island of Aghios Petros, Greece, in 1981. As well as obsidian tools (centre), artefacts of flint and chert (below) were found on the site of a Neolithic village, 7000 years old.*

RADIOCARBON DATING:1

Carbon 14 in moisture

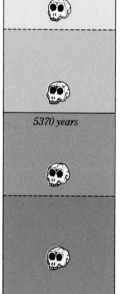

5370 years

NEUTRONS PRODUCED BY cosmic radiation interact with nitrogen in the earth's stratosphere to produce C-14 (radiocarbon or carbon 14), the radioactive isotope of carbon. Atoms of C-14 rapidly become incorporated into carbon dioxide and subsequently distributed evenly throughout the atmosphere.

As these radioactive atoms decay, they are replaced by new ones, so the proportion of C-14 in the atmosphere should remain constant. However, in modern times the balance has been somewhat affected through the burning of fossil fuels and nuclear explosions.

All living things take up C-14 during life, but the process ceases after death and the C-14 in the organism decays at a known rate. Radiocarbon has a half-life of 5730 (plus or minus 40) years – after that period has elapsed, half of the residual C-14 will have been lost by radioactive decay; after another 5730 years, half of the remaining amount will have been lost, and so on. Assuming that the amount of C-14 present in the atmosphere has remained constant, the amount of C-14 which is left in a dead organism should reflect the time elapsed since its death.

Professor Willard Libby, whose investigations of the upper atmosphere in the 1940s resulted directly in the development of radiocarbon dating, demonstrated its effectiveness by applying it to Egyptian antiquities of known historical date. The results showed a close correspondence between the historical and radiocarbon ages.

Radiocarbon dating can be used on a variety of materials, the best of which is charcoal, as that is mainly carbon. Other substances have to be

reduced to their carbon content before dating c be carried out. Wood also yields excellent resu particularly if only the cellulose fraction is used However, as in dendrochronology, there is the risk that the sample being analyzed may not be contemporary with the associated archaeologi material unless it has been carefully chosen. Shorter-lived plant material is also very suitabl and does not present any sampling difficulties.

Dating of human and animal bones has to be performed on their protein fraction, collagen, o which a relatively large amount is required. She pose problems, as they are easily contaminated Iron can be radiocarbon dated if charcoal or wo was used in the smelting, the method which wa common practice in the past. Occasionally, pottery will contain enough carbon to allow it to dated by C-14.

Analyzing the Sample

A sample for radiocarbon dating is first treated remove any contaminants, usually by repeated washing in dilute acid and alkali, and then reduc to a suitable carbon compound. If a gas counter being used to measure radioactivity, that will be carbon dioxide, methane or acetylene. Alternatively, when a liquid scintillation spectrometer is employed, the carbon will be converted to a some form of liquid, such as benzene.

A few routine tests must be performed on th sample. Sometimes, the carbon isotopes C-12, C-13 and C-14 separate out (fractionate) instea of remaining uniformly distributed. Measureme of the C-12:C-13 ratio using a mass spectromet allows the scientist to determine whether fractionation has taken place. The background radiation of the counting device is also measure and this is subtracted from the count rate of the sample – the result of this final calculation is its count rate.

Both the gas counter and the liquid scintillatic spectrometer measure the sample's present ra of radioactive decay over a period of hours or days, and from that its C-14 content can be calculated. The device also counts the activity c an artificial control, usually NBS oxalic acid (NB are the initials of the US National Bureau of Standards, who formulate it), which represents the C-14 activity of living tissue.

This artificial standard is devised to take into account changes in atmospheric levels of C-14 i modern times. Dates are calculated from the rat of the net count rate of the sample to that of the standard, allowing for the rate of decay.

All plants *and animals absorb radioactive carbon 14 during their lifetimes. When they die, the carbon 14 decays; after 5730 years it is at exactly half the original level, after another 5730 years it is a quarter the original level, and so on (right). Thus, measurement of the carbon 14 content remaining can be used to date any organic material.*

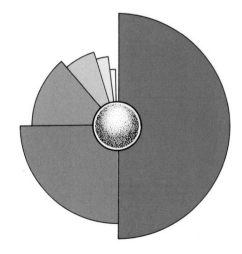

THE ORIGINS OF AGRICULTURE

THE REVOLUTIONARY IMPACT of radiocarbon dating can clearly be seen in the transformed picture it has given us of the origins of agriculture.

The earliest historical dates in the Near East are around 3000 BC, when civilized societies were emerging in Mesopotamia and Egypt. Both civilizations were founded on sophisticated agricultural technology, involving irrigation, and so it was apparent that agriculture was already no longer in its infancy. When had it begun?

Until the advent of radiocarbon dating, scholars generally agreed that agriculture was a radical innovation, readily embraced because it offered a secure way of life in place of the uncertainties of a hunter-gatherer existence. They considered that its development was rapid and suggested a date of around 4500 BC for its inception.

The accepted view was that postglacial climatic changes brought man into closer contact with plants and animals, leading to an awareness of the economic potential of controlling them. Once that awareness dawned, agriculture quickly spread.

Radiocarbon dating drove the first nails into the coffin of this theory. The initial dates obtained for the impressive early farming settlement at Jericho, 6250-5850 BC, raised a considerable storm. They were strongly challenged to begin with, but soon similar and even earlier dates were obtained for other agricultural sites in the Near East.

These indicated not only that farming was well-established in the Levant, Turkey, Iraq and western Iran 9000 years ago, but that the first steps towards it had been taken long before, in the final millennia of the most recent Ice Age.

In caves such as those of Mount Carmel and at open-air sites like Ain Mallaha, the appearance of sickles and pestles and mortars for harvesting and preparing cereals and other plants indicates an increasing interest in plant foods. In the early Postglacial period, settlements such as Jericho began to emerge in areas beyond the natural range of wild cereals. Their economies were partly based on the cultivation of cereals on well-watered land, although the inhabitants continued to gather and hunt, too. Gazelle were the main source of meat among these Near Eastern peoples, but gradually that role came to be filled by domesticated sheep and goats.

Some implications of this new information about the origins of agriculture are clear. The cultivation of plants and animal husbandry both began far earlier than was previously thought. However, they did not go hand in hand; plants were cultivated long before animals were domesticated.

Furthermore, food production was not a sudden discovery that was immediately acceptable, but the culmination of a series of changes in the relationship between man and his food sources *(see also page 112)*.

Excavations *of the ancient city of Jericho have revealed an impressive farming community which indicates that agriculture was well established there 8000 years ago. Other agricultural sites in the Near East have been dated even earlier. Farming spread gradually across Europe, reaching Britain around 5000 years ago.*

RADIOCARBON DATING: 2

Older Samples

The radioactivity of samples more than 40,000-50,000 years old is so weak that it is very difficult to measure. However, by passing the sample through thermal diffusion columns for several weeks, it is possible to concentrate the C-14 in the sample. This technique extends the date range to 70,000 years, but it is expensive, time-consuming and requires large samples, rarely obtainable from material of this age.

Recent advances, using an accelerator mass spectrometer (AMS), permit dating back to at least 70,000 years. The AMS directly measures the amount of C-14 present, and needs carbon samples of only 1-5mg, against 1-5g with the other techniques. Samples can be freed from possible sources of contamination much more effectively, as suspect portions can be discarded. And the AMS yields accurate results in a few hours.

After pretreatment, the sample is converted to graphite on tantalum wire. This is suspended in a caesium sputter ion source and the ions produced are accelerated through large electrical and magnetic fields. Ions of different mass are separated and counted in the process.

AMS is expensive, but it represents a major step forward and several laboratories are already experimenting with it. In the future, it may extend the range of radiocarbon dating to more than 100,000 years.

Striving for Precision

Libby originally calculated the half-life of C-14 as 5570 years. Later, it was more accurately determined as 5730 years, but by then many dates had been published on the basis of the earlier figure. It was therefore decided to retain the original for calculation and publication. These dates can easily be converted to their correct determination on the new half-life simply by multiplying by 1.03.

Radiocarbon dates are quoted in years 'before present' (BP or bp – see below). Convention dictates that 'present' in this context is the year AD 1950, so a radiocarbon date of 3976 BP represents (3976-1950)=1026 BC.

Even the updated figure for the half-life of C-14 is based ultimately on statistical probability. Radioactive decay is a random process, and cannot be predicted with certainty. So in giving radiocarbon dates, archaeologists qualify them according to accepted statistical practice, with a standard deviation (σ) such that in most cases two in every three readings will fall within it.

To obtain a standard deviation, a series of observations is first made of samples from the object to be dated. The average of these observations is calculated, and also the extent to which each reading varies from the average. By squaring the values by which each reading varies from the average, averaging them and then taking the square root, the standard deviation is obtained. The probability is that, in most cases, two out of every three readings will fall within the standard deviation.

For our date of 1026 BC, for example, if the standard deviation is plus or minus 120 years, the chances are two in three that the object dates from between 1146 and 906 BC.

Normally, radiocarbon date ranges are calculated to one standard deviation. It is possible to extend that to two or three deviations to encompass virtually all of the readings, but the spread of dates then becomes so great as to be of little value. The size of the deviation may be reduced, and the accuracy of the mean date improved, by dating a number of samples from the same deposit.

Calibration

It was initially assumed that the ratio of C-14 to C-12 in the atmosphere had remained constant. But disquieting discrepancies between some radiocarbon dates and historical dates eventually caused this assumption to be called into question, and the accuracy of C-14 dates was therefore tested using dendrochronology.

A sequence of datable trees was assembled in America, first using the long-lived giant redwood, *Sequoia gigantea*, and then living and dead bristlecone pines, *Pinus aristata*, which enabled sequence to be extended to 8200 BP. By comparing tree-rings (in 25 year blocks) with their radiocarbon date, it became apparent that the radiocarbon dates were consistently younger than the true dates of the wood before about 1500 BC. The discrepancy increases with time though there are indications that beyond the present range of dendochronology the discrepancy may have again decreased.

From data which has been obtained through dendrochronology, it has been possible to construct a calibration curve, by comparison with which radiocarbon dates can be converted to calendar years.

No one is certain what caused the changes in C-14 levels prior to 1500 BC, but it may be related to variations in the intensity of the earth's magnetic field. It has been suggested that this

THE MEGALITH BUILDERS

SINCE THE DAYS OF the earliest antiquarians, scholars have been puzzled by the many megalithic tombs of Neolithic date and impressive architecture around Europe's Atlantic seaboard. Although there are considerable regional variations in their form, there is a general over-riding similarity in design and, particularly, in their use of massive stones.

The construction of such large and architecturally complex collective tombs by European barbarians struck prehistorians as anomalous. The sea-faring civilizations of the Bronze Age Aegean, among whom collective burial and a diversity of stone-built tombs were known, seemed a probable source of inspiration. It was suggested that Aegean people had visited Iberia in search of metal ores and had introduced the idea of collective burial in massive tombs, which then spread northwards to Brittany, Britain, North Germany and Scandinavia.

Radiocarbon dates for the fortified settlement of megalith-builders at Los Millares in Spain appeared to confirm this picture, though dates for megaliths in Brittany seemed too early. When calibrated, however, it became clear that the radiocarbon dates were universally too early to support a Bronze Age Aegean origin. The oldest tombs in Brittany are now dated to the late 5th millennium BC, while megalith building became well-established elsewhere on the Atlantic seaboard during the 4th millennium. It is now clear that the megaliths are a western and northern European invention, not an introduced idea, and recent theories consider them in this light.

Massive stone tombs *such as this one near Plouharnel, Brittany, have been discovered in several areas around the coast of north west Europe. The tombs have been dated to 4000 - 3000 BC and were probably used as burials for tribal chiefs.*

magnetic field around the earth acts to deflect radiation arriving from outer space and that a decrease in its intensity sometime in the past had permitted an increase in the flux of cosmic radiation reaching the upper atmosphere. That in turn would have resulted in an increase in the -14 atoms produced.

In addition to the broad divergence, there were also apparently minor fluctuations known as wiggles, whose existence has been hotly disputed by scientists. The wiggles have yet to be explained, but may relate to changes in solar activity. Recent work on European tree ring sequences, particularly on oak trees from Irish bogs, tends to support the existence of the wiggles. Scientists are working to establish a wiggle curve, but in the meantime the smoothed calibration curve provides generally acceptable results. It is now archaeological convention to write uncalibrated radiocarbon dates with the notation bc/bp and the calibrated dates (now equivalent to calendar dates) as BC/BP.

THERMOLUMINESCENCE DATING

THERMOLUMINESCENCE (TL) IS THE dating technique archaeologists have long hoped for – the one that can date pottery. It can date material up to at least 35,000 years old and is also accurate for very recent material, unlike most other dating techniques.

TL relies on the presence in clay of tiny quantities of radioactive matter, which emits alpha and beta particles that in turn bombard quartz crystals, knocking electrons out of place. The displaced electrons become trapped in irregularities in the clay lattice.

If fired clay is reheated to a temperature above 380°C (most pottery is fired at more than 500°C), the electrons pop back into their original place. Light is also emitted. By measuring the amount of such light given off, and the quantity of radioactive material present, TL can establish the time that has elapsed since the clay was fired.

The technique applies to most clay heated to more than 380°C, and not just to pottery. So it can be used to date Palaeolithic clay figurines that were either accidentally or deliberately baked, and clay hearth surrounds. Recent tests have demonstrated that TL can also be used on flint tools heated during manufacture.

Testing the Samples

The first step in preparing a sherd for TL analysis is to grind it to powder, and to extract the quartz grains from it using laboratory separation techniques. The grains are then

heated on a graphite plate in an airtight chamber and the light that is given off is measured using a photomultiplier. A chart recorder prints out details of the temperature and the glow curves of the TL.

The material is heated again, when all the TL has been given off, to measure the background emission of the plate. The comparison of the two glow curves allows the amount of TL to be calculated. The radioactivity of the material is also measured with a counting device.

An important consideration in TL dating is where the pottery comes from. Radioactive elements in the environment emit gamma particles that vary in intensity according to local conditions. Although most of the TL that is measured is caused by the clay's internal alpha and beta particles, some may be due to the external influence of these gamma particles. If the source of the pottery is known, the level of gamma irradiation can be allowed for in the dating.

TL Completes the Picture

TL has been used to date several important archaeological cultures for which there are few or no radiocarbon dates, or for which the C-14 dates are of disputed reliability. One recent example is the investigation of the Neolithic and Chalcolithic cultures of Portugal.

To a large extent, these cultures are represented by a variety of Megalithic burials, but there are also hilltop settlements. On the basis of the finds, it was possible to work out a general picture of the stages in the development of the tomb architecture, but the actual dates involved were uncertain. Were the Portuguese megaliths as early as their counterparts elsewhere in western Europe? When did the settlements begin?

TL was called upon to answer such questions and 55 sherds were analyzed, from nine sites. The TL dates for the earliest tombs with pottery, the passage graves at Gateira and Gorginos, were around the middle of the 5th millennium BC – a good match with the radiocarbon dates for the earliest Breton passage graves.

Right through the sequence, TL dates from Portugal fitted radiocarbon dates elsewhere in western Europe, even to the surprisingly early rock-cut tomb at Carenque, which has exact parallels in Malta at the same date, around 4000 BC. The settlements were shown to have begun at the period of the largest Megalithic tombs.

Thermoluminescence *dating measures the emission of light from a sample which is heated in an airtight chamber in a special apparatus (above). The light emitted at different temperatures is plotted on a graph (right). Lines 1 and 2 represent the light emitted from two different samples. Line 3 represents the background light emitted from the chamber. This must be taken into account when calculating the TL of the sample.*

Thermoluminescence (TL)

Temperature °C

SURPRISES AT GLOZEL

A clay brick *(above) found at Glozel includes a swastika sign (on left in the 6th line from the top). Much of the writing on the tablet resembles Minoan and Phoenician scripts. Archaeologists declared the Glozel finds to be a hoax in 1927 but digging at the site continued, as shown in the photograph at left taken in 1928.*

IN 1924, A YOUNG FRENCHMAN, Emile Fradin, accidentally discovered a medieval glass furnace at Glozel, near Vichy, France. The local schoolmistress excavated it, and the schoolmaster encouraged Emile's enthusiasm by lending him books on archaeology.

Over the next three years, some very curious things appeared from Glozel: tools and carvings of prehistoric type, clay tablets bearing writing similar to Minoan and Phoenician scripts, and extraordinary vases with human faces.

Opinion on the authenticity of the artefacts was sharply divided. Some archaeologists believed the finds indicated that the Neolithic period in western Europe could not have begun until about 2000 BC, much later than generally believed. But in 1927 an international commission investigated the site and reported it to be a hoax.

In 1974, an international team of scientists decided to subject some of the Glozel artefacts to TL dating. To everyone's amazement, the series of dates obtained was neither modern, as the anti-Glozelians had supposed, nor very ancient, as the Glozelians had hoped, but clustered between 700 BC and AD 100. What was going on? The TL scientists were certain that there was nothing wrong with the TL dates. On the other hand, many of them were just as convinced as the archaeologists that the material must be forged.

Various suggestions were made. One was that the objects were originally undistinguished material of genuine antiquity but modified by the forger: old bones with modern 'Palaeolithic' carvings, modern 'writing' on tablets of genuine ancient fired clay.

More recent TL tests gave some support to this theory, since some of the pieces proved to be of medieval date. One of the later group of TL tests for a vitrified tablet produced a date of AD 1750. As for the curiously shaped clay objects, their softness suggested they could have been modified by soaking them in water and shaping them when wet.

Glozel remains a mystery. At present most experts believe that it was a fraud, but there are still a few French archaeologists who believe the site should be reinvestigated.

DATING EARLY MAN

HUMAN ANCESTRY extends back far beyond the range of radiocarbon dating. Attempts to date our earliest ancestors depend upon various other techniques, most of which apply to geological strata. Usually, archaeological remains occur in deposits above or below such strata rather than within them, so dating is indirect.

Potassium-Argon (K/Ar) Dating

The volcanic material from which igneous rock is formed contains both potassium (K) and an argon isotope (Ar-40). At the time of formation, all the argon is released. However, the potassium still present has a radioactive isotope, K-40, part of which becomes the inert argon isotope Ar-40 as it decays. The process of decay takes place at a known rate, so by measuring the Ar-40 now present, it is possible to gauge their age.

One method of doing this involves irradiating a sample with fast neutrons, converting the K-39 isotope to the argon isotope, Ar-39. By measuring this, it is possible to calculate the original K-40 content. The amount of argon present is measured with a sensitive mass spectrometer.

As it is impossible to exclude Ar-40 completely from the air during the measurement, the presence of two other atmospheric isotopes, Ar-38 and Ar-36, is also measured. The three occur in air in constant proportions, so the amount of atmospheric Ar-40 can be worked out.

Samples for K/Ar dating must be carefully selected, as the results can be affected if the rock is contaminated and also by the natural loss of argon through diffusion. The most reliable results are obtained by dating several crystal types from the same deposit and samples from scattered localities in the same geological stratum.

Fission Track Dating

The spontaneous fission of the uranium isotope U-238 produces submicroscopic damage trails in certain rocks containing uranium impurities, particularly volcanic 'glasses' such as obsidian. As U-238 decays at a known rate, the density of these fission tracks is proportionate to the age and to the amount of uranium present. When the rock is heated beyond a certain temperature, the fission tracks fade and disappear. It is therefore necessary to select materials for dating which have a high 'fading temperature'. The date obtained from these will be the date of formation of the rock.

The fission tracks can be observed in thin section under a microscope, particularly if they are enlarged by etching with hydrofluoric acid. The uranium content can be calculated by irradiating the sample to induce the fission of U-235 (which does not undergo spontaneous fission) producing a number of new damage trails proportionate to the uranium content.

Fission track dating can be used over a very considerable time range, from as little as 20 years to more than 1,000 million. Although it has mainly been applied to volcanic rocks, it can also be used to date man-made glass and pottery that contains suitable crystalline minerals.

Palaeomagnetism

In addition to short-term variations in the intensity and direction of the earth's magnetic fields, discussed previously, there have been longer periods when the earth's magnetic polarity has been completely or partly reversed. They have been identified in volcanic and sedimentary rocks and, more particularly, in deep-sea sediments, which contain a continuous record datable back to about 5 million years ago. This palaeomagnetic information provides a useful control for other dating techniques.

Ocean Sediments

Seawater contains the stable oxygen isotopes O-18 and O-16. Water molecules containing O-16 evaporate more readily than those with O-18, and are therefore preferentially incorporated into polar ice during glacial periods, altering the ratio between the two isotopes in the sea.

Planktonic foraminifera, minute ocean creatures, reflect this ratio in their composition. After death, the shells of foraminifera accumulate on the ocean floor, where they form a major component of the sediments.

Radiocarbon, K/Ar and fission track dating techniques are all applied to ocean sediment samples. This combination of techniques provides dates both for the earliest and the most recent sedimentary layers.

Biostratigraphy

Intensive work by palaeontologists has produced a widely accepted family tree for a number of animals, such as the ancestors of horses, pigs and elephants. Certain of these can be used as 'index fossils', providing a reliable date range for a geological deposit. Index fossils should be species that can easily be identified and which were abundant over a wide geographical area, but which existed for a short period of geological time.

The skull of Hom_ Habilis, *found at L_ Turkana, Kenya, b_ Richard Leakey (ab_ 1972 has been dated_ million years old – between Australopi_ and Homo Erectus.*

Zinjanthropus – _ of East Africa' – fou_ Tanzania in 1959 h_ been scientifically p_ in the Australopithe_ group and is believe_ between 1.7 and 1.9 million years old. T_ has been reconstruc_

THE ANTIQUITY OF OUR ANCESTORS

THE DATING OF fossil hominids, and thus their inter-relationship, has been a major source of dissension and acrimony among palaeo-anthropologists. The use of a variety of modern dating techniques has helped to resolve some of these controversies.

In 1972, Richard Leakey discovered a really impressive skull of *Homo habilis*, '1470', at Lake Turkana, Kenya. This lay in a deposit below a volcanic tuff, KBS, dated 2.6 million BP by K/Ar. Leakey therefore dated '1470' to 2.9 million BP. As previous discoveries of *Homo habilis* had been in deposits dated 1.8 to 1.5 million BP, there was a considerable stir in scientific circles.

Eventually, Basil Cooke, a distinguished palaeontologist, presented evidence that the type of pig (*Mesochoerus*) present in the same deposit as '1470' could not be older than 2 million years. The remains of forerunners of horses and elephants suggested the same.

Consequently, new attempts were made at dating. Fission track dates of 1.8 million BP were obtained from a vitric tuff below the KBS tuff. It was ascertained that there was some contamination in the KBS tuff; however, very carefully selected uncontaminated samples finally yielded K/Ar dates of 1.8 and 1.6 million BP. Thus '1470' was securely dated to the same period as the other *Homo habilis* remains.

A similar combination of dating techniques was applied at Hadar, Ethiopia, where the bones of Lucy and her relatives were discovered above and below a layer of black basalt, for which a date of 3 million BP was obtained. However, at Laetoli in Kenya, similar hominid remains had been found between tuffs dated 3.59 and 3.77 million BP. Could they be the same species at such different dates, or were the dates wrong?

The palaeomagnetic evidence showed that the Hadar fossils belonged to a period of reverse polarity, which the associated fauna, particularly the pigs, indicated should be the so-called Gilbert reversal of 3.8-3.4 million BP. Very careful collection of material for further K/Ar testing yielded a date of 3.75 million for the basalt, closely matching the Laetoli evidence, and permitting the classification of all these hominids as a single species, *Australopithecus afarensis*.

Five dating techniques *were used to determine the age of the fossils of Lucy and her relatives found at Hadar, Ethiopia. Some initial dating was possible solely through the geology of the site. Next, in 1979 and 1980, further fossils were dated by the palaeomagnetic record and the evidence of pig fossils (biostratigraphy). Potassium-argon and fission-track dating were also used to give a final date of 3.5 million years for Lucy.*

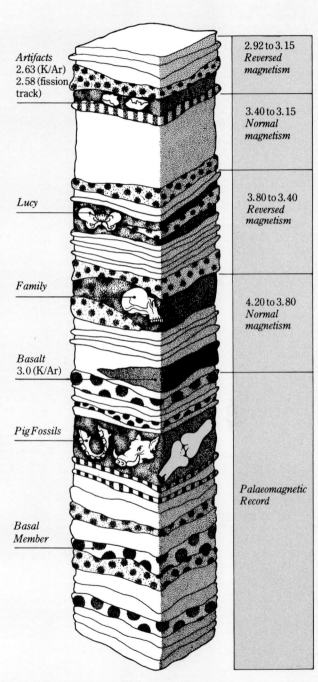

Artifacts
2.63 (K/Ar)
2.58 (fission track)

Lucy

Family

Basalt
3.0 (K/Ar)

Pig Fossils

Basal Member

2.92 to 3.15
Reversed magnetism

3.40 to 3.15
Normal magnetism

3.80 to 3.40
Reversed magnetism

4.20 to 3.80
Normal magnetism

Palaeomagnetic Record

----- PART 5 -----

UNDERSTANDING THE PAST

Opposite: *Excavation seasons are short and every moment is precious. This team has been digging all day in a sweltering Middle Eastern desert and they continue their work even as the last light fades.*

UNDERSTANDING THE PAST

IN A NOW-FAMOUS paper that appeared in *American Anthropologist* in 1954, Christopher Hawkes discussed the kind of inferences we are able to draw about the past. He concluded that they can be made at four levels.

The simplest inferences, in which we can place great confidence, concern ancient technology. Generally, it is easy to deduce from the physical examination of ancient artefacts how they were made. We have already seen the ways in which archaeologists tackle this relatively straightforward topic.

According to Hawkes, the second level concerns subsistence economics – how people have satisfied their basic needs for food, shelter, clothing and tools. Again, we have already seen that some information about that may be gleaned from physical analysis of archaeological remains. The movement of raw materials can be discovered, and the study of food remains gives clues about what people ate and at what time of year. Further indications of how past economies operated can be deduced using the methods of the economic prehistorian *(see page 156)*. Considerable confidence may be placed in the conclusions.

Hawkes's two remaining levels concern social and political organization and religion. They pose much harder problems. The organization of human societies is extremely varied, so how can we attempt to deduce organizational patterns of the past? Even more difficult, how do we recognize prehistoric religion and attempt to reconstruct it? Can we, in fact, do so?

All these aspects of the past are static, dealing with what a given society was like at a given time. But archaeologists are also concerned with how such societies interacted and changed. What mechanisms were operating, and were they the same as those that operate today?

It is to such questions, and the methods that archaeologists use in attempting to answer them, that the rest of this book is devoted.

Present into Past

Many theories have been put forward to explain observed archaeological phenomena, derived ultimately from the imagination, knowledge and experience of archaeologists themselves. But most of those archaeologists live in technologically advanced societies very different from the ones they are trying to reconstruct. Two important techniques in use today test their theories to see if they are reasonable or even possible, and may also yield information to extend the range of theories. They are experimental archaeology and ethnoarchaeology.

Experimental archaeology aims to test hypotheses – particularly, though not exclusively, those associated with function, technology or economic matters – about specific aspects of the past. Ethnoarchaeology entails the study of contemporary societies from an archaeological viewpoint for the light they may shed on their ancient counterparts.

Archaeological Experiments

Ethnographic information is often the source of inspiration for archaeological experiments. For example, pits are a common feature of prehistoric sites. Frequently, they now contain rubbish, but it is assumed that their original function was, in many cases, storage – in particular of grain, but also of pulses, nuts, green vegetables and other foodstuffs.

Further alternative uses can be suggested by examining the functions of similar pits among present-day groups. In parts of Africa, for instance, some pits are used in the manufacture of indigo dye. By experimenting with various uses in the environment inhabited by the prehistoric group under study, archaeologists can assess which of the uses are most likely.

Experimental archaeology can be used to demonstrate that explanations rejected in theory as impossible may not in fact be so – although, of course, practical proof that something is feasible does not prove that it actually occurred. One of the most famous experiments of this kind was the daring voyage of the balsa raft *Kon-Tiki* in 1947.

Across the Pacific

For many year, scholars speculated that the Polynesian islands of the Pacific might have originally been colonized from South America. However, the idea was generally rejected, because the boats available to the South Americans at the time colonization was supposed to have taken place were not considered capable of long ocean voyages.

The Norwegian anthropologist Thor Heyerdahl decided to challenge the received wisdom. He and his crew set sail from South America on a balsa wood raft of traditional design, the *Kon-Tiki*. Despite the gloomy prognostications of all who saw the raft depart, the *Kon-Tiki* landed safely about three months later, on the Pacific island of Tuamoto.

or Heyerdahl, the
orwegian anthropolgist
ft), sailed a balsa wood
ft, the Kon Tiki, from
uth America to
lynesia in 1947 in an
empt to prove that the
cific Islands were
ginally colonized from
uth America.
eyerdahl later made a
vage across the Atlantic
a papyrus-reed boat, the
a (below), to show that
peoples of the
editerranean could have
iled to Central and
uth America in similar
ssels. Heyerdahl's
rneys challenged
viously held beliefs that
ch colonizations were
possible.

Heyerdahl's achievement demonstrated that the grounds usually cited when discounting South American colonization of Polynesia were invalid. He did not, however, prove that such colonization took place. Indeed the weight of archaeological evidence is still against it, and overwhelmingly in favour of settlement from south-east Asia.

Exposing Flaws

The voyage of the *Kon-Tiki* exposed a false assumption. Experiments also sometimes reveal flaws in archaeological reasoning. For example, the accepted picture of food production methods in the Iron Age had to be revised dramatically when proper tests were carried out on storage pits of the period in Britain.

For a start, it had been believed that a typical pit could hold 5 bushels (0.18 cu m) of grain. Experiments showed that their capacity was actually no fewer than 44 bushels (1.58 cu m), indicating that the scale of Iron Age farming was far greater than had been supposed.

Archaeologists had also reasoned that the pits would have been lined with clay or basketry to protect the grain inside them, and that they would have a limited life – say, 10 years – before the soil soured and they were used for rubbish disposal. Work by Peter Reynolds, the British experimental archaeologist, demonstrated otherwise.

Grain stored over winter in unlined pits, dug in a variety of subsoils and well sealed with a clay capping, quickly became dormant. The germination rate after storage was high, between 60 and 70 per cent. The pits were easy to clean for reuse, and showed no signs of souring.

Finally, the tests revealed a hitherto-unrecognized fact. Careful study of the edges of such pits can provide clues about what they were used for. Although the idea seems obvious, it needed Reynolds's work to show that the pit-edges should not be neglected or treated superficially – exemplifying another role of experimental archaeology.

RECONSTRUCTING THE PAST

ARCHAEOLOGICAL EXPERIMENTS are today the recognized means of advancing our scienti knowledge of the past. They enable archaeologists not only to test established hypotheses, but also generate new ones, whic in turn can be tested.

One successful example of an experiment leading to a new hypothesis concerns the function of the notched ribs commonly found o sites of the American Basketmaker Indians. It was initially thought that they might have beer used for scraping hides, but when that was trie they broke. Further investigation revealed, however, that the ribs were very effective combs for extracting fibres from the leaves of yucca plants. It was known that ropemaking from these fibres was a major industry among the Indians, so it seemed reasonable to assum that the ribs were used in the process. The assumption was justified when a notched rib w found with yucca fibres and sap caught in it.

Most archaeological experiments relate to technology or to subsistence economics. They include such activities as: forest clearance, agriculture and food preparation; the reconstruction of buildings, earthworks and ships; manufacturing tools and weapons; pottery, weaving and painting, and the making musical instruments. Some researchers complain that, up to now, they have not been able to obtain human bodies to test ancient cremation and mummification methods.

Replicas for Research

Experimental reconstructions which are made ancient objects and activities can be done on several levels. These range from simple copies or reproductions, of ancient artefacts, perhaps for museum display, to reproductions made using only the technology, tools and materials available at the time the original was produced. furthur stage is to test the reproduction in simulated ancient conditions.

At the Lejre research centre in Denmark, fc example, a replica of an Iron Age plough, or ard found in a peat bog was used in experimental ploughing, yielding useful information. The researchers discovered that the original ard accidentally lacked a vital wedge between the ploughshare and the beam. They were able to study the ard's effectiveness in breaking groun the wear on the share, and the shape of Iron Ag ploughmarks. Experiments similar to the Dani ones have been carried out by Peter Reynolds Butser Farm in Britain.

Basketmaking *(above) has been practised by American Indians for 2,500 years. The craft originated in Indian cliff settlements similar to those at left which have been discovered at Mesa Verde, Colorado. They date from what is known as the Basketmaker Period (500 BC-AD 600).*

MILLIE'S CAMP

Reconstructions of incomplete remains of the [pa]st provide a fruitful area for experiment. [A]ncient houses, in particular, are often [re]constructed on the basis of surviving postholes [an]d other structural traces. They can then be [te]sted for structural soundness, and information [ob]tained on the time they must have taken to [bu]ild originally, and the materials used. By [al]lowing the reconstructions to decay naturally, [or] even destroying them by fire, archaeologists [ca]n obtain valuable insights into the signs such [de]cay or destruction may have left.

In another series of experiments, several [ba]nk and ditch earthworks have been dug, and [th]en left to decay. Periodically, a portion is [ex]cavated to observe the changes that have [ta]ken place.

[T]esting the Tools

[B]esides giving an insight into prehistoric [te]chnology, experiments allow us to appreciate [th]e skill and organization that went into a variety [of] activities, the time and manpower required [an]d the relative efficiency of evolving versions of [ea]rly tools – the comparative felling power of [st]one, bronze and iron axes, for example.

One constraint, however, is possible lack of [pr]oficiency by those carrying out the [ex]periment. Incompetent or unpractised use of [to]ols will obviously increase the time taken to [p]erform a task and reduce the quality of the [w]ork, inviting a risk of erroneous conclusions.

Despite that potential drawback, much has [b]een achieved. Not least has been the [d]emonstration, in many parts of the world, of the [a]bility of experimenters using simple technology [an]d large teams to carve, transport and erect [h]uge stone monuments. Their work shows that [su]ch feats were within the capabilities of ancient [m]an, and that neither supernatural nor [e]xtraterrestrial beings need to be called upon to [a]ccount for these works.

A FASCINATING and important extension of the experimental approach applies it to the interpretation of remains. In a pioneering study in the 1970s, the Canadian archaeologist Robson Bonnichsen examined a Canadian Indian camp that had been abandoned relatively recently; he interpreted the archaeological evidence he recovered in terms of the activities that took place there and the number, ages and sex of the inhabitants.

Bonnichsen then asked an Indian woman, Millie, who had once lived in the camp to tell him about the actual inhabitants and what they did. Bonnichsen's interpretations were shown to be erroneous in many respects, but the exercise was valuable in highlighting potential problems in such interpretations.

The approach used at Millie's camp combined experiment with ethnography, and the two are often closely connected in archaeological research. Many of the experiments made on archaeological material stem from ideas and possibilities derived from ethnographic data.

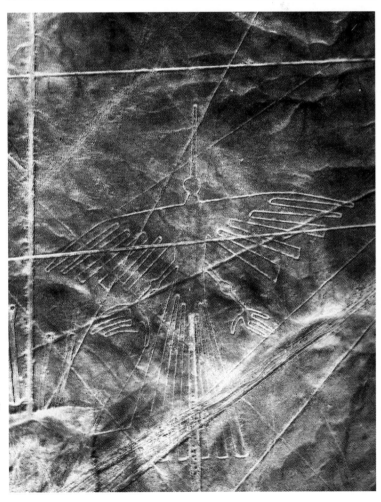

Line Drawings *such as this bird etched into the earth at Nazca, Peru, have provided a source of much speculation. Despite recent claims that the etchings were done by beings from outer space, most archaeologists believe that ancient man was capable of creating such drawings.*

ESTABLISHING RELATIONSHIPS

ANALOGIES BETWEEN THE present and the past have been drawn since the earliest days of archaeology. The realization in the 17th century that ancient stone tools were indeed human artefacts was largely due to observation, in the newly discovered Americas, of the native Indians using similar tools. By the 19th century, direct comparisons were being made between ancient peoples and contemporary groups such as the Australian aborigines, who were looked on as surviving relics of Palaeolithic life.

Gradually, however, the idea of such complete correspondence between ancient and present-day societies was abandoned. It has been replaced by a more specific and less generalized use of analogies.

Today, the value of ethnographic analogies is a matter of debate. Some archaeologists argue that, by drawing them to suggest elements in a picture of past lifestyles, we are limiting ourselves, because human culture is infinitely variable and nothing in the past need be mirrored in the present. The opposite view is that a comprehensive examination of present-day societies will provide us with a range of possibilities that broaden our outlook when considering the past.

Both contentions are valid. Ethnography provides a spectrum of ideas about how things may have operated in the past, but we must not allow ourselves to be limited in our reconstruction of that past by considering only those things we know to be true of the present day or of historical times. That is particularly important when looking at the aeons before the emergence of modern man. The behaviour of our hominid ancestors was probably very different from anything with which we are familiar from our own time.

Many archaeologists, however, believe that the value of ethnographic studies is greater when they are used to compare present and past groups in the same area.

A New Approach
In recent years, a new approach to the use of ethnographic data has been adopted; it is known as ethnoarchaeology. Some scholars believe that information about all the activities and interactions of ancient societies is encapsulated in the artefacts and other evidence uncovered by archaeologists – if only we can find ways of unlocking their secrets. Others are less optimistic, but no one disputes the fact that archaeological evidence can reveal valuable things about the past.

Many experts, of whom the eminent American Professor Lewis Binford is the chief exponent, are seeking to establish the relationship between the static archaeological

The Tsumkwe Bushmen *of Namibia are among the most primitive people alive today. Their nomadic, hunter-gather lifestyle closely resembles that of pre-historic man. Archaeologists disagree however, whether tribes such as the Bushmen should be regarded as relics of the Stone Age or as a unique people in the own right.*

PREDATORS OR VICTIMS?

MUCH OF THE DEBATE about whether certain of Man's early forebears qualify as hominids or as ancestral apes centres on their behavioural patterns. Raymond Dart's battle from the 1920s to have his *Australopithecus* accepted as a hominid *(see page 17)* encouraged him to search for evidence of specifically human behaviour, in particular the manufacture of tools and the regular consumption of meat.

Baboon skulls discovered in caves near the *Australopithecus* sites in southern Africa had depressions in them that Dart considered had been caused by blows from clubs. That implied to Dart that *Australopithecus* had hunted and killed game. Furthermore, the caves did not contain complete baboon skeletons, but only certain bones. Dart concluded that those had been retained because of their potential usefulness as tools.

In the 1960s, A South African archaeologist, C.K. Brain, tried to test the validity of Dart's assumptions, and to find out whether there were other ways in which the baboon bones could have accumulated. Brain studied a Hottentot village where the inhabitants kept and ate goats, and where dogs scavenged the food remains discarded by the villagers. The results showed a pattern that has subsequently been found generally characteristic of the combined operations of carnivores and scavengers – the bigger and heavier bones tend to survive their attentions, while the smaller and lighter ones do not.

Dart's baboon bones matched this pattern. In addition, the damage observed on them closely matched that inflicted by leopards on the bones of their prey. It seems therefore that *Australopithecus* was not the hunter of the baboons. Recent studies of Australopithecine teeth suggest that he was mainly vegetarian.

Two of the leading *experts on early man – Richard Leakey (left) and Professor Raymond Dart (right) – have devoted their lives to unravelling the mystery of human origins.*

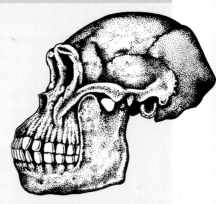

Australopithecus, *which lived about 3 million years ago, had a brain that was no larger than that of a modern ape, but he walked upright and probably used tools. His teeth resemble those of a primate; he probably ate fruit, berries or wild plants, and was not a hunter. The debate continues as to whether he was the first hominid or merely an ape.*

---

remains we study and the dynamic activities of the peoples of the past. It is a common assumption, for instance, that the pattern of artefacts recovered from a locality represent the activities that have taken place there. But do people really just leave things lying around, to be unearthed by their descendants?

To answer this and many other questions, archaeologists are increasingly studying ethnography directly, rather than relying on the accounts of anthropologists. Ethnoarchaeology is one of most promising fresh approaches to understanding the past.

The Garbage Project

In 1972, William Rathje and a group from the University of Arizona in the USA began trying to determine the extent to which variable factors influence the types of ordinary refuse that people discard. With the help of the health department in the city of Tucson (Ariz), the team analyzed the contents of the dustbins of more than 600 households and related the information to socio-economic data, such as the size of the household, the age of its members, their income and their ethnic group.

Among other things, the researchers found there were similarities in the material discarded by young and old people, and that considerably more food was thrown away by middle-class whites than by other ethnic groups. Much of the food wasted by the whites was not even unwrapped – and there was evidence that many households spent as much as $100 a year on steak which they never actually ate.

The archaeological implications of the study have still to be assessed fully. But it did establish that the archaeological premise that people make sensible economic use of the resources available to them is not always valid.

ARTEFACT VARIATION

WE HAVE ALREADY seen *(page 130)* the part that artefact assemblages may play in dating. They are also among the basic data from which archaeologists reconstruct the past.

Early antiquarians began to use variations both in the form and material of artefacts and in their associations to divide the past into chronological periods. By the early 20th century, scholars like Oscar Montelius and Paul Reinecke had refined and elaborated Thomsen's basic Stone Age-Bronze Age-Iron Age chronology into a detailed sequence of subdivisions, on the basis of variations in the forms of swords, pots, jewellery, axes and other artefacts.

In addition to chronological changes in the forms of artefacts and the composition of assemblages, variations between artefacts or assemblages found in different locations were also considered. The idea that geographically *archaeologist to* lages denote separate cultural groups came to be one of the major assumptions underlying archaeologists' views of the past.

Cultures and Peoples

This so-called 'culture-people' hypothesis derived from geographical variations still underpins much archaeological thinking, but today there are also many who question its validity, believing that other factors must also be considered, such as the availability of raw materials. This has encouraged the ethnographic examination of variations in artefacts and assemblages.

As long ago as 1939, Donald Thomson published a paper outlining the seasonal aspects of an Australian aboriginal economy, in which he noted that a single group occupied several widely separated sites in the course of a year. There were marked differences between the tools used at the different sites, as each season involved different activities.

The standard interpretation of Thomson's findings according to the 'culture-people' hypothesis would be that each site was occupied by a different cultural group. Nevertheless, despite the flaws in the hypothesis, ethnographic and historical data and our knowledge of present-day western societies clearly demonstrate that the expression of cultural differences through preferences in style of dress, hairstyles and body adornments, personal possessions, architecture and so on is a trait which recurs throughout mankind's history and spans not only geographical but also cultural boundaries.

Australian aborigines, *who move across the country as the seasons change, varying their lifestyle, provide an execption to the 'culture-people' hypothesis. While their tools and other objects differ from site to site, the artefacts all belong to the same cultural group.*

Tools of *the Mouster – the age of Neanderth Man – were fashioned from crude blocks of fl They have been found several parts of southe France.*

TOOLS OF THE MOUSTERIAN

THE GREAT FRENCH SCHOLAR of the Palaeolithic era, Francois Bordes (1918-1981), made an intensive study of stone tools from caves, rock shelters and open-air sites, particularly in south-west France. From them, he built up a generally accepted typology of tools of the Mousterian – the Middle Palaeolithic period that was the age of Neanderthal man. Assemblages from different deposits on these sites varied considerably in the proportions they contained of different types of tools.

Bordes himself divided the assemblages into four main groups. The so-called Mousterian of Acheulean Tradition contained hand-axes (as in earlier Acheulean assemblages), rare or absent in the other three groups. Denticulate Mousterian contained many toothed and notched tools, while the Charentian group (subdivided into Quina and Ferrassie) was abundant in scrapers. What Bordes termed Typical Mousterian had relatively few backed knives, but fairly balanced proportions of other types of tools. Bordes attributed each group to a different tribe, and the presence of all four groups on many sites to occupation by all of the tribes at various times.

Nevertheless, many archaeologists found the tribal explanation unacceptable. Was it likely that four cultures could repeatedly occupy the same sites, apparently at random, without influencing each other? One suggestion was that the variations were, at least in part, chronological. Another, by Professor Lewis Binford (*see pages 152-53*), proposed that Mousterian man constructed basic 'tool kits' that varied according to the specific task to be performed.

Binford and his wife Sally used a computer to analyze which artefacts tended to be regularly associated with each other, forming the tool kits. Bordes's four groups, it was suggested, each represented a different combination of the tool kits, and reflected the activities taking place at the site during each period of occupation. In their initial studies of such variation, among Mousterian tools in the Near East, the Binfords had isolated five main tool kits, interpreted as relating to toolmaking, butchering animals, processing food, hunting and specialized plant food processing. At the important French site of Combe Grenal, however, no fewer than 14 tool kits were isolated.

Finally, a factor that probably accounts for at least some of the variation was suggested by Dr David Clarke (*see pages 162-63*). The material recovered by archaeologists is only a fraction of what was once in use. Only some of the tools used at a particular location are likely to be discarded there, and of those only some will survive where they were left, while others are cleared away by man or removed by natural agencies. Of those that do survive, only a proportion will be found by archaeologists digging a small part of the site. So the variations in the Mousterian assemblages could be purely due to chance.

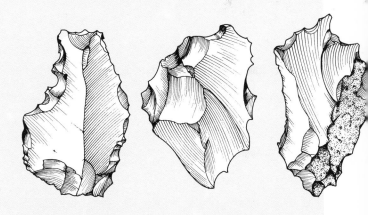

Mousterian tools *were often designed for very specific purposes. Primitive saws (left and centre) had notched edges. Boring tools (right) with sharp points were used like awls to pierce hides and drill eyes in bone needles.*

ECONOMIC PREHISTORY

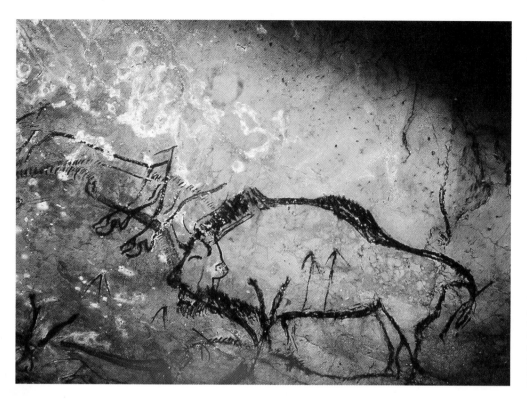

Cave paintings *dati[ng] from around 20,000 B[C] in the French Pyrenees, show bison wounded by arrows. Such paintings provide evidence that th[e] prehistoric inhabitants [of] the area were hunters.*

CERTAIN FACTORS are common to all forms of economic organization. People must obtain enough food and drink to sustain life and to reproduce, without expending as much energy in the quest for food as they get from the sustenance it yields. This means that subsistence economies must be efficiently organized to exploit productively the resources available within the limits of their technology. Societies may indeed indulge in 'uneconomic' behaviour, but if they do so to any significant extent they are unlikely to survive for very long.

Inevitably, the requirements of subsistence are reflected in the locations chosen for the settlements of small-scale, simple societies of hunter-gatherers, pastoralists and farmers who are self-sufficient in food. As societies become more complex, communities become increasingly interdependent economically, and the locations of their settlements reflect considerations other than subsistence alone. In attempting to reconstruct the organization of these more complex societies, archaeologists may use the techniques of locational analysis *(see page 158)*. The theory and methods of economic prehistorians are generally confined to subsistence economies, although they can be adapted to advanced economies, too.

Limits of Distance

Ethnographic and historical studies show that within subsistence economies, settlement are located to minimize the travel and effort involved in exploiting staple resources. As accessible distance depends on the nature of th[e] terrain, the presence or absence of natural barriers such as rivers or mountains and the transport available to the community, it is best thought of in terms of time.

A hunter, for example, generally operates within an area no more than two hours distant from his base. Pastoralists in general spend les[s] time than that on the move each day, to keep down the energy used by their animals in travelling. Arable agriculture imposes a genera[l] limit of about one hour's travelling-time from th[e] settlement. Within this, a radius 10 minutes distant from the site may enclose the area of intensive cultivation, growing important crops that require considerable labour, such as frequent watering or the application of manure. The gathering of plant foods, too, usually takes

lace within a one-hour radius. The considerable
nergy needed to collect and open shellfish, and
heir low calorific value, similarly restricts the
istance at which they can effectively provide a
ood source.

Territorial Analysis

Vith these considerations in mind, analysis of
he immediate environment of an archaeological
ettlement should suggest the economic reasons
or the choice of location. Allowing for other
onstraints, such as the availability of water or
he risk of flooding, sites tend to be located to
xploit efficiently those natural resources – wild
lants and animals, pasturage, arable land –
ppropriate to the economy of the community.
he resources considered to be of greatest
nportance are those most easily accessible
om the site.

Site territorial analysis is a method devised to
nvestigate the immediate environment of a
ettlement. The investigator makes four walks
om the site, each two hours long and in a
ifferent direction, noting such things as soil
ypes and vegetation.

Any environmental change since the site was
ccupied must be taken into account. For
nstance, in many areas, alluvial deposits have
een laid down in comparatively recent times, so
he present-day environment is not that
xploited by the people of the past.

Seasonal Changes

gricultural communities are dependent for
ost of their daily subsistence on the stored
uits of their labours – grain and other plants for
emselves, and fodder for their animals if that is
ot available locally all the year round. If they can
y down such stores, they can occupy their
ettlements permanently.

Except in a few rare cases where suitable food
ources are available throughout the year, the
hanging seasons force hunter-gatherers and
astoral communities to move periodically.
Hunter-gatherers may migrate between
ifferent ecological zones in which particular
oods are available at different seasons.
astoralists in Europe and elsewhere drive their
ocks upland in summer and lowland in winter,
r between inland and coastal pastures. Groups
ho largely depend for food on the hunting of
rge herbivores follow a similar seasonal pattern
f movement between pastures. Often, the
ocks kept by a settled farming community are
lso moved to seasonal pastures; some

members of the community accompany them,
while the rest remain at home.

When studying a settlement, therefore,
economic prehistorians consider whether such
seasonal migration was necessary. They
reconstruct not only the economic potential of a
site, but also the annual territories of its
inhabitants, by looking for similar sites in
complementary environments.

Because archaeological dating is relatively
imprecise, it is not possible to link two or more
sites together as successive habitations of a
particular community. But archaeologists can
identify the sites as part of the same economic
system, and they have successfully predicted the
likely location of complementary seasonal sites
using this approach.

The Tsomkwe Bushmen *of Namibia are nomadic
hunter-gatherers whose lifestyle has changed little over
thousands of years. Their pattern is to migrate to
different areas as food supplies vary according to the
season. By studying the life patterns of such primitive
tribes, archaeologists are able to gain valuable
insights into many aspects of prehistoric communities.*

SOCIAL ORGANIZATION

ONE METHOD of trying to find out about social organization in the past is through studies of pottery – so-called 'ceramic sociology'. The American archaeologists James N. Hill and William A. Longacre, working from the ethnographic observation that women are the potters in many societies, suggested that the patterns of distribution of individual pottery styles should reflect the social movement of women. In the pueblos they investigated, different pottery styles appeared in different parts of the sites, suggesting that each family or residential group had its own, the tradition of which was handed down from mother to daughter.

Ceramic sociology has been strongly criticized by both archaeologists and anthropologists who emphasise the complexity of kinship patterns and the fact that pottery styles are not necessarily transmitted from mother to daughter but may reflect many other influences. In any case, this approach may still have potential.

Locational Analysis

Another significant method of approach to reconstructing social organization is through locational, or spatial, analysis. Some aspects of settlement patterns, as we have seen, relate directly to economic factors – the availability of essential resources such as water, food or fertile land. But others are based on social considerations, the interactions within and between societies.

To choose an obvious example, a preference for easily defensible sites would seem to imply that conflict was an ever-present threat to the builders of the settlements. The proliferation of fortified settlements across central Europe during the 6th century BC may reflect growing competition and warfare in the face of environmental deterioration; in the east of the area, it also reflects the need for defence against nomad incursions from the steppes.

On the other hand, the promontory forts that appeared in the later Neolithic and were once thought also to reflect conflict are now interpreted by some archaeologists as corrals for confining herds of cattle.

Changing pottery styles *at an American Indian site in South Dakota during the 18th century, recorded in the chart at left, have been interpreted by the American archaeologist James Deetz as reflecting changes in patterns of social organization. The jug shown is a typical example of Indian 'black-on-white' pottery.*

The models used by economic geographers have been extensively borrowed by archaeologists as a way of looking at the human landscape. These allow the archaeologist to investigate whether sites are deliberately placed to make efficient use of certain interactions: the movements of goods in trade, access to centrally placed resources, control by centres over lesser centres through a hierarchy of settlements, communications networks linking centres to each other and, finally, to settlements which are subordinate to them.

This approach has successfully been applied to the archaeological evidence of many different times and places – Roman Britain and Near Eastern and Central American civilizations, for instance.

A major problem facing the archaeologist investigating the distribution of sites lies in knowing whether the picture he obtains is complete or even representative. Many sites have been destroyed entirely, while others remain undetected under modern towns, deep soils or thick forests. Another difficulty is that archaeological dating is generally too imprecise to give a definite picture of the distribution of settlements at a particular time. In many instances, sites considered to be contemporary with each other could easily be consecutive, making the interpretation of their relationship very different.

Distribution of Artefacts

Much information can be obtained by plotting the distribution of certain classes of artefacts and other remains on a site. Areas where artefacts of known, or at least highly probable, function are clustered could well have been used for specific tasks; for example, a series of heavy stone implements associated with large animal bones could suggest a butchering area.

Mathematics plays a large part in the study of archaeological distribution on all scales, as the object is to ascertain whether the distribution is random or contains a pattern, and, if so, what that pattern is.

Trade and Exchange

Another insight into the workings of ancient societies can be gleaned from studies of their patterns of trade – a field where, again, ethnographic research provides models. There are two contrasting mechanisms of exchange.

The first is based upon reciprocity, and is conducted between individuals and communities of equal status. Often, such exchanges are between members of a kin group, and are more in the nature of gifts to smooth the workings of the kinship network than economic transactions. The second exchange mechanism is redistribution. In complex societies, kinship exchanges are overlaid by politically controlled movements of goods and raw materials from their sources of origin to political centres, from which they are then redistributed. Concentrations of commodities appear in the centres, with lesser quantities in settlements lower in the hierarchy.

Market economies based on mercantile and, generally, monetary exchange seem to have emerged relatively late in the archaeological record. Markets may develop in various types of location – particularly at important nodes in a communications network, at sites where a wide range of goods is easily obtainable, or on safe neutral ground at the frontiers or boundaries dividing separate groups or societies. In contrast, the specific location of political centres tends to depend upon other factors in addition to that of trade.

In common with other forms of spatial analysis, exchange networks are often studied with the help of models borrowed from geography. These can be used, for instance, to predict the size of a centre or an industry that exported materials known to archaeologists from findings on 'client' sites. Similarly, the models can identify cases where the distribution of a commodity is either wider or more localized than might be expected, and assist in constructing possible explanations.

Pueblo Indians of the south west USA lived in cliff villages such as this one at Mesa Verde, Colorado dating from about AD 1200. The Pueblo were outstanding potters and the study of their ceramics provides clues to their social organization. Pottery traditions were handed down from mother to daughter and different styles have been found in almost every household. This suggests that residence was 'matrilocal' – husbands came to live in the households of their wives.

FROM THE GRAVE

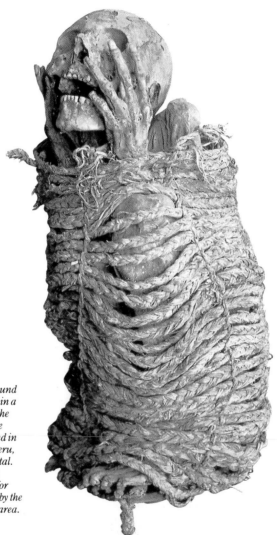

Inca mummies, *bound with rope and buried in a sitting position with the knees drawn up to the chest, have been found in caves near Cuzco, Peru, the ancient Inca capital. The bodies have been naturally preserved for more than 500 years by the dry conditions of the area.*

ARCHAEOLOGICAL ASSUMPTIONS about the significance of burials have included a belief that formal disposal of the dead and the provision of grave goods indicates a belief in an afterlife, and that the richness of grave goods reflect the wealth and social standing of the person buried.

Peter Ucko, now professor of archaeology at Southampton University in England, set out to test these assumptions by examining a range of ethnographic data. He discovered that some societies dispose of their dead merely to get rid of them. Others believe in an afterlife, but do not practise burial; one group, for instance, requires the corpse to be eaten by hyenas. The type and variety of grave goods proved to relate to many factors. Similarly, the method of disposal of bodies and the form of the tomb or grave varied widely between the societies for which Ucko had data. He therefore concluded that there are severe limitations to the information that can be deduced from the study of burials.

In England, Professor Lewis Binford took a more optimistic view, after he, too, had examined the ethnographic literature, and other scholars followed his lead. They noted a number of significant regularities. The form of disposal and the accompanying ritual, they found, are frequently of symbolic significance within the community, giving expression to the position held by the dead person within the society.

Binford isolates three important aspects likely to be given expression in funerary rites. First, there is what he calls the 'social persona' of the deceased, a sum of all the roles played by the person in his lifetime. Important variables in the social persona may include age, sex, kinship affiliations, rank and social position. Second, there is the size and composition of the social unit to which the dead person had belonged. The third criterion is the mode of death; distinctions may be made, for example, between the treatments accorded to suicides, executed criminals and heroes slain in battle.

Complex Variations

There is a considerable variety of ways in which a corpse can be disposed of, and in the rites associated with the disposal. Variables include the location of the grave and the form it takes, the position of the corpse within it, the treatment of the body (cremation or mummification, for example) and the selection of grave goods.

Recent ethnoarchaeological work, notably by Dr Ian Hodder of Cambridge University, England, indicates that the relationship between funeral arrangements and social structure are even more complex than Binford suggested. Religious beliefs, ideology and attitudes to death all play a part in determining details of funerary practices, rites and offerings, which do not therefore simply provide a mirror of social organization. Where social dimensions are expressed, they often reflect an idealized picture rather than the contemporary reality. Nevertheless, there is still guarded optimism among archaeologists that burials, one of the major sources of archaeological data, can reveal something about the way in which early societies were organized.

Slovakian Cemetery

he value of cemeteries in the reconstruction
prehistoric societies was elegantly
emonstrated in a paper by Sue Shennan, at the
me a research student at Cambridge
niversity, England, about a cemetery of the
rly Bronze Age Nitra group at Branc in
outhwest Slovakia.

Shennan analyzed the grave goods in 274
urials which, on the basis of radiocarbon dates
om the Nitra group, were made over a period
no more than 200 years, between about 2400
id 2200 BC. Anthropological data on the age
id sex of the skeletons were available and
iennan was able to isolate elements associated
ith these variables. Men and boys were
enerally buried on their right sides, lying south-
est/north-east or west/east. Women and girls
ere interred on their left sides, lying east/west
north-east/south-west.

Many of the associated grave goods were
viously part of distinctive clothing and
ersonal ornamentation. Women wore necklaces
id garters of bone beads, and copper willow-
af earrings. Men wore copper daggers,
illow-leaf knives, whetstones and a stone axe
ound their waist, presumably on a belt.
hildren wore willow-leaf rings as arm bands and
id miniature vessels instead of the full-sized
ots buried with the adults.

Shennan divided the graves into groups similar
their content and assessed the wealth of each
rial according to three criteria – the variety of
ave goods, the quantity of particular artefact
types and the objects' value. The value was
determined by allocating points according to the
distance of the source of the raw material, the
difficulty of obtaining it, and the time needed to
make the object.

Rich and Poor

Shennan thus isolated some graves that
were 'rich' according to all three criteria, and
various grades that were less rich. She then
looked at the age and sex distribution in the
different grades. She found that both adult and
child males were in some cases given wealthy
burials, while among women wealthy burials
were mainly confined to adults and adolescents.
More female graves were wealthy than those of
males, and in overall terms the female graves
were wealthier, too. Shennan used these
observations to make tentative suggestions
about social organization at Branc.

It was clear that the status of individuals
was to a large extent indicated by what they
wore. Wealth among the men seemed to be
hereditary, but the women could either have
possessed hereditary wealth or have acquired it
on marriage.

Since the community probably consisted of
only 30-40 individuals at any one time, the
complexity of its social organization implied
that it must form part of a much wider social
group. That conclusion was reinforced when
similarities with other contemporary cemeteries
in the region were noted.

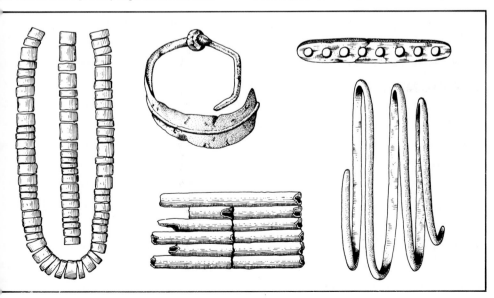

Grave goods *found in an
early Bronze Age cemetery
at Branc, Slovakia,
included clothing and
jewelery. Women were
buried wearing necklaces
and garters of bone beads,
copper willow-leaf
earrings, and other items
of personal
ornamentation. The
bodies of men and children
were also adorned.
Wealthier members of
society were afforded more
lavish burials, but
everyone in the community
appears to have been
honoured with at least
some grave goods,
suggesting a strong belief
in the afterlife.*

Iron-Age Farmers of Somerset

IN THE 15 YEARS following the discovery of the Glastonbury Lake Village in England's Somerset Levels in 1892, excavation revealed a waterlogged settlement built on artifical mounds beside the lake. The village, inhabited some 2000 years ago, had been defended on the landward side by a palisade and had contained a number of timber buildings. Preservation of plant and other organic remains was excellent, due to waterlogging.

In 1972, the brilliant British pioneer of 'new archaeology', Dr David Clarke, brought together the ideas of many of his students and colleagues in a book entitled *Models in Archaeology*. Clarke's own contribution to the volume was a study of the Glastonbury site, beginning with the individual buildings and working outwards to view Glastonbury within the context of the British Iron Age.

Clarke isolated a 'modular building unit' that occurred throughout the site, linked by lanes. This consisted of a pair of large round houses, a small house, and several subrectangular structures.

From the remains within these buildings, Clarke was able to suggest their functions. The pair of large houses faced each other across a courtyard. They contained artefacts relating to almost all the activities undertaken on the site, and from those it seemed likely they served as central stores as well as dwellings. Near them were one or two workshop huts, with additional outside workfloors that could be used in fine weather.

Segregation at Work

The material recovered from the workshop huts had been used to produce tools and weapons, including lathe-turned objects of wood – male activities. The courtyard between the large houses also contained items associated with male tasks, including manufacturing, threshing and dealing with horses.

The third, smaller house in each group resembled the larger ones, but was set at some distance from them. The material from the small houses seemed exclusively associated with women and their activities – jewellery, and tools for spinning, leather and fur working and food preparation. Among the structures near the smaller house was a bakery hut containing a row of hearths and an abundance of artefacts associated with female activities, suggesting that the women of the group congregated here to conduct their day-to-day activities, making clothing and preparing food.

The site also had a guard hut beside each of the two gates through the stockade. The gates and palisade bore impaled skulls, following Celtic custom.

A combination of different lines of evidence suggested each modular unit housed an extended family or lineage group of about 15-20 adults and children. Although the social status of each household appeared about equal, a unit at the centre of the village seemed possibly

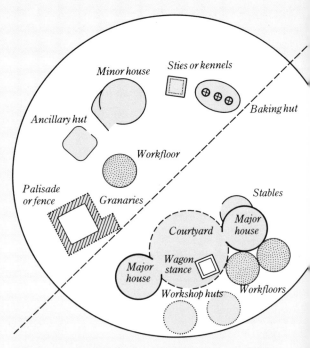

The 'modular building unit' *identified at Glastonbury Lake Village probably housed an extended family of 15-20 adults and children. Men apparently worked in the buildings around the courtyard; women worked separately around the minor house.*

wealthier than the others. It was flanked by two units rather poorer than average; perhaps these were the homes of families who were dependent upon a headman who lived within the central unit of the settlement.

Marriage and Migration

Clarke went on to make tentative suggestions about other aspects of social organization at Glastonbury. Certain imported items in the settlement could have been the property of women who had married into the community. They included the occasional spindle whorl of unattractive, non-local material.

Clarke next looked beyond the settlement to see it in the context of local economy and society. Glastonbury was set in low-lying marsh, subject to annual flooding but otherwise rich in arable land, pasturage and wild resources. Clarke outlined two ways in which such an environment could have been exploited: by small-scale, independent communities adapting to the constraints of flooding, and by farmers who grazed their flocks there in summer, moving elsewhere during the seasonal floods.

He argued from the data that the inhabitants adopted the second course, and had formed part of an extensive network linking the fenland with the nearby Mendip Hills. In particular, the material from Glastonbury showed close links with the large hillfort at Maesbury in the Mendips and its surrounding territory, from which Glastonbury obtained, among other things, stone for handmills, and fine pottery. The slopes around Maesbury probably provided the hill pasturage for the flocks from Glastonbury during the winter. The exploitation of the two zones allowed the area to sustain far larger flocks than could have been supported in either one alone.

Cloth and Crops

The evidence collected from Glastonbury indicated a well-developed textile industry. Woollen cloaks were a famous British export to the Roman world, and their manufacture could well have been an important activity at Glastonbury. Certainly, the flocks were large – perhaps as many as 1000 sheep.

Plant remains suggested that barley was cultivated in the area immediately around the settlement that did not flood in winter, while the main crop of wheat and Celtic beans was sown in spring on the more extensive summer lands. The inhabitants of Glastonbury could also draw on the rich natural resources of the fenland – fish and fowl, animals and plants.

Finally, Clarke examined the wider Celtic tribal area of Dumnonia, to which Glastonbury belonged. Maesbury, on the basis of the available evidence, fulfilled the role of local centre within the Glastonbury district. It would have provided goods such as luxury metalwork, as well as affording political protection to the smaller settlements.

A wooden God, *probably a fertility figure, from the Somerset Levels area shows the classic features of a hermaphrodite having both male and female sexual organs.*

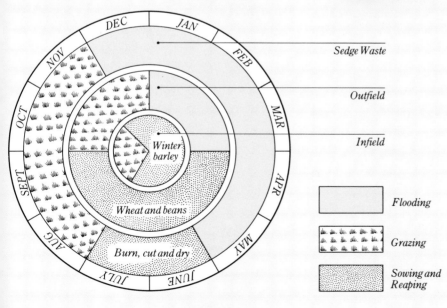

The Lake Village *at Glastonbury was an agricultural community that adapted itself to the changes caused by seasonal flood patterns. Here we see one possible yearly pattern. The whole site consisted of the infield, on the highest ground and within which the village presumably lay; the outfield; and sedge wasteland, low-lying and subject to the greatest flooding. To make best use of the natural cycle of flooding alternating with rich grazing and farming land, the sheep would have been brought in to graze in the outer sedge area in July and taken out in November, before the floods. This would have happened slightly later in the outfield.*

SILENT SENTINELS OF STONE

IT IS NOW generally accepted that the megalithic tombs of western and northern Europe *(see also page 141)* have nothing to do, as was once thought, with Mycenaean metal prospectors, but are the products of indigenous inhabitants of the region. Even so, they are still a subject of speculation and inquiry. What induced their builders to invest massive efforts in erecting such monumental tombs? How was the necessary labour force assembled? What underlies their striking similarities?

One answer to the last question was proposed by Professor Grahame Clark, one of Britain's greatest prehistorians. Investigating the megaliths of southern Sweden, he noted that one group was concentrated in coastal locations from which deep-sea fish such as cod, haddock and ling could have been caught in winter. Historically, much of the Atlantic was linked by the travels of fishermen and this could well have provided a mechanism by which the 'megalithic idea' and fashions in the style of tomb architecture spread between coastal Iberia, Brittany, Ireland, western England and Scotland and Scandinavia. The high concentrations of megaliths on coasts, and the surprising numbers on small islands may support a connection with fishing.

Professor Colin Renfrew of Cambridge University, England, however, views the similarities as similar responses to similar needs. At the structural level, the passage that forms a major element of many graves could have been devised independently in different areas to meet the need for repeated access to the interior of these communal tombs.

Other structural resemblances could be due to similarities in the raw materials available. In answer to the question of why the idea of building monumental tombs should arise independently in a number of areas, he cites the similarities in their backgrounds.

Territorial Markers?

Most megaliths occur in areas inhabited in the Postglacial period by Mesolithic hunter-gatherers. The adoption of agriculture through contact with Neolithic farmers, Renfrew argues, led to a population explosion in the region and consequent competition for farmland between neighbouring groups. In the face of potential conflict, the groups may have found it desirable to define and emphasize their territories and boundaries. The construction of megalithic tombs could have arisen in response to this need.

Renfrew has studied two circumscribed areas, the Scottish islands of Arran and Rousay, to examine this premise more closely. He found that a division of the arable land into territories, each containing one megalithic tomb, results in units that correspond in size to the individual crofting communities of recent times in the same area. Each unit supported between 10 and 50 people.

Massive slabs of stone, *some weighing as much as 50 tons, were dragged by teams of workmen and shaped with stone hammers to build this megalith at Carnac, Brittany. Dating from around 3000 BC, it is one of numerous similar stone tombs found scattered throughout western Europe, built to honour dead chieftains.*

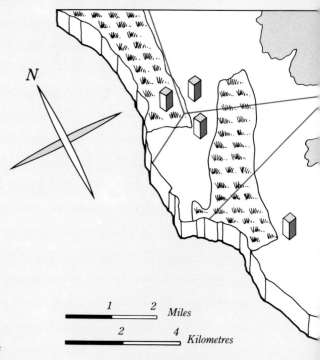

N

1   2   Miles

2   4   Kilometres

The labour needed to put up a megalithic tomb would probably be beyond the capabilities of a community of this size. But Renfrew argues, by ethnographic analogy, that the cooperation of other communities could be secured by some form of recognized social incentive – perhaps a period of feasting at which communal building was one of several activities.

Pastoralist Beginnings?

Recently, a further study of megalith distribution was made by members of a British group researching the early history of agriculture. This group demonstrated that although the megalith-builders may have practised some agriculture, it does not seem to have provided their principal economic base.

Instead, there was a close coincidence between the distribution of megaliths and that of good pastureland. Additionally, many megaliths occur along routes traditionally followed by pastoralists in their seasonal movements between summer and winter pastures, routes demonstrably of very great antiquity.

The economy of the megalith builders, the group argued, was probably based on keeping flocks. Nevertheless, it maintained, Renfrew's view of the megaliths as territorial markers still seems appropriate.

West Kennett Barrow, England (above), a huge collective tomb built about 2500 BC, consists of a long central corridor with four side chambers off it. Inside, the remains of 46 people have been found as well as jewellery, pottery and arrowheads.

This map of the southern portion of the island of Arran, Scotland clearly shows a large number of megalithic tombs. Some archaeologists believe that megaliths served as territorial markers for farming communities and, as can be seen here, many of them seem to be in close proximity to arable land. Hypothetical boundaries are indicated on the map by the straight lines; each area contains one megalith.

 Chambered tombs

 Land over 300 metres

 Modern farming land

ANCIENT BELIEFS

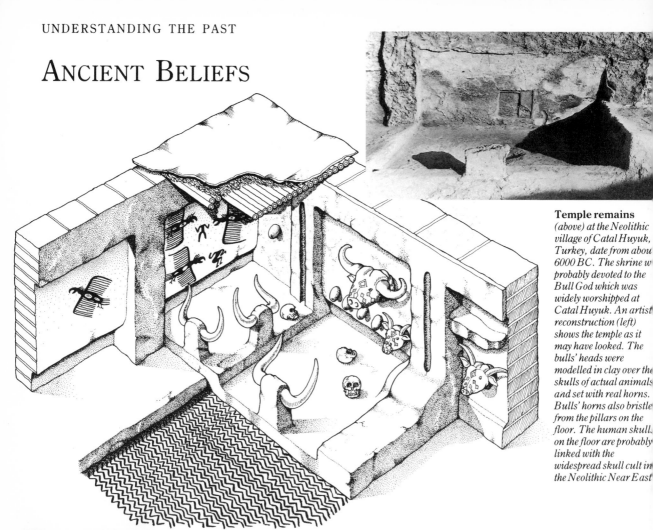

Temple remains
*(above) at the Neolithic
village of Catal Huyuk,
Turkey, date from abou
6000 BC. The shrine w
probably devoted to the
Bull God which was
widely worshipped at
Catal Huyuk. An artist
reconstruction (left)
shows the temple as it
may have looked. The
bulls' heads were
modelled in clay over the
skulls of actual animals
and set with real horns.
Bulls' horns also bristle
from the pillars on the
floor. The human skull.
on the floor are probably
linked with the
widespread skull cult in
the Neolithic Near East*

A seated god *carved in
white marble, found in a
Neolithic shrine at Catal
Huyuk, was probably a
cult statue. It is wearing a
leopard-skin cap and
multiple armlets.*

RELIGION IS the last refuge of the troubled
archaeologist – there is a well-known tendency
for anything that seems otherwise inexplicable to
the excavator or prehistorian to be interpreted
as 'ritual' in intent. The problems of
reconstructing past beliefs are twofold: to
identify the material symbols and to understand
the system of belief that these symbols
represent. The diversity of human thought and
imagination is infinite, and it is probably
unrealistic to hope ever to unravel the beliefs of
people of the past from archaeological data.

In many instances, though, some attempt may
be made to identify ritual structures and objects.
It seems reasonable to interpret the fish-faced
stone sculptures in the Yugoslavian Mesolithic
hamlet of Lepenski Vir as cult figures, and rooms
decorated with plastered bulls' heads in the vast
Anatolian Neolithic village of Catal Huyuk as
shrines. Large accumulations of fine Iron Age
bronzes in rivers appear more likely to be votive
offerings than the results of exceptional
carelessness, and sacrifical victims like

Tollund Man *(see page 93)* similarly point to Iron
Age veneration of watery places.

Where there is some historical continuity of
practice or belief, the interpretation is less
speculative. The magnificent temples of the
ancient Near East can be traced back to their
inception as small shrines. In India, there are
striking similarities between some of the
representations on Indus seals and the
iconography of later Hinduism, allowing us to
draw tentative conclusions about the beliefs of
the earlier civilization.

On occasion, evidence has been found in
Europe of an unbroken veneration of a particula
locality despite official changes of religion.
Christian churches are built over the remains of
pagan sanctuaries, and Celtic shrines lie beneat
the two Roman temples at Frilford in southern
England.

The clues to ancient ideologies and creeds ar
elusive and piecing them together must always
be largely a matter of guesswork, but the result
of religious inspiration are among the most

orious relics of the past. Magnificent temples
I over the world and exquisite religious art
reations attest the strength of man's
nagination and beliefs. Even though we may not
nderstand, we can appreciate the feelings that
spired them.

'enetrating the Palaeolithic Mind

ver since their discovery in the 19th
entury, the magnificent Palaeolithic cave
aintings of bison, horses and other animals in
rance and Spain have provoked speculation
bout their purpose and meaning. The
xplanations offered include several drawn from
thnography – that the paintings were associated
ith totemism, hunting magic or fertility magic.
can be argued that fertility magic is unlikely, as
xplicit representations of sexual activity or of
regnancy are rare. By contrast, frequently
und sculptured representations of pregnant
omen – so-called 'Venus figurines' – were also
feature of Palaeolithic art right across Europe.

The idea that the art was intended to ensure
uccess in hunting also seems improbable. The
nimals upon which the painters mainly
epended for food (reindeer in south-west
rance, for instance) are rarely represented. A
w beasts are depicted with lines or dots on
eir bodies, that some people interpret as
pears or wounds. But the rarity of these again
rgues against hunting magic as a universal
xplanation.

Recent work suggests that we should not in
ny case seek a single, all-embracing reason
ehind the cave art. Several different ones may
pply to different aspects of it. Detailed and
areful studies of the distribution, layout and
xecution of the paintings and engravings have
evealed interesting common features. Traces
re now being found of such art in the mouths of
ther caves and rock shelters where Palaeolithic
eople once lived. The greater part of this art
as been destroyed by the elements and by later
habitants, but enough remains to suggest that
was originally common. That may imply it was
tended as decoration of the home, although
hat does not preclude a ritual significance, too.

Rites of Passage

t the opposite extreme, many of the paintings
re located in the utter depths of the caves,
xtremely difficult and often dangerous to reach.
ne suggestion is that penetration of this hostile
egion may have played some part in initiation
eremonies, when children underwent rites

transforming them into full adult members of
their community. Sculptured clay bison deep in
the Tuc d'Audoubert cave are reached by a
tortuous route. Near the bison are the deep
heelprints of children's feet. The evidence from
many such caves indicates that the art was
visited only rarely.

A pattern has also been detected in the way in
which certain animals are regularly depicted in
the same parts of different caves. Annette
Laming and André Leroi-Gourhan, pioneers of
this investigation of the spatial distribution of art,
initially interpreted it entirely in terms of
opposing male and female principles,
represented chiefly by the bison and the horse
(the animals most frequently shown) that take
pride of place in the designs. Although that
interpretation seems unsatisfactory, it appears
that the paintings were often executed to an
overall formula, the purpose of which was to
divide the available space in a cave.

As data accumulates about the diversity of
artistic representations in the Palaeolithic, so the
complexity of the subject increases. Microscopic
examination, by the American scientist
Alexander Marshack, of engravings on a bone
has revealed minute representations of animals
characteristic of the spring; other scenes and
tally marks have been found on other pieces. He
interprets these as evidence of recording of the
seasons and other intervals of time, a primitive
calendar. Like the other theories, this is hard to
prove or disprove. We are left with a mystery
that will continue to fascinate and stimulate
people for many years to come.

Clay models *of bison
dating from 15-10,000
BC, at Tuc d'Audoubert,
France, are among the
finest of the many
spectacular examples of
Palaeolithic cave art
found in France and
Spain. There may have
been magico-religious
reasons behind such
artwork – the hunting of
bison was probably the
basis of the society's
livelihood and they
probably invoked divine
help for success.*

FORCES OF CHANGE

ONE OF THE MOST fascinating series of questions that archaeologists are incessantly striving to answer is what factors lie behind changes in the past. Principal among these are what Binford calls 'the Big Questions' – the transformation of society by the development of agriculture and the emergence of civilization. But change is of interest at every level, right down to the appearance in an area of a new style of pottery or an alteration in burial practices.

One school of thought approaches these topics by assembling data on the sequence of changes and studying it to try to discover the mechanisms involved. The rival school attempts to employ an explicitly scientific approach, by proposing a theory, assembling data to test it and discarding or modifying it if it is disproved.

The first approach generally seeks to explain change in terms of mechanisms familiar from history and ethnography, or predicted intuitively. Some exponents look to the internal workings of society, seeing cultural change as a natural human propensity. It can be due to random, almost accidental 'cultural drift', to progressively more complex cultural adaptations that have the appearance of inevitability, to shifts in fashion or to the inspired inventions of geniuses. Although individuals have undoubtedly shaped historical development, archaeology can rarely, if ever, recover evidence of such influences and, in fact, little is achieved by trying to search for them.

External factors are also cited. One is environmental change, for which independent evidence may be sought, for example, through pollen analysis or geological study. A second is the influence of other human groups, by trade, migration or invasion. Criteria used to identify migration are: the sudden appearance of traits new to the area; their previous existence in an identifiable source area; and subsequent modifications of some of the indigenous traits by the newcomers. Invasions show the same characteristics, with, in addition, evidence of conflict, such as the destruction of settlements or skeletons showing signs of violent death, and of the imposition of aspects of the alien culture. Though in principle these rules sound straightforward, they are not always easy to apply to archaeological data.

Archaeology as Science

In contrast to the traditional approach, which begins with a body of archaeological data and then attempts to draw conclusions from it, the 'scientific' approach begins with a set of theories and then sets out to prove them. The archaeologist proposes a series of mechanisms which may have operated in a given situation in the past and outlines the kind of evidence which would show whether they had done so. He then explicitly seeks this evidence and discards any theories which are refuted by the data obtained. He adopts as provisional explanations those theories which seem most consistent with the evidence, but continues to refine old hypotheses and formulate new ones, and seek new data by which to test them. Another approach which archaeologists have borrowed from science is General Systems Theory, which proposes that any organization can be studied as a system of inter-related parts. Using this approach, the operation and inter-relationship of different portions of the social system are examined to establish how they function, and the impact on them of new elements is studied. Explanations of changes which occur can then be advanced in the light of the results.

A Roman cemeter
Lankhills, England (above), excavated in 1967-68, was found contain the graves of several German immigrants who serv mercenaries in the R⟨ army in the 4th centu⟨ These German grave⟨ contained an abunda⟨ of burial goods, a fac⟨ which distinguishes t⟨ from Roman graves. ⟨ skeleton of a German soldier (right) is accompanied by grave goods which include ⟨ iron knife (1), a bron⟨ buckle (6), a bronze c⟨ bow brooch (3) and ot⟨ unidentified objects o⟨ bronze (4), silver (2) ⟨ glass (5).

LA-RIVIÈRE

A Palaeolithic burial *excavated in Gironde, France, shows how the body of a young woman was buried in a crouched position under the small stone monument which is shown behind her. Accompanying her in the grave are flint implements, a dagger of antler and a necklace of animal teeth. Her skull is coloured with red iron oxide.*

THE GERMANS IN BRITAIN

IN THE LATER DAYS of the Roman empire, from the 4th century AD, problems of defending its extensive frontiers induced the Romans to employ free German barbarians from outside the empire as mercenaries. Many of them subsequently settled within Roman territory, which then, of course, would have included Britain.

The British archaeologist, Giles Clarke, carried out a study in the 1970s to see whether the presence of these German mercenaries could be identified by looking for features of German origin amongst those of the native British culture of the time.

Clarke considered various aspects of the lifestyles of the immigrants as possible sources of such evidence. Many of those aspects, he argued, would have changed for purely practical reasons: the immigrant groups would be likely to adopt the locally available pottery, weapons and houses, for example. On the other hand, dress – particularly personal ornamentation – and religious practice might have remained distinctive. However, the personal ornaments were likely to have been valuable, well looked after and therefore rare, and, archaeologically, information could not be obtained on religion.

Clarke turned therefore to burials. He reasoned that the method of disposing of the body and the type of tomb would conform to local customs rather than maintaining those of the immigrants, again for practical reasons, but that the clothing and grave goods would reflect the beliefs and customs of the Germans.

He therefore studied 450 burials in a late Roman cemetery (AD 310-410) at Lankhills in Winchester. Most contained few or no grave goods. In addition, many of the skeletons wore hobnailed boots. But two small groups of graves showed a different pattern.

One group, of 16 graves dating from about AD 350 to 400, held an abundance of personal possessions including ornaments, and the skeletons did not have hobnailed boots. Many of the grave goods bore a strong resemblance to material found in graves in southern Bavaria. The six graves in the second group, dating from around 390-410, were diverse in their contents, but each had general Germanic affinities. Clarke concluded that both groups belonged to the Germans, and confirmed that the appearance of immigrants in an area can be detected by archaeology.

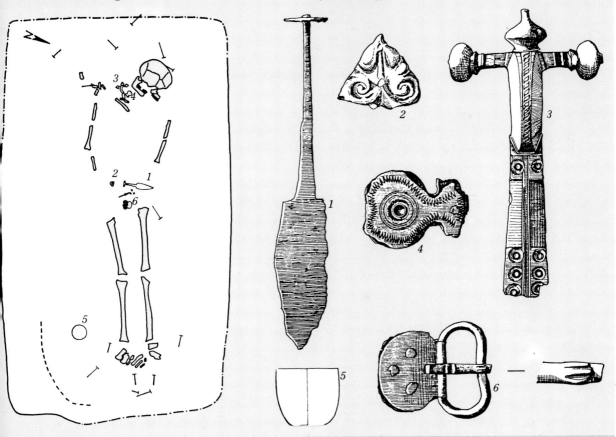

CIVILIZATIONS OF THE AEGEAN

Burial chambers of
*Mycenaean royalty (left) stand
on a hilltop in southern Greece.
When they were excavated by
Heinrich Schliemann in 1876,
these tombs were found to
contain rich treasures,
including a burial mask of
beaten gold (above) which
portrays the face of a
Mycenaean king.*

THE CAUSES BEHIND the emergence of the Minoan and
Mycenaean civilizations in the Aegean during the late 3rd
and 2nd millennia BC have intrigued scholars for years.
Until recently, most explanations attributed Aegean
development to outside influence, either in the form of
invasion of the area or by diffusion.

Civilization had emerged in Mesopotamia by 3000 BC,
and, some archaeologists argued, Mesopotamian trade
introduced civilized ideas and technological innovations
into nearby, less advanced areas. Others postulated an
invasion of the Aegean from some adjacent region, of
which Anatolia seems the most probable.

Professor Colin Renfrew approached the problem from
a different viewpoint. He contended that the scanty
available evidence for invasion or immigration from
Anatolia into Greece in the early Bronze Age showed that,
at most, such incursion was limited, and that it could not
be deemed responsible for the transformation of society
there. Trade, though clearly documented, was also an
inadequate explanation in itself.

To understand the major changes in social organization
and complexity that took place, it was necessary, said
Renfrew, to study the workings of late Neolithic society in
the Aegean, to examine the fresh variables that emerged
in the early Bronze Age and to determine the impact these
may have had on every inter-related aspect of the local

social system. The two major new developments he
considered were changes in the subsistence economy and
the introduction of bronze metallurgy. Renfrew examined
the resultant impact of both of these developments on
population growth, economics, craft technology, social
organization, trade and communications.

From Subsistence to Surplus

The subsistence economy of Neolithic Greece was
based on mixed farming. In addition to wheat and barley,
pulses and flax were cultivated, while sheep were the main
animal raised.

Early in the 3rd millennium BC, cultivation of the vine
and olive also became important in southern Greece and
the Aegean islands. Both crops were eminently suitable
for storage, in the form of olive oil and wine, and for trade.
They were grown on the lower slopes of hills, within easy
reach of the villages, on land that was not suitable for
arable farming. Their cultivation required work at a
different time of year from that needed by cereal crops,
and much of this work, such as harvesting, was light
enough to be done by children.

As a result, agricultural yields were substantially
increased without disrupting established agricultural
practice. That in turn allowed, or stimulated, population
growth, and for the first time there was enough

demand for specialized crafts and services to justify the existence of full-time craftsmen, who could be supported from the extra agricultural output.

The Coming of Bronze

Some copper artefacts were made during the 4th millennium BC, but there were not many of them and they had little economic or social significance. When, in the 3rd millennium, copper began to be mixed with tin to produce the relatively hard alloy bronze, demand for metal goods grew. Bronze could be used to make a range of useful new tools and weapons, and a variety of impressive ornaments. The demand for metalwork stimulated specialization in crafts such as metallurgy and jewellery-making, while the new tools promoted the development of other crafts, like carpentry and shipbuilding. Competition for prestigious or useful craft products and for control of their producers helped to heighten both social differences within communities and conflicts between them, resulting in the emergence of local chieftains who were also in many instances warriors.

These chieftains regulated agricultural and craft production, operating a redistributive system through which the farmers could obtain tools or ornaments they needed or wanted. The organizational demands of controlled redistribution made it necessary to develop methods of measurement and recording, which culminated in the emergence of writing.

Renfrew argued that any single innovation would have had a limited or negligible effect on social organization, because the inherently conservative nature of societies acts to minimize change. However, the interaction of several simultaneous developments created a 'multiplier effect'. In the Aegean, increased agricultural productivity provided the means to support craft specialization, while bronze metallurgy supplied the motive, setting in motion a series of changes in other sub-systems of society.

Those changes in turn resulted in what, in a term borrowed from the jargon of electronics, are called 'positive feedback loops' – alterations in the workings of a social system that serve to reinforce themselves. Thus Aegean society was transformed from one consisting of basically self-sufficient, equal and egalitarian farming villages to one of prosperous, hierarchical chiefdoms, with palace-dwelling rulers and actively competing with one another both at home and in international trade.

The Snake Goddess *was regarded by the Minoans as the source of all life. Also known as the Mother Goddess, she was the focus of Minoan religious worship. Effigies of the goddess, such as this one in faience (a form of glazed earthenware) were common in Minoan homes.*

The Royal Palace *at Knossos was the heart of the Minoan civilization of ancient Crete in the 2nd millenium BC. As well as being the home of the king and queen, the palace was a religious centre where priests and priestesses lived. It was decorated with elaborate wall-paintings reflecting the Minoans' love of nature.*

CLUES FROM PLACE NAMES

THE NAMES OF settlements, hills, fields and other features of the landscape can provide valuable clues to the possible location of sites of archaeological interest. The principles outlined here and illustrated with examples from Europe and North America are applicable generally.

Place names, like historical documents, are the preserve of the specialist. Superficial resemblances between words with entirely different meanings may mislead the unwary, and a grounding in philology and etymology is needed for accurate interpretation.

At the simple level, names indicate the former existence of features in the landscape, or the use to which a particular area or natural feature was put. In England, for example, field names containing the element 'town' suggest that the field was once the site of a now-vanished village. Other names may derive from prehistoric monuments that disappeared only in historical times. In many languages, the monuments may be linked with the devil, or with dragons or other mythical entities – and by extension with the dragon-slaying St Michael, if a pagan site was subsequently taken over by the Christian church. At Carnac in Brittany, for instance, the biggest tumulus in the vast complex of megaliths and mounds has a chapel of St Michel on top.

Sometimes, a name may show that the purpose of a feature was remembered, with its builders, long after it fell into disuse. 'Rath', a common component of place names in Ireland, denotes a fort surrounded by a bank and ditch. 'Wic' and its variants in several northern European languages come from the Latin *vicus* and indicate a Roman settlement.

Patterns of Settlement

At a deeper level, place names provide vital clues to the pattern and chronology of land settlement. In Britain, the names of many towns and villages reflect the Roman presence. The most common is the suffix *-chester*, a derivation of the Latin *castra* (a fortified camp). The city of Chester itself was a major Roman fortress built in AD 76-78. Much of the city's Roman wall survives.

One of the most grandiose of the many public baths built by the Romans in Britain is reflected in the name of the city of Bath. A great complex of Roman baths was built here in the 1st century AD, attracting tourists from all over the Roman world. Many Roman town houses have been uncovered and the Sacred Spring, around which the original baths were built, can still be seen.

An interesting hybrid which reflects both Roman and British settlement in an area is the place name *Wickham* – a combination of the Latin *vicus* and the Old English *ham*, both of which mean 'settlement' or 'village'. Thus West Wickham and East Wickham are both built on the site of an earlier Roman-British settlement.

After the Roman period, the relationship between colonizing Vikings and Anglo-Saxon peasants can be gauged from the distribution of village names containing Viking elements. Such place names abound in the north and east of England, the region designated to the Vikings under the Treaty of Wedmore in 878.

The most common Viking element in place names is the suffix *-by* (farmstead or village). There are literally hundreds of names ending with the *-by* suffix in northern and eastern England. Another extremely common Viking element is the suffix *-thorp* (a small settlement which is dependent on a larger village).

In the south of England, Saxon place names tend to be the most common. The suffix *-ham* (place or village), for instance, is widely used, as are *-tun* and *-ton*, both later Saxon words which also denote a place or village.

Hybrid names in which a Scandinavian personal name is combined with a Saxon suffix are quite numerous in areas where the Vikings settled but were never dominant. Examples of such names include Oulton, Branston and Thurgarton in East Anglia.

In Scotland, an interesting feature of many place names is the prefix *-pit* which indicates the presence of the Pictish people who settled in parts of Scotland between AD 200 and 700. Such names include Pitlochry, Pitcastle and Pitscottie.

The influence of European settlement in North America can be gauged to a great extent simply by examining the distribution of place names derived from English, French, Dutch, German, Spanish and other languages. So although New York's Dutch origins are concealed by the name-change from Nieuwe Amsterdam, they are revealed in names such as Bowery (originally *Bouwerij*, from the Dutch word for farm) and Harlem, named after Haarlem, the town in Holland.

The examples above give a glimpse of the way place names can provide valuable insights into a region's history. The inter-relationships between linguistic groups, the order of settlement, and changes in patterns of land-use are the most common questions to which place names may help provide an answer.

BARBARIANS ON THE MOVE

THE BEGINNING OF THE END for the Roman Empire came in AD 406, when hordes of barbarians of quite diverse tribal origins moved westwards across the Rhine and started to settle in the lands on its farther shores. Some stopped only briefly in Gaul before moving on; the Vandals, for example, devastated Iberia and founded a kingdom in north Africa. Others, notably the Franks and the Burgundians, chose to stay in Gaul itself.

Another group, the Visigoths, initially settled in southern Gaul, where they founded the kingdom of Toulouse. But early in the 6th century they were defeated in a conflict with the Franks. Many migrated into what is now Spain, where the Visigoths had already established military outposts.

Much of our knowledge of these population movements and settlements comes from the study of place names. For instance, the Alans, a group driven by the Huns from an empire on the Caspian Sea, settled on the River Loire for a time, and names such as Allaines bear witness to their former presence there. The distribution of place names that now end in -*ans* or -*ens* (originally -*ingos*) chronicles Burgundian colonization of much of French-speaking Switzerland, the Jura and the plain of the River Saone in France itself. Names also support the traditional belief that the Burgundians originally came from Scandinavia – Borgund in Norway and Bornholm (once Borgundarholm), an island in the Baltic.

From the North

Increasing pressure from hostile tribes, particularly the Scots in the west and north, drove many Britons from south-west England across the sea to Brittany (Bretagne). Breton regional names such as Dumnonia (as south-west England was then known) and Cornouaille (Cornwall) show the widespread influence of the immigrants. So do names which reflect a land division into parishes around monasteries, rather than the organization by estates then practised in the rest of Gaul.

Place names indicating land tenure also yield information about early Visigothic settlements in Spain. The invaders seized about two-thirds of the Roman land-holdings there, and those became known legally as the *Sortes Gothicae* (the Gothic lot or portion), preserved in names such as Sort and Consortes. The Roman third, or *Tertiae Romanorum*, gave rise to names like Tercia. Towards the end of the 6th century AD, the Visigoths gained control of the whole Iberian peninsula, but that expansion is hardly discernible from place names, for by then the Visigoths had largely adopted Byzantine Roman language.

A Shifting Frontier

On a larger scale, place names indicate fluctuations in the frontier between people speaking Romance, the language of Gaul, and those speaking Germanic languages. By the 7th or 8th century AD, the linguistic frontier more or less followed the same course that it does today. However, on either side there were enclaves where people spoke the language of the other region.

Among those was the area around Boulogne, on the Channel coast of France, which was strongly Germanic. Latin place names there evolved differently from those in most of the rest of Gaul, where Romance was dominant. The Roman settlement name of Cessiacum became Quesques to the German-speakers, but Chessy to the French. Similarly, Gilliacum became Guelque in Germanic, but Gilly in Romance. From the 9th century onwards, the Boulogne enclave was gradually 'reconquered' by French, but the legacy of German can still be traced.

The location of the German-French language frontier can be shown to have derived from two factors relating to the barbarian invasions – distance from the borders of the original Germanic territories, and the degree of devastation the invasions caused in a given area. The frontier runs roughly parallel to the Germanic boundaries as they existed during the 4th century, about 100km (180mi) beyond these boundaries.

In Bavaria, in what is now southern West Germany and was part of the Roman Empire until the barbarians overran it in the 5th century, only insignificant pockets of Romance-speakers survived. Their settlements are often denoted by the element *walah* in the name. The term, in Germanic tongues, means 'foreigner', and it is also preserved, for the same reason as in Bavaria, in the place names Wales and Wallonia, the French-speaking region of Belgium.

In Gaul itself, which was predominantly Romance-speaking, the evolution of place names subtly indicates the mingling of Roman and Germanic cultures that ultimately led to the emergence of the Merovingian kingdom in the late 5th and early 6th centuries AD (Merovingius is a Latinization of the Germanic personal name Merowig, the traditional founder of the dynasty). In particular, this can be seen in the proliferation of place names that combine a German personal name and a Latin affix. Early examples ended in the Latin -*acum* or -*iacas* (for example, Athanacum), but by the 7th century the Latinate element was generally *ville* or *court* (for example, Villeurbanne and Agincourt), both of which are still popular in the coining of place names in France.

The linguistic evidence of some degree of synthesis between Roman and Germanic cultures in Gaul is borne out archaeologically by the emergence of row grave cemeteries between the 5th and 6th centuries, combining elements of both. The dead were buried with their jewellery and weapons, as was customary in the Germanic world; they were buried lying east to west in the Christian custom, and many of the burials were in stone sarcophagi, a Roman feature.

PART 6

BILLINGSGATE
DIARY OF AN EXCAVATION

By

JOHN SCHOFIELD

(Field Officer, Museum of London)
with Steve Roskams

HISTORY, THEORY, TECHNIQUE – archaeology is all of this. But it is much more. Every site represents thousands of hours of back-breaking labour by a team of dedicated people, contending not only with the vagaries of weather and the inevitable tensions that build up when groups work together for a sustained period under pressure, but also with the complications presented by local inhabitants and government bureaucracy and the unforeseen problems that must be dealt with swiftly so the actual work can proceed.

Every moment on a dig is precious and fraught with the desire to maximize its potential, but an archaeological dig is also exciting and exhilarating. There is the constant exposure of mankind's past existence, the solid contact with the lives of people who lived on the exact spot one is digging.

The only way to understand the fascination of archaeology is to experience digging in the field. But it is possible to glimpse this by living through the experiences of actual field workers. Here we present a diary of one such group, recording the 1982-83 excavations at Billingsgate in the City of London, where 16 centuries of history were laid bare.

Opposite: *So often all trace of the past is wiped away by modern redevelopment – a fact which has led to the growth of rescue archaeology. Here the Billingsgate excavation team uncover a Saxon river embankment.*

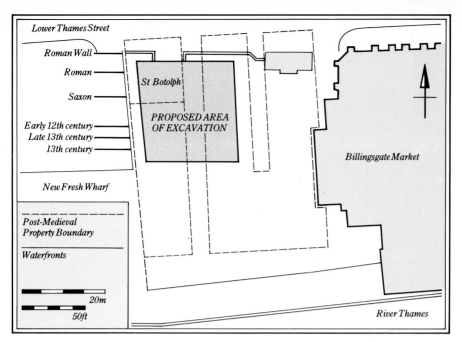

This overall plan *shows the whole of Billingsgate Market, bounded by Lower Thames Street on the north and the River Thames on the south. The actual excavation site was about one-quarter of the parking area (just outside the market building). The positions of historical walls or revetments were known from an adjacent excavation, and records indicated the location of the church of St Botolph Billingsgate, which had been destroyed in the Great Fire of 1666, along with nearly four-fifths of the City of London (i.e. the square mile that delineates the original London). There was access to the street and spoil heaps and huts could be placed to the south of the site.*

THE ORIGINS OF BILLINGSGATE MARKET famous until 1982 as London's main fish market, go back to a time in the Saxon period when it was a place for general trade. In medieval times its centre was an inlet in the packed riverfront of London; this was later built over for the fish market building of 1875 and all archaeological layers in that part destroyed. But next to the market building was a large open space, used in recent years as the parking area for the fish market, beneath which lay 2000 years of London's archaeology. Plans were drawn up to move the fish market to another site and sell both the market building and its adjacent land for redevelopment. The Museum of London began to plan a major excavation in advance of the destruction which the new office block being developed on the site would cause.

The site lay south of Thames Street, between the street and the present north bank of the River Thames. Its importance lay chiefly in that it contained the remains of previous quays and waterfront buildings, back to the line of the 3rd-century Roman quay, which ran from east to west immediately south of the northern edge of the site, 10 metres (32½ feet) below street level. The alignments of the Roman and later Saxon and medieval riverside quays or revetments could be predicted from excavations on an adjacent site several years previously. Waterlogged conditions would ensure good survival for timber structures such as the Roman and later revetments, and objects made of organic substances such as wood, leather and bone. The strata were probably not greatly much damaged by later basements or foundations. Even though this was to be an ambitiously large project, the Museum could not hope to excavate it all. So with time and financial constraints in mind, an area forming only about one-quarter of the site which was to be destroyed for redevelopment was chosen.

PREPARATIONS

IN THIS CASE priorities dictated that the area, about 20 by 25 metres (65 by 81 feet), should be in the north-west corner of the site, where the richest cross-section of archaeological features could be expected: the Roman quay, Saxon and medieval embankments and revetments, the parish church of St Botolph Billingsgate (destroyed 1666) and other buildings on the medieval and early modern waterfront. This was termed Area A and had to be excavated at all costs. Areas B and C, to the east and south of the main trench, would be excavated only if time allowed. If this were not the case , we would have to make detailed plans to ensure that the destruction of these areas was monitored during redevelopment.

Plans for the budget begin up to two years before the site starts (i.e. Month 1): many opinions must be sought, many permissions gained, and much money accumulated. Brian Hobley, Chief Urban Archaeologist, asks for two years on the site after the closing of the market, but *before* the developers move in with their earth-moving machines. Meanwhile I design the excavation. It is clear that the excavation requires a large team of professional archaeologists, machinery (cranes and dumpers), and three particular pieces of civil engineering: a roof over the site, a public viewing gallery and, most important of all, the intended excavation to 10 metres (32½ feet) below street level requires that we delimit the area of excavation with a cofferdam of sheet piling to resist the tidal pressure of the adjacent river and to hold up the surrounding land. This must be square or rectangular to get up into the corner of the site where most of the objectives lie stacked on top of each other beneath the ground.

With seven months to go, the main grant from the Corporation of London is announced; the largest grant so far for a single site excavated in the City of London. The Department of Environment have also confirmed their own substantial contribution. We now have a working budget for the whole exercise.

Six months before the projected start we visit the fish market building and look for facilities to exploit. We note the position of the electricity supply, water supply, floodlights – all present and installed, a good sign for an archaeological excavation. We must obtain permission to use subsidiary buildings of the market as our own offices: the Crab Boiling House, for cleaning and processing of the finds – a certain amount of cleaning out will be necessary to remove, or at least alleviate, the ingrained fish smell; and the Billingsgate Porters' Changing Rooms, below the surface of the parking area, away from the actual site of the excavation, to serve as our own comparatively palatial changing rooms.

It is also clear that we must acquire a suitable computer before the excavation starts, so that the information can be recorded as it is excavated. We buy a minicomputer and a number of microcomputers as outstations for data collection. It is proposed that two of these computers be used on site; they will require a hut for themselves, preferably dust-free.

Three months to go – the date of starting is confirmed. Specifications are prepared for a temporary roof to cover the area of excavation. A custom-made design by our own engineer seems the best of several alternatives.

Two months before the start of the excavation, we appoint Steve Roskams as Site Supervisor. He has directed the excavation of several other sites in the City and will write the most detailed 'archive' report: the layer-by-layer history of deposition on the site, from which all subsequent analyses of buildings or finds must begin.

With one month to go, we begin to arrange for excavation and finds staff to transfer to the new site. The numbers are to be increased by employing 35 temporary staff under a Manpower Services Commission scheme. The MSC, which funds unemployment relief schemes, has funded archaeology in Britain in recent years to an amount equal to that put in by the Department of the Environment. We have secured a scheme for two public relations staff or guides, two computer personnel, two photographers, two administrators, and 27 archaeologists (including diggers, finds staff and environmental analysts). The whole team will comprise over 50 staff.

The BBC wish to make a programme about the excavation. This will be done by coming down every couple of months and filming whatever is going on, along with special filming sessions for notable discoveries or important visitors.

MONTH 1: *Excavation Begins*

ON THE 20TH of the month, the excavation starts with machines (*see page 76*). We must break through the surface over the future area of excavation and cart away the 3 metres (10 feet) or so of post-\war rubble, down to the 19th century cellar floor. While this is going on the various sections move in furniture and equipment; we wire up the temporary conservation and environmental laboratory. Two small mobile cranes and two dumpers arrive for use on site. One crane will travel along each of the long sides of the excavation, removing spoil in large metal buckets which are then tipped into the dumpers. The spoil heap lies behind the site huts, and is taken away every few weeks by bringing in a mechanical digger and large trucks or lorries. The computer is installed, but much work is still required to perfect the programs ('software') we are to use for our special purposes. We should be able to input site information about the layers by Month 3. By then the rubble will have been cleared and the excavators will need to begin inputting their site data if they are not to have a large backlog.

Other sponsorship for major items of equipment is still being sought. A supermarket chain has donated several large deep freezers for conservation of the large amounts of waterlogged wood and leather which are expected to be unearthed during the course of the excavation.

The Billingsgate excavation *was filmed by the BBC for its 'Chronicle' series, making the whole project a matter of immediate public record for millions. Here, as the basement level is being emptied of rubble, the camera crew are interviewing site supervisor Steve Roskams, who is giving an up-to-the-minute progress report.*

MONTH 2: *More Than We Thought*

IT BECOMES CLEAR THAT there is more archaeology here than we expected. The basement floor is found to be slightly higher – only about 2.5m (8 ft) below the level of the parking area. This will mean that more historic archaeology survives beneath it. In addition, the site was bisected north and south by an alley which seems to have determined the cellar arrangements of the 19th-century warehouse. Trapped in the middle, between two cellars, is a piece of older, upstanding wall. It is of stone, very thick and burned along the top. This must be the east end of the church of St Botolph. It rises several feet above the general level of the archaeology, which itself looks extremely promising. We are in luck.

An enormous crane arrived in the middle of the night with a police escort and the piling of the excavated area can now take place. The piles will themselves cross over some features of archaeological interest, and these must be investigated before the piles are driven in. Within the church a floor of medieval tiles can be seen, along with evidence of human burials. It becomes clear that we have the southern third of the church in the area of excavation; the northern two-thirds lie under the pavement of Thames Street. Our viewing gallery will be built over the north side of the excavation. But just now anybody can see through the gates directly onto the south aisle of the church, where human bones are being excavated. So as not to cause any offence to members of the public, a light shelter is erected over the area.

MONTH 3: *17th-century Finds*

THE PILING HAS finished, and two huts have been installed on the southern edge of the excavation area, facing both the excavation and the street. One will serve as a site office and the other is intended to house the site computer.

One of the former fish market buildings is commandeered as a staff mess room. I am able to beg the entire furnishings of seats and tables from a small cafe which is closing down; triumphantly we unscrew them from the floor and transport them to Billingsgate.

Now that a full team has arrived on site, we are making significant progress. The pre-Fire surface of St Botolph's Lane, which divided the site into two north-south parts, is presently exposed, along with 17th-century buildings on both sides. On one side is the church, in which burials are being excavated; evidence of wooden coffins, iron coffin fittings and burial shrouds is recovered. One coffin lid had the date 1666 clearly outlined in nails punched into it. The earliest burial in what must be the south aisle of the church, by contrast, contains the lead papal seals of Pope Gregory XI (1370-76).

The Great Fire has left an indelible mark: the stones are charred and blackened, the lead from the windows has melted and become distorted, the painted medieval glass is warped and shattered by intense heat.

South of the church and across the lane are the houses and warehouses which stretched from Thames Street to the river both before and after the Great Fire.

A cofferdam is created around *the excavation area by driving in piles (left) to a depth of about 9m (30ft). When this has been completed, the site is cleared for the first photograph (above). Already it is possibly to distinguish separate buildings. The trench, delimited by the cofferdam, is cut from the floor of a warehouse basement, whose walls can be seen around the trench. It is sited over St Botolph's Lane, whose location is known from maps.*

The 'Chronicle' team view a skeleton from one of the many graves excavated in the south aisle of St Botolph's Church. The burials span the time from late medieval to the early 17th century, and examination of the remains provides archaeologists with a way of learning more about conditions during that period. From skeletal remains we can determine such facts as sex, age, and general state of health. We can even observe the development of dentistry.

MONTH 4: *Getting Earlier in Parts*

WORK ON THE BUILDINGS erected after the Great Fire is almost finished, though some of their sequences were longer and more complex than expected. In the eastern half of the site, the brick floors and drains of the post-Fire building have been investigated and removed. One of the cesspits has proved so noxious that the excavators were forced to wear breathing apparatus. To the north, possibly medieval surfaces are appearing.

In St Botolph's Lane the excavators are down to the 15th or 16th century. An odd consequence of having this lane running down the middle of the site is that those who are excavating the buildings on either side use it for access to their work areas, just like the original owners did five centuries ago. But the excavators who are in charge of the lane area strongly object – their colleagues are walking over archaeological strata! This sort of trespassing would not be allowed elsewhere on the site. Chastened, we keep to the plank walkways.

MONTH 5: *Into the 15th Century*

THE PUBLIC VIEWING GALLERY is now being built at the north end of the excavation, next to the street. It is very rare in British archaeology that resources are available for such ambitious public display of a site during excavation, and there are few previous experiences of this kind of thing to profit from. The iron gates of the parking area are replaced by a ticket office. A series of talks are given, allowing the public to view the finds.

In the south-west corner of the site, excavation of the 18th century building has meant the emptying of deep drains. When these drains were removed, medieval walls were revealed. This means that this part of the excavation

will be slightly ahead of the other parts, due to the destruction of the 16th- and 17th-century strata by the 18th- century building. There will be a danger that this corner will always be excavated ahead of the rest of the site. This is not a great problem, but it does mean that the excavators in this area will be digging an earlier period than the rest of the site. Being 'out of phase' means that the overall photographs will not show features which were in use at the same time. Perhaps Steve will slow down in this area until the rest of the site catches up.

Within the church of St Botolph, excavation is down to 15th-century levels. It is now clear that inside the limits of the excavated area we have the south aisle of the church. The church's relationship with the merchant's house to the south seems to have been remarkably predatory. At first it was separated from the house by a cobbled area or pathway; but then the cellar or undercroft of the house was incorporated into the body of the church, with some modification to its stone walls and vaulted ceiling, and the intervening space also made internal within the church. It may have been a private chapel; in the floor was a prominent brick tomb with a man's skeleton in it. We know that in 1449 John Reynewell bequeathed his house, next to St Botolph's, as a vestry; the house we have found to the south of the vestry was his. It is fascinating to see the interaction of church and local community demonstrated so graphically – the structural alterations, the moving of doorways, and the enclosure of space which had previously been open to the sky.

The site as it appeared *during Months 5 to 6, showing 15th-17th century structures. The south aisle of St Botolph's, where burials were found, appears top left; south of it is the undercroft, the lower storey of a house later incorporated into the church.*

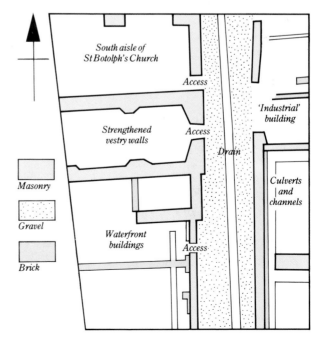

South aisle of St Botolph's Church

Access

'Industrial' building

Strengthened vestry walls

Access

Drain

Masonry

Gravel

Culverts and channels

Brick

Waterfront buildings

Access

MONTH 6: *Have We Enough Time?*

EXCESSIVE RAIN THIS MONTH, affecting progress.
Fifteenth- and 16th-century levels of St Botolph Lane have
been removed, disclosing 15th-century walls of buildings
on the west of the lane, south of St Botolph's church. The
building south of the church with its undercroft is now
revealed: walls over 3 metres (9¾ feet) high, remains of
vaulting and two windows flanking steps up to the lane. To
the north it seems that there was an external space
between the house and the church, later incorporated into
the south aisle of the church; we have uncovered the older
south wall of the church much further to the north. By the
end of this month Steve intends that all the later medieval
stone buildings will have been removed from the site, and
it will look very different: slighter foundations of timber
and clay to the north, with timber revetments bordering
the medieval river on the south. The only stone building in
this period, possibly the 13th century, would be the
church. Here our progress is slower than elsewhere due
to the care required over human burials.

Within the 12 months allowed for the excavation, we
hope to be on the waterfronts and the reclamation deposits
behind them shortly, allowing four months for the
medieval revetments; two months then for the Saxon
embankments buried beneath and to the north of them,
and three months after that for the original Roman
quayside beneath that. The extra work involved in the
recording and removal of the unexpected strata at the top
of the sequence has caused problems of timing, but this
tight schedule is possible, given no further serious hitches.
The public viewing gallery is opened by an Under-
Secretary of the Department of Environment this month;
we mount a small exhibition in the gallery itself. The
Under-Secretary makes a stirring speech about

Twelfth or 13th- century
*wooden revetments, excavated
during the 7th month of the
project. They stand over 2m
(6½ft) high in a marvellous
state of preservation. They are,
in fact, reclamation dumps held
back by the diagonal posts which
would have sloped down to the
foreshore. The landward side of
the revetment, which cannot be
seen in the photograph, showed
carpenter's marks in the wood,
indicating some evidence of
prefabrication (i.e. it was
probably done in sections for
quick assembly). The infill
behind the revetment walls,
consisted of both domestic
rubbish and the sort of coarse
fabric used for sacking. The
latter was atypical of the
clothing remains found in other
City excavations and this is
probably due to the industrial
nature of the site.*

A special element of the Billingsgate excavation was its accessibility to the public. For many, a trip to the site was an important learning experience. Here one of the Museum's Communications staff gives an on-site talk to absorbed youngsters.

government support for archaeology. Unfortunately, we are told the next day, the government inspectors in charge of archaeology had promised the City Corporation that nine months' excavation would be sufficient, and thus the City gave us a licence for nine months. The Museum had, in fact, asked for two years. We need at least one year, and this is already Month 6. There is at least another 6 months' work to do. A contingency scheme of some brutality may have to be introduced from the end of Month 7.

MONTH 7: *Medieval Finds*

THE FIRST MEDIEVAL REVETMENT appears at the south of the site. We shall sample it for dendrochronology, but first indications from pottery suggest it is of mid or late 13th-century date. It formed the riverwards end of properties south of Thames Street. Well preserved in waterlogged (anaerobic) conditions, it stands over 2m (6½ft) high. It has to be constantly kept wet by spraying because the Conservation Department hope that it can be removed piece by piece and conserved for future display. A noble idea, but while the conservator sprays the timbers once or twice a day, the surrounding archaeologists prefer a dry environment to continue their work. One or two strained smiles can be observed.

Soil and rubbish used to reclaim the land by being dumped behind these timber walls are spectacular in condition, quantity and variety. They are mostly domestic: wooden bowls, spoons, knives, broken pottery jugs, shoes worn beyond hope of repair, buttons and buckles, harness fittings. Others are industrial in character: tools, fishing gear or industrial waste. Unlike finds from other sites in the City, the Billingsgate textiles do not seem to be clothing fragments such as frayed collars or cuffs, but coarsely woven tabbies and twills suitable for sacking. Each of these objects is carefully drawn, described, and given initial conservation.

MONTH 8: *Into the 11th Century*

THIS MONTH THE ROOF IS erected; summer is about to come to an end, and the approach of the English autumn and winter strongly urges the necessity of a canopy over the whole excavation. The gallery will abut the roof structure and look down the length of the site.

We have now excavated some distance down the depth of the cofferdam sides, so that extra supports now have to be inserted in the piling structure. This means, among other things, a horizontal girdle of steel around the cofferdam halfway down. As the excavation has followed the lie of the land, the remaining strata are higher at the north end and lower at the south end. Steve and his team must therefore dig, by hand, the trenches through their beloved strata towards the north to accept the steel beam around the edges.

Negotiations for an extension have succeeded in gaining time until the end of Month 14, at least in principle - but this is not confirmed in writing. We wait for this before cancelling the contingency plan, which now swings into operation. It involves digging the eastern half, where there are more complicated deposits, very carefully; but digging the western half, particularly the waterfront reclamation dumps, at high speed.

On site, the top of an embankment, possibly Saxon, may have been located in the north-west corner of the site, with timbers to its south. Steve intends to reach the Roman levels by the end of Month 11.

Staff in the finds *shed, formerly the Crab Boiling House, carefully sort through everything, cleaning and examining each find for subsequent recording and analysis.*

MONTH 9: *Time Becomes Critical*

DISCUSSIONS ABOUT THE EXTENSION have not produced the required letter of assurance. So we are trying to finish by the end of Month 11, the present termination of our permitted occupancy of the site. The team are working very long hours to achieve the impossible. Various backlogs build up; particularly scores of little soil mountains over the untouched surface of the parking area, each with a label stuck in the top – environmental samples waiting to be sieved. We begin to plan even more drastic solutions; fortunately we have access to another large open space a mile upstream, an as yet undeveloped site. I arrange for the rubbish there to be levelled by a bulldozer to produce a flat surface; we can then bring our waterfront dump deposits to that site and spread them out to examine them for artefacts using our metal detectors and other recovery techniques.

On the site, a whole series of successive revetments can now be seen. In the south part of the site, they have been photographed and drawn, and will be lifted next month. Towards the centre, their forerunners are totally exposed and are being recorded before they, in their turn, are removed. The earliest waterfront so far exposed is showing through at the north end of the site. The contingency plan means that the structures showing in the eastern area are considerably later than those which show elsewhere; but consistent and careful recording will ensure that their true sequence can be recomposed in the course of post-excavation analysis.

MONTH 10: *11th-century Buildings*

STILL NO WORD FROM THE DEVELOPERS or the City about an extension. Brian Hobley takes the decision to carry on excavating until the end of Month 13, as intended; we therefore drop the contingency plan to finish by the end of Month 11. Although of relatively short duration, executing the contingency plan was a serious disruption.

At the north end all trace of the church of St Botolph has gone; beneath lies the embankment of 11th- or 12th-century date over which it was built. To the east, in the half being investigated less swiftly, 12th-century timber buildings are being excavated. Interestingly, there is more development on this side, nearer the medieval centre of Billingsgate. It may be that pressure for waterfront development radiated out of the Saxon public landing place and impromptu market of Billingsgate.

In the southern part, excavation has reached the deepest it need go, since we have arrived at the 12th-century river foreshore and riverbed. The revetment structure here is being dismantled carefully; it contains parts of reused 11th- or 12th-century timber buildings. We know very little of early medieval timber building techniques (the buildings of this age on dry land in London having long disappeared), and this is a real bonus. From now on excavation can proceed from the south edge of the site northwards in a horizontal direction, picking out the successive revetments in reverse order of building as we unravel the process of land reclamation around the time of William the Conqueror.

Among the many *prominent visitors to the Billingsgate excavation was Prince Charles, who has had a longstanding interest in archaeology, which he studied at Cambridge. Here the Prince is shown, after having toured the actual site, speaking with finds and conservation staff as they record and study data in the Crab Boiling House, commandeered for the project as a work area.*

The Saxon embankment (which may, in fact, date from the mid 11th century) is being drawn and will be dismantled in the west of the site, hopefully to expose the Roman quay. In the east we are also in 11th-century levels. Elsewhere in the parking area, timbers from the embankments and revetments are drawn and sampled for species. Some of them are laid in specially built tanks for conservation, or put aside for dendrochronological sampling by chain-saw. Sieving of waterfront dumps is providing much artefactual and environmental material and is catching up with the backlog from previous months. During Month 12 we hope to catch our first glimpse on this site of the Roman quay.

From work on previous sites, we expect that the time-gap between the Roman quay of the 3rd century and the first Saxon bank will be shown only in silts enveloping the Roman structure as the river rose and the quays went out of use. But when was the first Saxon embankment erected and, with it, the rebirth of international trade for London? With luck, we should be about to answer the main question posed by the Billingsgate investigation.

Initially the Saxon embankments appear as a mass of green-grey clay and haphazard branches. However, as we begin to dissect it, more order can be seen. Unexpectedly, we are not dealing with a sloping beach at all but with a massive vertical revetment, tied back to the clay dumping with large horizontal members. Clearly the first waterfront to be erected in post-Roman times, whenever it took place, was a considerable investment in time and money.

In the closing stages *of the excavation, the pace increases as the Saxon embankment is recorded and excavated. In the embankment were timbers reclaimed from land use. The vertical posts are slim trunks chosen specially for the purpose, but their comparative youth makes dendrochronology difficult. The dating of this embankment will provide the date of the establishment of Billingsgate as an international port, probably by King Alfred in the years after 886.*

MONTH 11: *The Origins of Billingsgate*

AT LAST AN AGREEMENT FROM the developers allowing excavation to continue until the end of Month 13.

Winter draws on and the site must now be floodlit; not only large lamps in the roof for general coverage, but mobile tungsten-halogen lamps on tripod stands which excavators can place over their own piece of work. The photographers who are working on the site have to bring their own extra illumination; after dusk the whole site seems to sparkle brilliantly from the many lights. Freak winds damage the plastic sheeting of the roof, and this must be replaced.

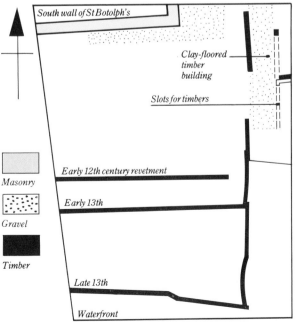

South wall of St Botolph's

Clay-floored timber building

Slots for timbers

Masonry

Gravel

Timber

Early 12th century revetment

Early 13th

Late 13th

Waterfront

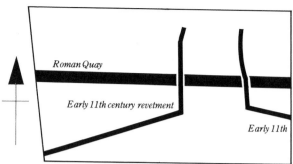

End of the journey: *the early 3rd century Roman quay, 8.5m (28ft) below street level. In structure it is a timber wall of beams, braced by an arrangement of tie-back braces and piles, which may have supported quayside buildings. The working surface of the quay was provided by the dumped soil and debris packed inside the structure; it was originally some 5 or 6 beams high. The view shown is to the North, with the Roman foreshore in the foreground. Analysis will tell what happened to it in the Dark Ages. It may have fallen into disuse before the end of Roman Britain.*

MONTH 12: *Roman Quay Appears*

STILL NO WORD FROM the developer; Steve and his team dig on. To many of them Christmas is incidental. The various Saxon embankments are complicated and time is getting short. I transfer extra staff to Billingsgate to provide more excavators. Now the excavation is concentrated in the northern half of the site, deep inside the sheet piling cofferdam. As examination of the southern half has finished, the spoil from the north is taken by wheelbarrow and piled against the south wall of the trench.

A few days before the end of the month, the Roman quay is exposed over half the width of the site and stands up to one metre (39 inches) high; squared black baulks of timber forming a quay wall, braced back to large piles with horizontal beams. The structure was partly dismantled or robbed in antiquity; silt accumulated around it. Presumably ships were no longer using it, indicating a decline in the fortunes of London. The first action thereafter on this site was the building of the rubble bank found already on top of the silted up Roman quay.

In planning the overall photographs of the quay structure, Steve uses the presence of the roof as a shelter. His staff expose and clean the timbers carefully over the whole area, working late into the night. Despite the bad weather, the site can be left dry and clean overnight; our photographer comes in at the crack of dawn and takes his pictures. The staff return and set about recording and dismantling the structure.

As this main site comes to a close we must ensure adequate provision for the watching brief on the other three-quarters of the site. We can only arrange to observe the machines as they remove many cubic metres of archaeological strata.

MONTH 13: *Hectic Last Days*

THE DISMANTLING OF THE Roman quay continues with the help of a tree surgeon who takes large slices from the timbers with a chain saw. These are carefully bagged and removed for dendrochronological analysis. Some timbers are removed by crane for individual drawing. A 3-metre (9¾ft) section of complete quay is removed, timber by timber, to be conserved and perhaps displayed in the museum. Many Saxon timbers are removed to the other nearby site, to be drawn in comparative leisure. As the end of the month approaches we begin to withdraw. The Visitors' Gallery closes and is boarded up; we start to ferry out hundreds of boxes of finds, scores of carved stones from the church of St Botolph, site and office equipment. Other sites absorb the well-used tools. Because of the pressure of the last month, some material is still to be recorded and drawn in its new home.

MONTH 14: *The Rest of the Site*

THERE IS NO FORMAL BACKFILLING of the site as it is to be occupied by the developers and the remaining part of the parking area removed for their own purposes. The team largely disbands; most of the excavators and finds staff are employed on other sites in the City, but a few drift away. The development, which we were assured would happen immediately, does not. But we begin to make plans for the observation of the excavation and bulk removal of the remaining three-quarters of the site by contractor's machinery.

DURING THIS TIME Steve checks the site records and the site matrix diagram, which records the relationships of all the layers; he sorts the layers and features into stratigraphic groups and begins to assemble the history of the site, layer by layer, starting from the bottom. The site divides into many periods of ancient occupation, beginning with the Roman quay. Meanwhile the last of the thousands of finds are registered, their particulars computerized, sorted and transported to the Museum for storage. The pieces of St Botolph's church are carefully drawn. The pottery dates from several thousand layers are entered into the computer. The dendrochronological samples are sent off for analysis. Archaeologically, we sift information and wait for specialist reports.

On the site, also, we have to wait. Negotiations with the developers to observe and record during their earth-moving operation are difficult. In Month 22, with the bulk excavation of the site only weeks away, Brian Hobley manages to arrange a meeting with the developer and his representatives. They agree to a watching brief under very strict conditions.

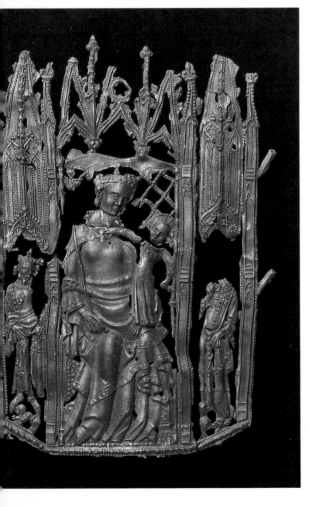

DESPITE THE FACT THAT ACCESS is granted late in the building works, spectacular discoveries are made during the watching brief. Five further medieval revetments are seen south of the excavated area, forming land reclamation units of the medieval and Tudor periods. With the help of the Society of Thames Mudlarks and Antiquarians, who use metal detectors along the foreshores of the present river, many further small finds are recovered. From the Roman period come decorated dress fittings and pendants, leaden seals for merchandise, and a flagon lid in the form of a duck; from the medieval period, pilgrim badges, dress accessories, tokens and cloth seals, knives and tools, miniature toys, shoes, fishing equipment, weaponry and a unique medieval trumpet.

Among many small finds *uncovered during ground-breaking and construction, was this 26mm (1in) toy bird (right) made of pewter. It would have been attached to a small pin and parts of it, including its tongue, were able to be activated to simulate natural movement. The large pewter pilgrim badge (left), about 7.6 x 12cm (3 x 4⅘in), was found in spoil from the site. It was probably from a pilgrimage to Canterbury.*

What Has Been Learned

THE EXCAVATION AT BILLINGSGATE will take many years to analyze. There were nearly 10,000 layers and hundreds of thousands of individual finds. The site supervisor writes the archive report which forms the basis of all subsequent analyses, and of any publications which result. The site will contribute to the publication of several thematic studies which will cover a number of excavations of recent years; the Roman and Saxon waterfronts, the church, the medieval buildings and their finds will all see the light of day in separate volumes. The excavation has been a great addition to our knowledge of all periods of London's history, and perhaps its main purpose – to find out the date of waterfront development in the City as it emerged from the Dark Ages into the early medieval period under King Alfred's guidance – will be successfully achieved. But Dark Age London itself is to be found elsewhere; this much has now been confirmed. Another piece of the jigsaw has fallen into place.

INDEX

Acknowledgements

Picture research Liz Eddison

Key: (t) top; (b) below; (l) left; (r) right; (c) centre.

The Paul Press Ltd and the authors would like to thank the following persons and organizations, to whom copyright in the photographs noted belongs:

6 Vision International; 8 Salisbury and South Wiltshire Museum; 9 The Illustrated London News Picture Library; 10(t)(b) The Mansell Collection; 10(c), 11 C M Dixon; 12 The Mansell Collection; 13 French Government Tourist Office; 14 Ann Ronan Picture Library; 15 The Mansell Collection; 16 The Illustrated London News Picture Library; 17 Bruce Coleman; 18 The British Library; 19(t) Ronald Sheridan; 19(b) The Illustrated London News Picture Library; 20(tr)(tl) BBC Hulton Picture Library; 21 Michael Holford; 22 The Mansell Collection; 23(bl)(br) BBC Hulton Picture Library; 24(t)(b) The Mansell Collection; 25(tl) Ronald Sheridan; 25(tr) Michael Holford; 26, 27(t)(b) Robert Harding Picture Library Ltd; 28(t)(b) Paolo Koch, Vision International; 29 Robert Harding Picture Library Ltd; 30 Werner Forman Archive; 31(t)(b) Salisbury and South Wiltshire Museum; 32 The Illustrated London News Picture Library; 33 Stephanie Colasanti, FIIP; 34 Royal Commission of Historical Monuments of England; 35 Griffith Institute, Ashmolean Museum; 36 Topham Picture Library; 37(t)(b) Robert Harding Picture Library Ltd; 38 Dr Georg Gerster, John Hillelson Agency; 39 Planet Earth Pictures; 40 Dr Georg Gerster, John Hillelson Agency; 42, 43 Michael Holford; 44 Michael Holford; 45 The Public Record Office; 46 Aerofilms; 47 The Mansell Collection; 48 Dr Georg Gerster, John Hillelson Agency; 49 Aerofilms; 50 Robert Harding Picture Library Ltd; 51 Ronald Sheridan; 52 B. Norman, Sheridan Photo Library; 53 Jane McIntosh; 54 Museum of London; 55 Jane McIntosh; 57 Mike Gorman; 59 Daily Telegraph Colour Library; 60 Ronald Sheridan; 62, 63(b) Robert Harding Picture Library Ltd; 63(t) Michael Holford; 66, 67 Mike Duffy, York Archaeological Trust; 68, 69 Dr Georg Gerster, John Hillelson Agency; 72, 73 Leslie Alcock, Camelot Research Committee; 74 Museum of London; 75 Michael Holford; 76, 77, 78, 79, 80 Museum of London; 81(t)(b), 82 Robert Harding Picture Library Ltd; 84, 85(r)(l) Museum of London; 88(l) Museum of London; 88(tr)(br) Jane McIntosh; 89 The Illustrated London News Picture Library; 90 Topham Picture Library; 91 Michael Holford; 92 Conservation Dept, Museum of London; 93 The Illustrated London News Picture Library; 94(t) Jane McIntosh; 94(b) Ronald Sheridan; 95 Fishbourne Roman Palace, Sussex Archaeological Society; 96 Michael Holford; 97 Photoresources; 98(t)(b) Planet Earth Pictures; 99(t)(b) S.J.K. Photographic; 100 Dr Brian Bracegirdle; 102, 104, 105(b) Conservation Dept, Museum of London; 105(tr), 106(tr) Daily Telegraph Colour Library; 106 C.M. Dixon; 107 Dr Georg Gerster, John Hillelson Agency; 109 Museum of London; 110 John Coles; 113 C.M. Dixon; 115(t) Ronald Sheridan; 115(b) Wellcome Institute; 116 C.M. Dixon; 117(tl)(tr) The Illustrated London News Picture Library; 118 Robert Harding Picture Library Ltd; 119 John Hillelson Agency; 120 Science Photo Library; 121(t)(b) Reading Museum and Art Gallery; 122(t) C M Dixon; 123(b) Ronald Sheridan; 124(b) Ronald Sheridan; 125(t) Michael Holford; 126(t) Larry Mulvehill, Science Photo Library; 126(b) Museum of London; 127(t)(b) Ronald Sheridan; 128(t) Topham Picture Library; 128(b), 129(b) The Illustrated London News Picture Library; 129(t) Victoria and Albert Museum, John Sparks Ltd; 131(t) Jane McIntosh; 131(b) Mary Evans Picture Library; 132(t) Topham Picture Library; 132(b) The Illustrated London News Picture Library; 134 Topham Picture Library; 137(t)(c)(b) S.J.K. Photographic; 139 Topham Picture Library; 141 Ronald Sheridan; 142(l) Topham Picture Library; 142(r) The Illustrated London News Picture Library; 145(t)(b) Bruce Coleman; 146 Vision International; 148(t)(b) Topham Picture Library; 150(t) Tropix; 150(b) Werner Forman Archive; 151 H.R. Dörig, Vision International; 152(t) Bruce Coleman; 152(b), 154(b) Robert Harding Picture Library Ltd; 154(t) Michael Holford; 156 C.M. Dixon; 157 Robert Harding Picture Library Ltd; 158, 159 Werner Forman Archive; 160 H.R. Dörig, Vision International; 163 Michael Holford; 164 Jane McIntosh; 165 Michael Holford; 166(t)(b) The Illustrated London News Picture Library; 167 Robert Harding Picture Library Ltd; 168, 170(r) Photoresources; 170(l) Michael Holford; 171(l) Ronald Sheridan; 171(r) C.M. Dixon; 174, 177, 178, 179, 180, 181, 182, 183, 184, 185 Museum of London; **Illustrations** 58 Leslie Alcock, © Camelot Research Committee; 65 Prof. Keith Branigan for his technical assistance; 87 Museum of London; 119 Jane McIntosh; 130 Mortimer Wheeler, © Archaeological Survey of India; 136 BT Batsford Publishers Ltd; 158 from *Stylistic Change in Arikara Ceramics*, by James Deetz (Illinois Press); 169 (The Antiquaries Journal 1970) The Society of Antiquaries London

Note: the publishers have made every effort to trace copyright holders for illustrations which appear in this volume and wish to offer their apologies for any unintentional errors or omissions.

Front cover
UK edition: Main photograph – Brian Brake, John Hillelson Agency
Bottom left – Museum of London   Bottom right – Michael Holford

US edition: Main Photograph – Michael Holford
Bottom left – Museum of London   Bottom right – Michael Holford

SUGGESTED FURTHER READING

L. Alcock, *'By South Cadbury is that Camelot...' The Excavations of Cadbury Castle 1966-1970* (Thames and Hudson, 1972)

L.R. Binford, *In Pursuit of the Past, Decoding the Archaeological Record* (Thames and Hudson, 1983)

D. Bothwell and E. Higgs, (eds), *Science in Archaeology* (Thames and Hudson, 1969)

K.W. Butzer, *Early Hydraulic Civilization in Egypt* (Chicago, 1976)

J.M. Coles, *The Archaeology of Wetlands* (Edinburgh University Press, 1984)

    Experimental Archaeology (Academic Press, 1980)

    Field Archaeology in Britain (Methuen, 1972)

J.M. Coles and B.J. Orme, *Prehistory of the Somerset Levels* (Somerset Levels Project, 1980)

G. Dalton, *Tribal and Peasant Economies* (New York, 1967)

Glyn Daniel (ed), *Archaeological Atlas of the World* (Thames and Hudson, 1975)

Glyn Daniel, *A Hundred-and-fifty Years of Archaeology* (Duckworth, 1975)

Liam de Paor, *Archaeology, an Illustrated Introduction* (Penguin, 1971)

E. Doblhofer, *Voices in Stone* (Souvenir Press, 1961)

J. Doran and F. Hodson, *Mathematics and Computers in Archaeology* (Edinburgh, 1975)

R.W. Ehrich (ed), *Chronologies in Old World Archaeology* (University of Chicago Press, 1971)

K.V. Flannery, *The Early Mesoamerican Village* (Academic Press, 1976)

P.V. Glob, *The Bog People* (Paladin, 1971)

C. Green, *Sutton Hoo, the Excavation of a Royal Ship Burial* (Merlin Press)

E.S. Higgs, *Palaeoeconomy* (Cambridge University Press, 1975)

D.C. Johanson and M. Edey, *Lucy, the Beginnings of Mankind* (Granada, 1981)

K. Muckelroy, *Maritime Archaeology* (Cambridge University Press, 1978)

C. Orton, *Mathematics in Archaeology* (Cambridge University Press, 1980)

M. Pope, *The Story of Archaeological Decipherment from Egyptian Hieroglyphs to Linear B* (Thames and Hudson, 1975)

C. Renfrew, *Before Civilization, the Radiocarbon Revolution and Prehistoric Europe* (Jonathan Cape, 1973)

D.N. Riley, *Aerial Archaeology in Britain* (Shire Publications, 1982)

M. Rule, *The Mary Rose, the Excavation and Raising of Henry VIII's Flagship* (Conway Maritime Press, 1982)

M. Shackley, *Environmental Archaeology* (Allen & Unwin, 1981)

A. Sherratt, *The Cambridge Encylopedia of Archaeology* (Cambridge University Press, 1980)

C. Taylor, *Fieldwork in Medieval Archaeology* (Batsford, 1974)

C. Wells, *Bones, Bodies and Diseases* (Thames and Hudson, 1974)

H.V.F. Winstone, *Uncovering the Ancient World* (Constable, 1985)

DATE DUE

MAR 24 1999			